152.47
B288c

W9-CHY-356

MAY   '09

CONELY BRANCH LIBRARY
4600 MARTIN
DETROIT, MI 48210
(313) 224-6461

JUL   10

PLEASE DETROIT PUBLIC LIBRARY

MAR   2008

CREATIVE ANGER

CREATIVE ANGER

Putting That Powerful Emotion to Good Use

Rhoda Baruch, Edith H. Grotberg, and
Suzanne Stutman

Westport, Connecticut
London

Library of Congress Cataloging-in-Publication Data

Baruch, Rhoda, 1925–
    Creative anger : putting that powerful emotion to good use / Rhoda Baruch, Edith
H. Grotberg, and Suzanne Stutman.
      p.   cm.
    Includes bibliographical references and index.
    ISBN 978–0–275–99874–5 (alk. paper)
    1. Anger.   I. Grotberg, Edith Henderson, 1928–   II. Stutman, Suzanne.
III. Title.
  BF575.A5B373   2008
  152.4′7—dc22   2007026122

British Library Cataloguing in Publication Data is available.

Copyright © 2008 by Rhoda Baruch, Edith H. Grotberg, and Suzanne Stutman

All rights reserved. No portion of this book may be
reproduced, by any process or technique, without the
express written consent of the publisher.

Library of Congress Catalog Card Number: 2007026122
ISBN-13: 978–0–275–99874–5

First published in 2008

Praeger Publishers, 88 Post Road West, Westport, CT 06881
An imprint of Greenwood Publishing Group, Inc.
http://www.praeger.com

Printed in the United States of America

The paper used in this book complies with the
Permanent Paper Standard issued by the National
Information Standards Organization (Z39.48–1984).

10 9 8 7 6 5 4 3 2 1

MAR   2008

CONELY BRANCH

Contents

Acknowledgments		vii
Chapter 1	Skills for Creative Anger: RETHINK	1
Chapter 2	RETHINKing Anger Is Good for Your Health	21
Chapter 3	RETHINKing Anger Is Good for Your Relationships	37
Chapter 4	Recognize Anger in Yourself and in Others	57
Chapter 5	Hear with Empathy	73
Chapter 6	Anger in Couples	87
Chapter 7	Anger in the Family	107
Chapter 8	Anger in the Workplace	127
Chapter 9	Friends and Anger, and Anger in the Community	147
Chapter 10	The Anger-Violence Connection	163
Chapter 11	Cultural Differences	181
Chapter 12	Change Comes from Practice	197

Chapter 13 Regaining a Sense of Personal Power   215

Further Reading   233
Index   235

Acknowledgments

If we could we would acknowledge all the people, organizations, media professionals, and publishers who have made this book possible. But that would take a chapter in itself! So, we have selected a few from a variety of professions and disciplines to describe the scope and wealth of resources available to the authors.

The media has been a major partner in disseminating RETHINK information, including conferences with writers, producers, and technicians. The outstanding figure in that area is Leonard B. Stern. His background in television, including three Emmy Awards, a Writers Guild of American Award, and many others, was instrumental in incorporating RETHINK into television programming. He formed Tallfellow, Inc., in 1996, which functions as an independent story department for studios, publishers, and independent production companies. He was Media Editor of *Dialogue: Insights to Human Emotions for Creative Professions*, a quarterly publication of the Institute for Mental Health Initiatives (IMHI), founded by Rhoda Baruch, with Suzanne Stutman and Edith Grotberg as colleagues. And Laurie Beckelman merits special thanks, as she helped us communicate our messages to the public through her exquisite writing for *Dialogue* and other materials. The supplementary work of art director and designer Ellen Shapiro helped *Dialogue* win repeated awards, including several from the National Association of Mental Health Information Officers, NAMIO.

In the area of cognition and emotions, i.e., thinking/feeling, two views are drawn on by the authors. One is from Aaron T. Beck, M.D., and the other is from Stanley I. Greenspan, M.D. Dr. Beck (*Prisoners of Hate: The Cognitive Basis of Anger*, Harper Collins Publishers, 1999) stresses the importance of thinking about a disturbing situation, such as one that is anger-producing, in another, more constructive way so that the feelings can change. RETHINK has drawn on that concept, but not totally. Dr. Greenspan stresses the importance of the basic interaction of thinking and feeling in dealing with an anger-producing situation, viewing thinking and feeling as functionally inseparable. Empathy, for example, can change thinking from critical to compassionate (*The Growth of the Mind: And the Endangered Origins of Intelligence*, Addison-Wesley, 1997) and RETHINK has drawn on this concept as well.

The authors have been involved over the years with the following who made major contributions to RETHINK development and application: Parents Anonymous Association, Jewish Social Services, District of Columbia Police and Schools, 4H Clubs, Boys and Girls Clubs of America, National Center on Families and Fathers of the Casey Foundation. And appreciation is extended to Research Press, Champaign, IL, for publishing and distributing RETHINK manuals and videos on anger management for parents, children, and teens. Special appreciation is extended to Dr. Ayman EI-Mohandis, M.D., Chairman, George Washington University School of Public Health and Health Services, Washington, DC, who brought IMHI into the School in 2000 to continue its work.

CHAPTER 1

Skills for Creative Anger: RETHINK

Anger is an emotion. Anger is energy. Using anger creatively is putting that powerful emotion/energy to good use. And good use is incorporated in the acronym, RETHINK: seven skills that can help you learn how to manage your anger and use it creatively. More than ten years of research, workshops, and programs with school systems, adult groups, and the media, make it clear that using RETHINK anger management skills assures creative outcomes that enrich relationships, resolve conflicts, and contribute to physical and emotional health.

RETHINK consists of these seven skills:

R—Recognize your anger and what triggers it.

E—Empathize with the other person and put yourself in the other person's shoes (in other words, listen with your heart).

T—Think about the situation and your anger and try to reframe the situation in a less angry way. Humor can help to reframe a situation and reduce tension.

H—Hear what the other person is communicating with words and nonverbal actions. Hear (listen) with your complete attention.

I—Integrate respect with your responses. Use "I" statements.

N—Notice how your body reacts to your feeling angry. Notice how you calm yourself.

K—Keep your attention on the present problem.

Anger is a universal emotion. It is expressed in many different ways, such as in body posture, called attitude; on the road, called road rage; in the workplace, called harassment; and in schools, sometimes in the form of bullying. You experience anger at home, and in the extreme form it is called domestic violence. You see it in the government, called dissembling. And, around the world, in the most destructive expression, it is called terrorism. Anger is expressed in every form of communication, including newspapers, television shows, as well as information and entertainment programming.

We know the damage that anger energy can generate in terms of health and human relationships. We also know that the same energy can be useful when actions are taken to recognize the sources of the anger. RETHINK skills provide many ways to end conflicts, and help improve health and human relationships. Anger is needed to alert you that you are in danger, and that you are vulnerable, and that you are being mistreated. Anger is needed for a response to what is making you feel fear.

The RETHINK skills are both useful in managing your anger and in improving your interpersonal skills. They will pave the way for you to function more effectively in a variety of settings at home, at school, at the workplace, and in the community with family and friends. RETHINK is also a creative act as it provides the skills to see the anger producing situation in a different light. Here are two examples:

There was a long line at the security section of an airport and people were becoming angry as the process was held up repeatedly because someone did not have the right papers or tickets and it took what seemed an eternity to get the problems resolved. As the frustration grew, a new problem emerged. Here came a man, rolling his baggage, passing people in the line who were in no mood for this intrusion. He added to the anger. But, as he passed people, he had a smile, and explained that his plane had arrived late and he needed to make a connection that was leaving in ten minutes. The people in the line, hearing his explanation, now felt empathy for the man—they had the same experiences—let him through and even wished him luck!

This is what is meant by seeing an anger producing situation in a different light. The skills used in this scenario were Empathy, and having information in order to Think about the situation differently. It also required the skill of Hearing the explanation.

A cartoon by Tom Toles of the *Washington Post* captured the frustration and anger generating experiences at airport security lines by drawing a security line going directly to the plane. Humor can also be used as a RETHINKing tool. It is well known to break tension, and anger certainly includes tension.

If conflict is unresolved, anger can last a lifetime, forming ghosts that haunt you as they reappear to influence reactions to new causes of anger responses. Using RETHINK as a tool to change your perspective on situations that have roused your anger can be used to address experiences you had many years ago, even back to childhood. Here is one story adapted from Anne Tyler's novel, *Dinner at the Homesick Restaurant* (New York: Ballantine Books, 2005).

For the past thirty-five years, Cody Tull has been furious with his father, Beck, who had "ditched" the family when Cody was still a boy. When they finally met again, after the funeral of Cody's mother, the son began to vent his long held anger. "How could you do that? How could you just dump us on our mother's mercy?" The mother, Pearl, had had fierce rages, often terrifying to the children. "We were kids, we were only kids. We had no way of protecting ourselves. We looked for your help. We listened for your step at the door so we'd be safe, but you just turned your back on us. You didn't lift a finger to defend us." Cody had bent closer to his father as he unloaded his pain and misgivings.

After a long pause, Beck's reply was poignant: "She wore me out," he began. He had married "up" and as he told his story, he explained how his life's goal had been to make his wife happy. He had succeeded at first, but later on he said:
"She saw my faults. No matter how hard I tried, it seemed like everything I did got muddled, spoiled, turned into an accident."

If he would bring home a toy to cheer up the family, his wife would say it was too expensive. Cody and Beck remembered together the archery set the father had brought home. His plan for a family trip to the country never worked out. A quarrel between their two children ended up with an arrow getting shot off accidentally and hitting Cody's mother in the shoulder. When Beck returned from his next trip, his wife told him that the wound had become infected and she had nearly died.
"For me, it was the last straw. . . . I said, 'Pearl, I am leaving.'"

Beck went on to tell his son about how he had checked on his children from afar, reluctant to reopen a relationship with Pearl. And he hoped that now he and his children could have a relationship missed for so many years.

After this information, Cody saw his father in a totally different light. Actually, his father was a fragile, pathetic man, needing his support just as Cody had needed his father's, not at all the all-powerful Dad whom he had imagined and toward whom he had felt so much anger.

A change in perspective (how you think about the situation) can modify the feeling of anger. Can you remember having such a change in your perception that ended your anger? Have you seen a film or read a book that shows a character transform how he thought about a person, thus seeing him in a different light?

One Skill at a Time

There are not a lot of experiences involving anger where a change in perception is made, a change in behavior is seen, and we are able to find a way to calm ourselves, and the anger producing situation cannot be resolved. Frequently, however, anger is either left to fester or acted out in nonproductive ways. Understanding the underlying forces of anger and knowing the RETHINK skills provide tested ways to deal with anger producing situations. These skills are not something learned in one hour or even from one reading. In order to be able to incorporate the RETHINK skills into your daily repertoire of responses, you need to be patient with yourself, to practice, and not to fear mistakes. But most of all you must practice.

The Components of Anger

Anger has three components. One is physiological: how the body reacts to angry feelings. Another is cognitive: how the brain reacts (that is, what automatic thoughts make us angry?) The third is behavioral: what actions or inactions are taken when we are angry? The Table below describes the components of each category:

Body/Physiological	Thoughts/Cognitive	Action/Behavior
Heart races	It's not fair!	Hit spouse/spank child
Headache	She's out to get me!	Drive fast
Stomachache	No one loves me!	Yell, cry, and throw things
Tension in shoulders	I hate my life!	Walk out, or run away
Blurred vision	I can't see straight!	Get drunk
Throat feels tight	Everything always goes wrong for me!	Sulk, get depressed

Do any of these features fit you? How does your body alert you when you are getting angry or when you have already reached a full state of anger? Do you feel tension? Where? Does your stomach start to ache? How about a headache? We know people who say that until they start to cry they don't even realize that they are angry. Others say that the mounting tension in their shoulders is the cue that they are feeling angry. And still others say that tightening their lips and squinting their eyes are their cues to anger. What about you? (Write down your responses.)

When you are angry, what do you think about?
What do you tell yourself?
Do you have a secret conversation with yourself?
What do you say?

In these conversations, are you negative or positive? That is, do you say "I'm not going to let that jerk do this to me!" or do you say, "I've got to work this out!" Negative thoughts fuel and escalate anger. And what about your behavior (your actions) when you are angry? From your experiences, what sort of actions do you find most constructive. That is, which actions do you find:

Communicate your dissatisfaction?
Create an atmosphere most conducive to resolving or avoiding conflict?
How does your body react when you become angry? And when you become very angry?
Is there a difference? Can you feel it?

Keep your notes and at some later time in your reading they will be referred to again.

Learning the Skills That Help to Resolve Conflict: RETHINK

Start with an "R"

Let's begin with the first letter of RETHINK—R. R stands for Recognize. Before you do anything else you need to recognize when you are angry. What triggers your anger? Can you remember what you were thinking the moment when your body started to give you signals that something was not right? What did you do? In order to recognize your anger, you must first pay attention. Establish an Early Warning Detection System. Noticing what is happening in your body is a way of understanding and utilizing the physical changes that occur from experiencing anger. Each person has his own unique body signals. What body signals alert you that you are feeling angry?

In Chapter 2, you will read more extensively on the relationship between anger and your health. It is important to recognize anger signals from those around you. A group exercise that is fun is asking teens to talk about how they know when their parents or teachers or siblings are angry. "My mom gives me the pointy eyebrow!" one will say. "My dad's muscles twitch!"

says another. "My teacher pulls her lip way down and frowns, like she just tasted something awful!" says a third. Learning to recognize anger and what may trigger it in others is as important a lesson as any. In Chapter 4 you will read more extensively on the importance of Recognizing anger in yourself and in others. Please note that with the exception of the first skill (Recognize), there is no required order for using the rest of the seven RETHINK skills.

Learning to Use the T: Think

"Man is not disturbed by events, but by the view he takes of them."
(Epictetus)

It seems paradoxical that the key element in managing the powerful emotion of anger is the dispassionate action of thinking. It is strange but true—thinking is the cornerstone of anger management. How we perceive events, how we interpret a word or a gesture, are as important to the anger process as the reality of the situation, as any disinterested objective witness can attest. However, perceptions and interpretations may well be accurate as to what has made a person angry, and in that case, creative anger is used to deal with the situation without escalating the anger. Using RETHINK skills can alter the outcome. It is important to keep an open mind to Think about the situation in other terms. You may well have misinterpreted the situation as you respond with your own anger. Learning to Think before reacting to a situation is crucial to a more desired productive outcome. There are numerous ways to Think about a situation.

Use of Self-Talk

As you Recognize your anger alarm sounding off, think about what you do or tell yourself. Self-talk can be calming or upsetting. Do you have an alternative action to take? Do you speak positively to yourself? Optimistically? "Okay, this traffic can't last forever," or "I came here to dine, so I'm in no hurry—I'm going to sit back and enjoy this meal," or "I can handle this. I will not blow up at anyone or myself—that would only make matters worse."

Or, do you think in the negative? Get exasperated. Think the worst. Generalize. "I'll never catch up on the work with that lazy secretary." Or "Why can't my wife ever match my socks, ever?" Or "Why does this always happen to me?" Or "I know he/she is out to get me." Such thoughts add fuel to a situation that may not have been incendiary at all. Positive thoughts can dampen an explosive situation and calm your bodily responses. Examples of how people RETHINK and channel their anger:

1. Depersonalize the situation (or person) that is triggering your anger.

   Example: Zak wrote his final exam on the computer only to learn that his roommate borrowed his computer and erased his paper. All of his work was lost. He was furious! Rather than become discouraged or take his anger out on his roommate, he decided to use his anger energy to rewrite the exam. He began to think of the version that was lost as the first draft, which had been awkward and unclear. When he handed in the paper, he used Think skills to consider that this paper was a finer rendition of the first paper he had written and lost. He smiled at how curious fate was in helping him improve his product. His grade A+ convinced him that he was not just smart, but that he had Good Thinking on his side.

   This did not mean he saw his roommate's act in any way less than it was—a direct violation of friendship and decency. It meant that Zak, realizing the paper was lost, saw no value in attacking his roommate, but rather to get busy writing another paper. He would talk with his roommate and see if they could find some way to deal with this detrimental behavior so it wouldn't happen again.

2. Redirect the aggressive energy. Use the energy. Find a mission.

   Example: Nancy was feeling envious of the beautiful clothes her sister Christine had bought for the holidays. Nancy could not afford to buy even one new dress for this season. This feeling of envy was not a new experience. There had been a long history of the parents favoring Christine by giving her more clothes than Nancy during childhood and the teen years. The parents gave no reason for this, except to occasionally say that Christine was insecure socially and needed help.

   Nancy decided to use her anger energy from this continuing disparity by going to the homeless shelter and helping people less fortunate than she to have an enjoyable holiday. She recruited a crowd of young and fun-loving friends to join her. Instead of thinking, "How unfortunate I am! My sister always gets everything she wants! It's not fair!" she found herself changing her way of thinking. "How lucky I am to be able to bring a little joy to these people facing real tragedy." She felt enriched by the experience and felt her earlier thoughts were shallow in judging herself the "poor sister." The joy of giving and the pleasure of friends made for a magical and memorable day. She was not unaware of the unfairness that her sister was given clothes and she was not, but she did not want her life to be limited by that knowledge. Her parents weren't going to change so she would turn her interests and skills into helping others. Another example of redirecting the aggressive energy:

Example: Walter was furious as well as sad when his wife Charlotte died. He felt certain that her doctor had been negligent and that the hospital had actually made mistakes in her treatment. He could find no one at that time who would take an interest in his case, no lawyer, no medical association, and no hospital authority. His anger mounted with each frustrating encounter. He decided to enroll in law school at the age of fifty-five and enlisted the advice of many of his professors as he continued to focus on the case of his wife's unnecessary death. After he earned his degree, he sued and won the largest settlement on malpractice charges up to that time. He founded a law firm, from which he has since retired, which is now preeminent in such cases; also he has established a foundation to work for patients' rights. This is creative anger!

3. Use your head: Practice restraint and responsiveness, and save face.

Example: Karen was presenting to a class of new recruits at the counseling center on the latest research on the numbers of people who were suffering from eating disorders. Bonnie, a colleague, interrupted and said, "You are wrong! The figures are exactly the opposite of what you said." Karen felt angry and attacked, but managed it well. She responded, "Perhaps we have been reading two different journals." Then she turned to the new recruits and said, "Let us check our figures on the rates of occurrence and we, Bonnie and I, will get back to you on this."

4. Commit yourself to letting go of your anger.

Example: Nadine broke off the relationship with Joe five months ago. Joe was devastated. He had finally found the perfect mate for himself, he thought. He couldn't believe she didn't feel the same way. Then he learned that she was dating another man. He was furious. How could she, only five months out of their relationship? He started to feel crazed. All he could think about was Nadine. Soon he found himself in and out of the internist's office with stomach pains. His physician recommended medication to calm his nerves and psychotherapy. Joe learned to think about his relationship with Nadine in a different way. He realized that staying with Nadine would have always been a struggle. She was not his soul mate. He set out to find his true love. Remember, holding on to your anger can be hazardous to your physical as well as emotional well-being.

5. Distinguish between an honest mistake and an aggressive act meant to harm you.

   Example: Someone took your seats at an opera. Probably it was an honest mistake. Thinking it's an unintended mistake defuses the anger. But if you experience an intentional affront; for example, someone cuts you off to take a parking space you were maneuvering to take, you see this as intentional. While you can't change the situation, and you are angry, you can use the anger energy creatively and tell the person you are sorry he took the place you were to take and hoped he wouldn't do that to someone who might retaliate in undesired ways. You express your anger. You warn him that his behavior would not be tolerated by everyone and you move on to find another parking space.

6. Make a good "no call."

   Referees do this in a basketball game when they let play continue because they have decided that what may look like a foul wasn't one after all. Anyone watching basketball games sees situations that would make most people furious. There are acts that are called "fouls" and they happen frequently in games. The players surely experience feelings of anger, but their training prepares them for these situations and they do not allow anger to change their behavior. No one is going to get them to stop playing their best in order to respond in anger to a foul. Besides, they get a free throw! Sometimes, two, and occasionally, three!

   Example: You are about to get in the checkout line at the grocery store with a basketful of groceries, when a woman with just a few items scoots in front of you. As they say in New York, "Fugetabout" it. It's not worth the upset.

   Give yourself credit for not "blowing your stack." Give others credit for the same thing.

   Example: The elevator broke this morning. Sam decided to walk the seven flights of stairs and consider it his exercise for the day. And he said to himself, "Good thinking, self!" This is also known as making lemonade out of lemons.

7. Fantasize.

   Write the letter you dream about, "telling that so-and-so off," then burn it. Write a second version, then a third, etc., until you write a version that feels balanced. Even then, you may decide not to send it.

8. Search for the humor in the situation.

Example: Because the city failed to notify him by mail that his driving license was nearing expiration, Richard was forced to go to City Hall to renew his driver's license personally. Upon entering the room, he was confronted by a line snaking along the wall of similar applicants and realized that he would lose the better part of his morning getting this simple task done. His blood began to boil with anger. He started a conversation with the next person in line and soon the two of them and others in the line were laughing at the absurdity of the situation. The poor guys and gals who had caused them this trouble had to work today, while they were swapping jokes that they had received on their e-mail or remembered. And everything sounded funny to them. We might say they were a bit hysterical! They had to be shushed by authorities in the office, who were working while they were enjoying a holiday spirit.

9. Put things into perspective.

"One of the nice things about feeling rotten is having a good excuse to stay in bed tucked up with an entertaining book" (Alex Guinness, English actor and writer).

Example: Say to yourself, "In the year 2025, this won't even matter."

H and E or Hear with Empathy Are the Next Skills to Learn

It is almost impossible to Hear what another person is saying without incorporating Empathy as part of the process. And Chapter 5 expands on these two critical RETHINK Skills.

Empathy is the ability to understand what another person may be feeling, that is, putting yourself in the other person's shoes. The RETHINK skill of Empathy is closely allied with the skill of Hearing. To fully appreciate what another person may be feeling requires attentive listening to both the words and the feelings behind the words. Nonverbal cues, such as stiffening the body in anger, can mean as much or more than the actual words a person speaks. To Hear with Empathy requires giving up judging the speaker and stifling the natural impulse to impose your own thoughts and feelings. This does not mean that you must agree with what is being said—good listening does not require hypocrisy. Just listen with your heart as well as an open mind—paying full attention and attempting to understand the other person's point of view. When you listen with empathy, your objective is not to change the other person's point of view (although that may happen). Your objective is simply to put yourself in the other person's shoes. Only when you can do this can you have an opportunity to understand why other people feel the way they do or why they experience a situation differently from you. Besides, just being heard helps the other person calm down and feel less angry. We often yell when we are angry because we want to be Heard.

Answering the following questions will help you Hear more effectively and defuse the anger: What is the person upset or worried about? Can you let the person know, by words, gestures (or a combination of both) that you understand the feelings by just repeating what he has said? Can you identify some of the feelings the person might be experiencing?

Example: A waitress has just been rude to you, triggering your anger. Imagine that her last customer has stiffed her for the tip. Tell her you see the restaurant is busy, and that perhaps she is having a rough day because it is so busy. What can you order that will be quick and easy?

Empathy takes effort, and a little selflessness. It is time-consuming, at least at first. But it is also true that the short-run cost creates a long-term profit in the form of better, stronger, personal and business relationships, and less personal stress. Besides it is a very caring way to be with another person and has a magical way of diffusing anger.

Naturally, when you Hear with Empathy you don't ask many questions. In fact, cross-examination-like questioning is the opposite of empathic listening, because it measures only knowledge of facts as opposed to feelings and thought about facts. The key to empathic listening is what is called "reflective listening"—where the listener "reflects" back the feelings that are being expressed through words, gestures, or tone of voice. To hear with Empathy means the ability to identify the speaker's feelings: to give them a name. Sometimes naming feelings can be difficult. Many people were never taught how to express their feelings and even adults have trouble articulating what they are feeling. Many counselors teach struggling couples to practice reflective listening. It is an extremely helpful and empowering tool. When used properly, reflective listening not only defuses anger but it can also bring people together, reinvigorate love, and energize a relationship. Here are some suggestions of how to phrase reflective listening statements:

It seems like you are feeling . . .
It sounds like you are feeling . . .
I wonder if you are feeling . . .
I get the impression that you might be feeling . . . Is that right?

Empathy is used when we feel compassion for other people or recognize that they are having a problem or a bad day. Identify with the predicament. Surely you've been there, done that, at least once or twice. As soon as you realize that the other person's anger may be about their predicament, and not you, you begin to manage your own anger.

Example: Dad was exploding after feeling very powerless to control his son, frightened that his son would get into trouble and develop a bad reputation. After the explosion, Dad gave himself some time to calm down and reflect. He remembered that his son, Matt, is a good kid and was doing what kids do. He, as a young boy, also did things that drove his parents up a wall and was bitterly reprimanded for relatively innocent things. He decided to reengage with Matt, to hear his side of the story and work out an after-school plan that was less troubling to Dad and consistent with Matt's need for being with his friends. Dad felt a bit foolish for reacting so strongly and rescinded the grounding.

Example: Martha swung her car around into the parking lot of the symphony hall, as she had done for the past ten years. She knew where to park and timed things just right. "Hey, YOU! Where do you think you are going? Wanna get us all killed?" The parking attendant was blasting her. Martha was very angry! Who was he to talk to a trustee like that? And she had never so much as dented a fender in this garage. So why should he growl and preach at her? She took a deep breath, calmed herself, and decided that maybe it was really his problem.

"I bet you had a rough day today," she offered instead of justifying her driving, or demanding an apology, or threatening to have him fired. It could easily have escalated in to an "incident."

"Boy, did I ever," replied Jim. He came closer and began to recount an awful day through Martha's open window. "First thing this morning, my boy was hit by a car as he was cycling to school. His arm is in a cast and he can't play football for the rest of the season. Then the sink overflows, and . . . "

Martha sat there and listened. This man had had a terrible day and he needed to tell someone who could sympathize, empathize. His angry outburst had been inappropriate, but understandable, given his stress level. She locked her car and went to her meeting, waving to Jim as she walked toward the elevator.

Now, Martha and Jim exchange warm greetings whenever she comes to a concert or a meeting. They always take a few minutes to tell each other some news, like how the boy's arm is doing and how the team is getting on without him. Martha enjoys these chats and tries to get there early enough to just talk to Jim. And he is always helpful and courteous. Empathy and Hearing what he had to say defused a potential messy blowup.

Notice is the Next Skill to Learn

When you feel angry, you feel agitated. Notice what that feels like in your body. Where does the energy go? —To your head and you get a headache, to your stomach and you have a stomachache, to your legs and they feel wobbly, or to your shoulders that feel stiff. Notice also what calms you down, and learn how to calm yourself. Learning how to quiet your body will help to quiet the anger, rather than escalate it. Look at the difference between helpful and harmful calming techniques. For example, abusing alcohol or food as a reaction to anger is not helpful; indeed, it is potentially harmful to the individual and others.

Intense anger has potential for danger. Work to make anger a *temporary* feeling. It takes a millisecond to get angry, one minute to notice it, and twenty minutes or less to really cool down if you make the effort. During this period, you don't have to swallow it, explode, or suffer with a migraine headache. There are many techniques to help you calm yourself down. Here a just a few.

Some Calming Techniques

Use Relaxation techniques and visualization to let go of your anger and calm yourself. Although these behaviors may sound either too simplistic or "hokey," some classic relaxation techniques are tried and true ways for reducing or defusing anger:

a. Visualize your anger in a balloon and let the anger fly away.
b. Visualize your anger far away on the horizon.
c. Think about your life in the distant future without anger.
d. Throw your anger into a body of water and watch it float away, or symbolically put it or throw it away. (You can even tell yourself that you can retrieve your anger at any time!)
e. Do breathing/relaxation exercises or just take some deep breaths.
f. Do physical exercises: take a walk; do some yoga.
g. Meditate. Buddhists label their anger and repeat it over and over.
h. Think of a relaxing phrase and say it to yourself.
i. Relax in a warm bath.
j. Pray.
k. Put yourself in "time out," and walk around the block.
l. Count to hundred backward.
m. Listen to relaxing music, and sing along. Better still, dance along.
n. Call or e-mail a close friend.

Again, the Use of Self-Talk

Once you are able to calm your body's responses, then it is time to engage your head and start thinking. Remember the discussion above about self-talk when we discussed the skill of THINKing? What do you tell yourself when your anger is triggered? Actually, talking to yourself is a very normal activity. Do you try to calm yourself by being positive: "Okay, I may not like this situation but I need to be thoughtful about my reaction. I don't want to lose my job. Why does this always happen to me? My boss is out to get me. I hate everything about him." Notice how the first thoughts can serve to reduce the level of arousal, while the second series of thoughts can only serve to heighten the anger.

Remember the Last Straw Principle

Be aware of the last straw principle when you are overwhelmed by fatigue and stress. Will the next little annoyance cause you to blow your cool? We suggest you first practice Recognizing your anger and then Noticing how to calm yourself down before you respond in any way to a provocation. We also recommend that you be aware of additional stress and pressure in your life that may arouse your ire more quickly than usual. Look for additional support for yourself at these times rather than lose your temper and regret your actions.

Integrate is the Next Skill to Be Learned

Another RETHINK skill is I—Integrate your feelings of love and respect for the other person, and into the anger-filled moment. It may call for you to acknowledge your own responsibility in the situation.

The ability to express grievances effectively involves integrating seemingly contradictory feelings of love or respect with the anger. You have probably heard people say, "Be assertive, not aggressive." That means being in control of your anger, making "I" statements rather than "You" statements (which are blaming statements.) A helpful format to express "I" statements is:

I feel . . . (say what you are feeling)
When . . . (describe the situation)
Because . . . (tell something about yourself).

You may feel so hurt yourself that all you want to do is strike back—regardless of whether you think it would make you feel better, stop the pain, or end the onslaught of aggression. The reality, however, is that attacking on a personal level rarely if ever has a favorable or positive effect in an argument. Just the opposite usually occurs. The anger increases, the destructiveness magnifies, and the conflict turns into a lose-lose situation for both parties.

Example: Vicki and Sally have been friends for many years. Recently, Vicki began to feel resentment toward Sally. She felt judged, manipulated, and misunderstood. When Sally refused a request that Vicki made, Vicki stopped calling Sally. She refused to join her in any activities. Finally Sally pushed Vicki to talk. Because the anger had been building for so long, when Vicki finally spoke her mind, she made accusations: "You are judgmental, controlling, selfish!" Her final words were: "I'm just expressing my feelings."

In that example, Vicki makes aggressive, accusatory, and critical attacks on Sally. Not once did Vicki acknowledge her own responsibility for the situation. She made no "I" statement. If she did, it might sound something like this: "Sally, I am feeling hurt and angry because you didn't want to write the reference letter for me and I felt let down. It was especially hard for me because I respected your opinion so much." This would give Sally an opportunity to express her reasons for not wanting to write the letter as well as to express her regret that she hurt Vicki's feelings.

Making a *direct, honest* "I" statement about your feelings is difficult. It is important to be able to express your emotions while at the same time being sensitive to the other person's feelings. Being articulate when expressing anger is very difficult. Sputtering and emotional outbursts often result from the frustration of not being able to express angry feelings, until we learn better management skills.

When we speak, we expect that our words and actions actually have measurable effects on other people. Accidental or negligently spoken words also effect the listener, especially so when the words are hurtful or disrespectful. Since "I" statements are about the speaker, not the listener, they reduce the likelihood of accidental harm. Remember, hurtful statements once spoken are like feathers let loose from a ruptured pillow—impossible to take back. Using "I" statements forces each of us to take responsibility, and not load onto others our own emotional baggage with "you" statements.

In angry exchanges, it is absolutely essential that you differentiate between the offending act and the overall character of the offender. There is much to commend the aphorism: "mistakes are events, not an entire person." Emotional energy focused on rectifying the action or fixing the problem that needs to be addressed is much more productive for any relationship than attacking the overall character of the offender. Plotting revenge or getting even, name calling, judging, or unfairly criticizing or blaming, doesn't solve any problem. Nor, in the end, can any of it provide lasting satisfaction.

You may feel so hurt yourself that all you want to do is strike back—regardless of whether you think it would make you feel better, stop the pain, or end the onslaught of aggression.

The reality, however, is that attacking on a personal level rarely if ever has a favorable effect in an argument. Just the opposite usually occurs. The anger increases, the destructiveness magnifies and the conflict turns into a lose-lose situation for the involved parties. If you find yourself, however, chronically disrespected or someone chronically blows up or loses control with you, it does not mean that you allow that person to abuse or hurt you. As a matter of fact, if you are in an abusive situation, find help, get out, and make sure to protect yourself. Integrating love and respect in anger exchanges has its time and place.

Keep to the Problem

Finally, let's focus on the letter K, which stands for "keeping to the present problem at hand" and "Keeping in present time." It could also stand for "Kitchen sink" as in "Don't throw the kitchen sink into an argument about the bedroom." Keeping to the present involves maintaining your focus on the immediate issue. Do not use the occasion to bring up old grudges from the past. Don't use statements beginning with, "You always . . . ," or "You never. . . . " Or, as a parent, do not remind your child that she always leaves her clothes on the floor. When you stay in the present tense, anger management and conflict resolution is made possible.

Staying in the present situation means you face the reality of the situation without bringing out all the old baggage. This skill involves effective problem solving techniques. Define the actual problem. Whatever the immediate problem, look for ways to resolve it by asking yourself what else can you (we) do? Restrain from backing away or from being overly aggressive. Look for alternative ways of thinking about the problem. Be committed to finding a workable solution even if your first idea is unsuitable or even irrelevant. Brainstorm for ideas and evaluate the options. The more options you think of the better. Then take the best suggestion. Try it. If that doesn't work you can always go back to the drawing board and come up with another solution or pick up on your second-best solution.

Example: Dianne was so angry she could hardly contain herself. She wanted to hit someone, throw something, or scream. Paul was drunk again! He had promised he would stay sober and now she felt betrayed as well as embarrassed at this public disgraceful behavior. She was angry and every memory of previous lapses, previous humiliations, flooded her mind. She was tempted to begin her tirade and review all the previous time she had been through this same scenario, but she knew how futile that routine was. Now she must KEEP to the present problem and look for solutions. She needed help and Paul needed help. She would get him settled in bed, and while he was sleeping, she would contact his brother and mother, his best friend Tim, his partner at work, and try to decide where the best treatment center was for him. They would help her decide how to get him into treatment, how to handle the costs, and how to persuade him that a new approach was necessary. Perhaps they would hire one of those intervention specialists. If she could just keep everyone focused on the problem at hand, they would come up with some options for solving it—the problem had become repetitious and made everyone mad at Paul at one time or another.

Example: You call your mother-in-law and the greeting you get is: "Oh, it's you. I haven't heard from you in so long that I forgot your name. You never call me anymore, not for the holidays, not when I was so sick and I nearly died, not when you receive my gift, etc." If she could learn to KEEP to the present time, it would be so much easier to call her. This would be a more desired greeting: "Oh it's you, finally! I must admit I was feeling lonely; even angry and needed a call form you. I love hearing from you; it makes my day."

What NOT to Do when expressing anger and trying to resolve a situation:

Blame, blame, blame (directly or indirectly).
Hurt yourself and/or others.
Break things.
Punish someone close to you, or go out of your way to make them furious.
Take drugs, drink alcohol, or overeat.
Sink into a deep depression.
Drive your anger away in a "big Rig down I-95."
Intentionally provoke someone else's anger.
Conclude you know what the other person is thinking without asking the person.
Pretend you aren't feeling angry (denial).

Putting the Skills Together

David is an experienced trial lawyer who coaches his twelve-year-old son's basketball team, "for relaxation." In the law court, he is aggressive, tenacious, but suitably respectful of judges and counsel, and in control. On the basketball court, however, he has trouble keeping in control. David continually questions referees' calls, and gets called for technical fouls on a regular basis. He hollers rapid fire and inconsistent instruction to the boys. When confronted by one of the other parents, David justifies his behavior by saying, "the boys play too hard to be beaten by stupid referees." Publicly, he laughs off his outburst, saying that he wants to "teach the boys how to compete in the real world." But privately, David confides in his wife that he is worried about his excesses, but just can't control himself: "It's like a fireball forms in the pit of my stomach and my anger takes on a life of its own." What's worse, David thinks that he is "hard wired" this way, and that change is impossible. During and after the season, he was in and out of doctors' offices complaining of chest and stomach pains. Even David's son has asked his father to "chill." "Chill" is one of those remarkable idiomatic expressions that exactly captures the essence of what it suggests—cooling off, turning down the heat. So, how is it that David can't manage his acute reaction to the highly emotionally charged situation represented by an athletic contest?

What advice would you give David after reading this chapter? Would you tell him to RETHINK how he experiences his son's basketball games? A good idea. David can begin by seeing himself as different from his son; he can try to Think of the games as what they are supposed to be—fun, not torment—for the boys. He can learn relaxation techniques when the referee makes the inevitable bad call or one of the boys makes a stupid foul. He can Recognize and interrupt some obsolete automatic thoughts that pop into his head; for example, "That big bully is out to shame me again and make a nothing of me." Before he goes off he can try to Empathize with the boys who are, after all, doing the best they can; he can Think about how embarrassed he would be at his behavior if he were in his son's sneakers; he can pay attention to his own body signs and when he feels the rush inside his body he can take a "time out" from the tension and let another Dad take over. The point is that David has options. We all do. His anger does not need to consume him or the team. David has the power to take control, live more happily (and possibly longer), and, overall, to improve his relationship with his son.

You too can learn to RETHINK your anger. It will take time and practice. You may want to focus on each skill separately, or combined—whatever helps you master the skills. Everyone makes mistakes while learning. Be tolerant of your sometimes clumsy attempt and reread sections that you think might help. In the following chapters, you will have opportunities to draw on your experiences and see how they might benefit from the skills of RETHINK.

CHAPTER 2

RETHINKing Anger Is Good for Your Health

How can a basic human emotion such as anger be associated with either good or bad health? Many readers will view this idea with skepticism. Even if you ask your physician about this notion, he may well encourage your doubting. Yet the idea has been getting more attention and research over the last several decades. We (the authors) first became interested in this relationship when the National Institutes of Health held a conference on anger that they called, "The Disabling Emotion." Since then we have been monitoring the mounting body of evidence that relates mismanaged anger to cardiovascular disease and a growing number of ailments. Notice that we use the word *mismanaged*, because anger, or more accurately, the energy, the adrenaline, which anger generates, can be used creatively so that the source of the anger is not only resolved, but may also enrich life's experiences. Well-managed anger can be good for your health, and can in fact be enabling to health. That anger is related to health, and that it may be destructive or empowering, is the premise of this chapter.

The Role of History in the Mind/Body Connection

You may find it hard to believe, but there continues to be resistance to accepting the mind/body connection. And history certainly played a role in that resistance. It was in the beginning of the seventeenth century that an arbitrary division of mind and body was made in Western cultures.

The medical sciences were free to explore the physical body, leaving the mind under the control of the church. The mind was viewed as being more spiritual than physical and the church seemed the appropriate institution to tend to it. The resistance to change in thinking is expected in some areas of human endeavor. There is a sense of comfort and familiarity with the accepted and tested ways of viewing the self and the world. Change can rouse fear. What is going to happen to me? What is going to happen to what I believe? What is the risk of trying new medicines, new ways of dealing with things that frighten me? And anger may well be tapped when the belief is threatened.

But to wait over two centuries for Western cultures to begin to study the interconnections between the mind and the body is staggering to consider. Yet, it has only been in the last thirty-five to forty years that scientists around the world are studying these interconnections.

How Does It Work?

Anger, like fear or joy, is a basic human emotion. All people experience it, some more frequently, some less, and some more intensely than others. Anger is a feeling that usually occurs with other feelings such as sadness, guilt, fear, frustration, and even love. As discussed in Chapter 1, anger is fueled by our thinking.

Anger is an inevitable reaction to perceived threats of harm. It is an emotional reaction that can cause the body to react in as quickly as eight seconds. Anger's effect on the body begins in the central nervous system. The major players in the nervous system are the brain and spinal chord, but there is more going on in peripheral systems. One such system, the somatic nervous system, directs sensory and motor components, primarily serving the skin and voluntary muscles. Another, the autonomic nervous system, primarily serves internal organs through the sympathetic nervous system and the parasympathetic nervous system. The nervous system also contains billions of cells called neurons that give off an electrochemical charge, releasing chemicals called neurotransmitters. The neuroendocrine system consists of glands controlled by the nervous system that secrete hormones that have immediate effects on specific organs. The pituitary works with the brain and produces a hormone called adrenocorticotropin (ACTH), which is released into the blood stream and plays a central role in directing a response to anger and, in turn, acts on the two adrenal glands. One adrenal gland secretes two major hormones: alderstone and cortisol. Cortisol is a steroid hormone that increases the rate and strength of heart contractions and affects every organ in the body. The other adrenal gland secretes hormones norepinephrine and epinephrine (commonly known as adrenaline), which are neurotransmitters. It is this glandular action releasing hormones that says, "I want to pump you up," and prepares the body for stress. The body's emergency response system is thus activated. Norepinephrine and epinephrine raise the basal metabolic rate, increase the force of the heart's contractions, cause dilation of the pupils and bronchi, and constrict blood vessels. There is also a decrease in blood flow to the gut, digestive activity, kidney activity, blood flow to the skin, and the activity of gastric glands and pancreas.

Many people have great difficulty recognizing or dealing with this emotion, anger, which sets off all these body reactions. And if the anger is not resolved, the energy remains, causing serious health problems.

But it is this same energy that is used in RETHINKing an anger-producing situation to reach a satisfactory resolution and a restoration of the body to balance and more positive feelings.

The important lesson is: Anger can play havoc on our bodies and on our health; but anger can also be used in nondestructive and creative ways that enhance our health, both mental and physical.

RETHINKing Your Anger

How do you view anger? Have you had some good experiences with anger whereby showing your anger, you have been able to stop the undesired or even dangerous behavior of someone you know or a member of your family? Think of one of those experiences:

What triggered your anger?
What did you do?
How did you feel?
What were you thinking?
What did the person you were angry with do in response?
How did that person feel?
What was the end result?
Was there resolution?

Use those same questions to describe a situation where showing your anger had some undesired results, such as: you lost a friend, a job, or you came down with the flu. You might even have been physically injured.

Anger can be helpful in alerting you that something is wrong, perhaps even threatening, or that something is unfair, or something is dangerous. How you respond to these threats can be a problem when:

It triggers a desire to hurt someone else.

It jeopardizes your health, safety, or opportunities for love, friendship, and success.

It drains your empathy, blinding you to the feelings or reasoning of others.

It turns everything into a fight—even things you and your opponent usually agree upon.

It targets your opponent's person as well as his or her ideas.

It prevents you from relating to someone as an individual rather than as a member of a group, whose position angers you.

It causes you to value winning the fight above all else, even the preservation of the relationship.

Anger As a Tool for Change

Anger has a mixed reputation. It is seen by many as a good thing because it lets the one you are angry with know something is very wrong and needs attention. Power adjustments between two people are often needed. It is seen by others as a bad thing because it is used to hurt others verbally, and sometimes, physically. But anger in and of itself has little relationship to its reputation. Anger need not be destructive. When you manage anger rather than allow anger to manage you, it becomes a force for positive, creative, changes in your life. It is not a feeling to avoid. It alerts you, both physically and mentally, that something needs to change. This is the paradox of anger. When out of control, it can destroy. But when used creatively, it can be a formidable tool for change and growth.

At no time was the productive use of anger more apparent than in the days following the terrorist attacks of September 11, 2001. The world, and especially the people of the United States, roared with fury at the wanton destruction and loss of life. For some, fury led to mindless revenge. They torched Arab-owned businesses and attacked Arab-looking people. The number of workplace discrimination complaints filed by Arab-Americans, Muslims, and Sikhs more than doubled during the three months following the attacks. These workers were victims of anger out of control. Their attackers were no longer focused on the appropriate target, the terrorists. Anger was often acted out on someone who had some of the characteristics of the persons who engaged in terrible acts. But for many more people, anger provided the energy for creative anger responses. It galvanized their will, their talents, their resources, and their courage. They responded in countless ways. Some, such as police and firefighters (many of whom continue to suffer from health problems as a result of breathing in the contaminated air), politicians, and health workers, provided direct services for disaster relief. Others reached out to families and friends who might have been affected. One family reported receiving phone calls and e-mails from relatives and acquaintances in twelve different countries. Communities gathered for candlelight vigils to express their shared grief, anger, and renewed commitment to freedom. People flew the American flag. Almost immediately, thoughts turned to the victims and their families. People gave blood. They donated money. Empathy and caring quickly supplemented their rage. These combined emotions contributed to a steady, continuing response. The nation is still living with the effects of those events.

Anger Is an Important Emotion in Developing Emotional Health

Aristotle had a phrase for it:

> Those who do not show anger at the things that ought to arouse anger are regarded as fools; so too if they do not show anger in the right way, the right time or at the right person.

This concise statement makes it very clear that not only is anger an important emotion, but it is also a universal emotion, necessary to function as a human being. Further, it makes it clear that the way anger is displayed and used requires intelligence, caring, and skills. And, William C. Menninger, in his famous list of *The Criteria of Emotional Maturity*, includes a statement relating to anger, which he refers to as "hostile energy." The Emotional Maturity list is consistent with body/mind linkages as well as expressions of negative feelings. He states: "The capacity to sublimate, to direct one's instinctive hostile energy into creative and constructive outlets is part of emotional maturity." Menninger, in his definition of emotional maturity, is referring to a person who can anticipate that hostile energy will surface in an anger-provoking situation, and has the (RETHINK) skills to transform that energy into creative and constructive acts. How one manages the anger is an important ingredient in all our relationships throughout the entire life span. (The other characteristics of emotional maturity are: The ability to deal constructively with reality; a relative freedom from symptoms that are produced by tensions and anxieties; the capacity to find more satisfaction in giving than receiving; the capacity to relate to other people in a consistent manner with mutual satisfaction and helpfulness; and the capacity to love.)

Temperament and Anger

Temperament is our natural disposition. Research indicates that specific areas of the brain play a crucial role in the development of temperament. Temperament determines how fast you react to a situation that you view as threatening to your physical safety or your emotional well-being; that is, to an anger-generating situation. Do you react very quickly or very slowly to the situation? You are born with your temperament and it shows up in infancy: How does an infant react to noise, movement, light, and handling? How is the baby calmed down or energized? By the end of the first year of life, specific patterns of brain activation differ among infants. These patterns are associated with dispositions and become the foundation of a personality, as well as the starting point of emotional illness or emotional wellness.

When babies who had cried a lot and had more difficult temperaments matured, they have more difficulty regulating their anger as adolescents and as adults. In a safe environment where ways of thinking about provocation are treated calmly, thoughtfully, and as experiences to be learned from, children will grow to manage their anger. However, when a child is the target of harsh, frequent, and intense anger, and especially when a child is very reactive, these circumstances will be reflected in a child's thinking, feeling, and behavior. Chronic anger reaction patterns represent a learned style of coping with stressful life experiences.

The Case of David: A Short Fuse

David loves sports and loves being around kids. He knows, however, that he has a short fuse when an unfair call is made: especially if the unfair call has to do with his son's team! The score was twenty-two to twenty-three when the buzzer sounded and the game was over. The other team won! David went wild, screaming at the referee for calling the game and at the timekeepers who had mistakenly moved the clock ahead by three seconds. He was so out of control that it took three men of the team fathers to restrain him. Although he was correct about the time issue, his son was humiliated, imploring his father to cool it.

David maintains it is his nature and he is partially right. In biological terms, he is hardwired for certain characteristics. But that is certainly not the whole story. Different parts of the brain "talk" to each other; they form neural network relationships. The dialogue between the brain's different regions occurs in much the same way as the dialogue between the brain and the motor areas. The brain trains these areas to react in a certain way. Similarly, the "thinking" part of the brain fires millions of neurons, and links up with and trains the "emotional" part of our brain. Over time we learn, through repetition, to connect certain thoughts with specific feelings. These associations are made early in our life and are repeated over and over until they become second nature, a habit. But new connections can be made and new skills acquired. Your basic temperament seems to influence whether you become a risk taker or are more cautious and reflective. Each end of the temperament scale comes with strengths and weaknesses. The risk taker does not always think of consequences before acting, loving to feel the adrenaline rush when testing limits or challenging the line between danger and safety. The cautious person does not always take action when it is necessary or even crucial. RETHINKing anger involves temperament.

Consider Your Temperament

To use anger energy creatively, it is helpful for you to be familiar with your own temperament. If you tend to respond quickly, almost impulsively, to an anger-generating situation, do you find that you take actions you are later sorry for? Do you tend to go right into action, or do you stop and think first? If you respond with action, how do you know you are not going to contribute to a problem you have not analyzed? Do you shout, threaten the person, or even become physical with the person? Or do you accept what the person is doing that may make you angry and suffer the consequences of retaining the anger energy? If you take a long time to respond, what are the consequences? Perhaps the situation just continues? Here is where RETHINKing skills come in.

Remember the RETHINK skills discussed in Chapter 1. Let's review them again. A quick analysis of the situation will help you:

RECOGNIZE what is making you angry.
EMPATHIZE with the other and see if you can understand what is causing the anger. Can you find words of comfort?
THINK to make sure you have assessed the situation correctly. Think again about the situation. Can you change the way you are thinking about the triggering event?

HEAR what the other person has to say.

INTEGRATE your love/caring and respect for the other. Can you make "I" statements?

NOTICE what calms you down, especially if you have a quick-responding temperament.

KEEP the attention on this situation without referring to other offences.

Your temperament is part of you; you will always have the same temperament. Age can slow down the speed of response to a stimulus, but people in their seventies are still known to have a temperament that responds to a stimulus almost immediately. It is mastering RETHINK skills that can provide the opportunity to slow down taking action, even though the energy is already there for action. Impulsive behavior is often the most dangerous way to respond to an anger-provoking situation. Be familiar with your temperament and decide how soon you need to manage your response.

Anger and Illness

> "A doctor has published evidence that hostility is hard on the heart. I hate that" (George Will).

Everybody knows that when your anger gets out of control it can result in someone getting hurt. But did you know that the first victim of mismanaged anger is often the person holding the anger? Did you ever wonder why, when you get really angry, your eyes bulge, and your heart rate increases? That some people stutter or sputter? We have already described how anger has such a powerful effect on the human body and that scientists have shown that chronically angry and stressed people are more vulnerable to specific diseases. Anger can produce biological changes, muscle tension, changes in vascular flow, and other changes in your body.

Exploring the physiological and psychological sources of anger can help in greater understanding of what is going on in the body and mind as feelings of anger are experienced.

The body-mind connection is referring to the body as the physical part of each person and the mind as the thinking-feeling part of each person. However, historically, the thinking-feeling part of the brain has been separated into cognitive (thinking) and emotional (feeling.) This separation is still accepted in some professions, especially as the thinking is viewed as controlling or managing the feeling.

The work of Stanley Greenspan (*The Growth of the Mind*, Addison-Wesley Publishing Company, Inc., Reading, MA, 1997) makes a convincing case that to separate thinking from feeling tends to take away the humanity of individuals. He also points out that the study of the brain, a focal topic for the decade of the 1990s, demonstrated the physiological relationship in the brain that brings thinking and feeling together. That connectedness impacts on the effects of thinking and feeling on health, both mental and physical health. Your thoughts can affect how you feel emotionally as well as physically; your feelings can affect how you think, and how you assess your health. And the growth in understanding of these interactions has added immeasurably to understanding the amazing complexity of human behavior. These interactions have special meaning as you recognize the role of anger in affecting physical and emotional health. Negative feelings—hopelessness, suspicion, hostility, depression, distrust, and resentment—are seen to have a great impact on the health of people. A common emotion in people harboring negative feelings is usually a high level of anger.

Recent research by Debra Vandervoort (Developmental Learning, Personality, Social, *Current Psychology* 25(1) (Spring 2006): 50–66) provides information from her studies with college students. She was investigating the relationship among hostility, health, belief systems, and ways of coping with anger, anxiety, and sadness in a college student sample. Those students who scored high on a test to measure hostility (an emotion including anger) had poorer physical health than students low on the test of hostility. Those with high hostility scores tended to be vindictive, pessimistic, have unrealistic expectations of themselves and others, and a desire to avoid difficulties. Clearly, these students had no effective skills in dealing with anger. Illnesses associated with hostility include coronary heart disease, anxiety, depression, and general mortality.

Timothy W. Smith has an article in the *Annual Review of Clinical Psychology* (The Effects of Anger/Hostility on Health and Longevity, 2 (2006): 435–467), which underlines the connection between anger/hostility and physical health, including longevity. He points out that while it is difficult to study the complexity of factors affecting health, the connection between anger/hostility and physical health are clearest. And a recent publication, *Educating the Human Brain*, is based on studies of the interaction of feelings and health so that the effects can be noted (Michael I. Posner and Mary K. Rothbart, *American Psychological Association* (2007): 263). It is important to note the increased interest and concern about the thinking/feeling of the mind with the body's health status.

The Harvard Medical School added to this increased interest in the body/mind connection by holding a three-day Medical Continuing Education Program (November 3–5, 2006) on Anger, Irritability, and

Aggression. One of the goals was to provide information on the impact of negative feelings on the physiological health of individuals.

And the American Psychological Association has provided a comprehensive list of the body's reactions to stress, recognizing anger as a stressful state. (Reprinted in the *Washington Post* (January 23, 2007): F2).

1. The nervous system
   When stressed, physically or psychologically, the body suddenly shifts its energy resources to fighting off the perceived threat. In what is known as the "fight or flight" response, the sympathetic nervous system signals the adrenal glands to release adrenaline and cortisol. These hormones make the heart beat faster, raise blood pressure, change the digestive process, and boost glucose levels in the bloodstream. Once the crisis passes, body systems usually return to normal. However, this "fight or flight" response, which at one time in our history was crucial to our survival, appears to be signaled on a daily basis. Thus, ironically what was once considered a survival response, has now become a threat to our health and can have long-term consequences, depending on frequency, intensity, and duration. The body's "adaptive reserves," that is, its ability to return to normal, can be depleted and the body unable to recover. When these responses persist over the long run, immune functioning itself becomes impaired and illness is the result.
2. Musculoskeletal System
   Under stress, muscles tense up. The contraction of muscles for extended periods can trigger tension headaches, migraines, and various musculoskeletal conditions.
3. Respiratory System
   Stress can make you breathe harder and cause rapid breathing—or hyperventilation—which can bring on panic attacks in some people.
4. Cardiovascular System
   Acute stress—stress that is momentary, such as being stuck in traffic—causes an increase in heart rate and stronger contractions of the heart muscles. Blood vessels that direct blood to the large muscles and to the heart dilate, increasing the amount of blood pumped to these parts of the body. Repeated episodes of acute stress can cause inflammation in the coronary arteries, thought to lead to heart attacks. Frequent, intense anger, hostility, and cynicism are correlated with heart disease, the number one killer in the United States, accounting for 40 percent of all deaths. "Hostility is a stronger predictor of death than any other risk factors, like smoking, high blood pressure and

high cholesterol." (D. Goleman, *Emotional Intelligence*. New York: Bantam, 1995.)

5. Endocrine System

When the body is stressed, the brain sends signals from the hypothalamus, causing the adrenal cortex to produce epinephrine—sometimes called the "stress hormones." Liver: when cortisol and epinephrine are released, the liver produces more glucose, a blood sugar that would give you the energy for the "fight or flight" in an emergency.

6. Gastrointestinal System

Stress may prompt you to eat much more or much less that you usually do. If you eat more or different foods or increase your use of tobacco or alcohol, you may experience heartburn or acid reflux.

Stomach: Your stomach can react with "butterflies," or even nausea, or pain. You may vomit if the stress is severe enough.

Bowels: Stress can affect digestion and which nutrients your intestines absorb. It can also affect how quickly food moves through your body. You may find that you have either diarrhea or constipation.

Thus, given body chemistry and quick to anger or more aggressive tendencies, those people whose thoughts automatically trigger anger are at a higher risk of serious illness and even death. If this is not bad enough, there is evidence that people high in hostility are also more apt to engage in risky behaviors such as smoking, drug abuse, overeating, and alcohol use. In turn, each of these unhealthy behaviors can lay the groundwork for a host of diseases.

Anger and Stress and Health: How You Think Makes a Difference

We have pointed out some health issues. But here is a broader picture of the linkages between the mind and the body. For example, people who live in poverty, people who are dissatisfied with their jobs, are objects of prejudice, have been alone for a long time, or lose a loved one suddenly, are far more likely to become ill or die compared to people who are happy, and fulfilled in their lives. Just the act of worrying can elicit body responses, including tears, increased heart rate and blood pressure, increased muscle tension, and irregular breathing. It should be noted that these are also physical reaction to anger-provoking experiences. One thought can cause millions of cellularbiochemical reactions (http://www.womensmindbodyhealth.info/conn31.htm). How you feel, what you believe, CAN affect your health. Fear, anger, cynicism, hopelessness, and helplessness can harm health. Now, this list of the negative reactions to stress and anger should not conceal the fact that some of our best times involve stress. Watch the people at a football game. They are having a great time, the stress is high, but the adrenaline is delightful! And watch children at a carnival as they ride the Ferris Wheel. The stress is high, but the adrenaline is delightful!

Books are read and movies watched that stimulate the adrenaline to flow, but the watchers know they are safe, so it is a secondary thrill. Similarly, when people are angry, they are in a state of stress, adrenaline is high, and they need this adrenaline as energy that can help deal with what had made them angry. What is important is how we use this energy, stimulated by the adrenaline, so that the use of this energy is positive rather than negative. Because we now know that optimism, good humor, a sense of control, and courage can help to improve health or the recovery of health.

Eastern Medicine View of Health and Use of Energy

It is the energy concept that underlies body/mind medicine, contrary to the model of western medicine where physics and chemistry is the basis of much medical research, that is the energy model of eastern medicine (C. Hiew, *Tao of Healing*. Lincoln, NE; Writers Showcase, 2000). This body/mind connection is predicated on the concept of energy as the underlying pattern and force of the universe. And it is assumed that when there is illness, mental or physical, it is because of the energy being out of balance in the individual. The goal of those providing guidance is to help the person restore the energy balance and therefore, restore mental and/or physical health. For example, stress that exceeds manageable limits can contribute to illness. And balance can be restored by relaxation, meditation, and by finding more effective ways of dealing with what has caused the stress. The energy must be throughout the body; when it is focused on the heart rate because of a fear- or anger-rousing experience, it is necessary to think in terms of redistributing the energy. This is often done simply by thinking of the energy going away from the heart and being sent to the limbs. This way of thinking is known as meditation. And the effects of meditation on health are being investigated throughout the United States, in universities, and at the National Institutes of Health in the Alternative Medicine Division.

Additionally, Dr. Herbert Benson, a cardiologist at Harvard University Medical School, found that meditation and yoga could create a physiological state characterized by lowered blood pressure, heart rate, respiration, and metabolism. Dr. Benson emphasized the "relaxation response" as an antidote to illness.

Homeostasis

The body/mind connection has an ally in the homeostatic power of the body. Homeostasis simply means the body wants to get back to a normal, healthy state. And most western medicine depends on that as people recover from operations and illnesses. Those who have the belief, the expectation of getting better, tend to have a greater recovery rate than those who fear they will get worse. And when the fear generates anger, the obstacles to recovery are increased.

Health, Health Services, and Management of Anger

It is one thing to know about the anger-health connection; it is quite another to know about the anger-health *services* connection. You have probably had a number of unpleasant experiences in the process of receiving services that have roused your anger.

Most people have experiences with health care professionals and most are aware of the tendency to submit to the advice of the professionals. The anger they feel at being put in a submissive role is countered by the fear of not receiving the care they need. And the professionals often reinforce that fear as they protect their roles. Sharon Ramey, Stephanie DeLuca, and Karen Echols (Resilience in Families with Children Who Are Exceptional. In: *Resilience for Today: Gaining Strength from Adversity*, ed., E. H. Grotberg. Westport, CT: Praeger Publishers, 2003, 81–104) found that when she wrote an article telling parents about the many problems and limitations of both professional judgment and the services available, and tried to do so in a way that would help parents fulfill their role as a true partner in making judgments about treatment, her writing was not published. The editors thought the information would be too discouraging to parents or would confuse them or cause them not to respect professional judgment. This, in spite of the fact that parents responded to the writing by saying they wished they had been able to read something like that even earlier, to help them in understanding the world of professionals and why they received such differing opinions and attitudes.

There has been a long history of patients having somewhat of a dependency relationship with service providers. Many patients are reluctant to challenge what a doctor says, even when they do not understand the reasoning behind the advice. They become passive and accepting, and whatever anger they feel about being treated like an ignorant child is sti-fled by fear of not receiving treatment. A kind of false loyalty develops between the patient and the doctor, as the patient accepts her role.

Recognizing Pain

The experience of pain and how it is dealt with in the medical associ-ation is a good example of the passive relationship that can develop with service providers. Pain, because it is not measurable, was dismissed as an unimportant vital health indicator. Pain is subjective, and it was not until 1999 that the Veterans Health Administration added the word *pain* as the fifth vital sign to the four major health indicators: pulse, temperature, respiration, and blood pressure. Patients no longer had to assume they must bear the pain that accompanies so many illnesses. Of course, pain is a subjective feeling, not a measurable condition—and involving feelings has been contrary to medical science, where objectivity and measurement dominate. The fact that pain is recognized, without measurement but with just the simple question: "Are you experiencing pain?" is a dramatic change. Subjective experiences are accepted, which suggests to a patient some expression of empathy and caring, the E of RETHINK. Empathy and caring, then, are being recognized as good for your health!

Anger and Medical Care

But conflicts between health providers and clients still exist. And many of these rouse anger. Here are four major conflicts clients have had with providers of health care. As you read these, place a mental check mark next to the ones you have experienced:

1. Objective (cure-oriented) versus subjective (care-oriented) focus on the health problem.
   The professional looks at the problem objectively. He wants to know what the health problem is and what the symptoms are. The condition is considered independent of the person. This model stems from the medical model: diagnose and treat only the illness. The patient as an individual is somewhat lost in this formula. You, however, are more likely to look at the problem subjectively. You probably ask yourself questions such as: "Am I in serious trouble? Will I be able to do the things I want to do? How long will this condition last? What is the prognosis? Will this affect my job, my loved ones? This way of thinking is care-oriented, while the other is cure-oriented. Many

patients deal with a great deal of anger that they cannot express for fear of not being taken care of. That in itself is not conducive to good health!

2. Verbal versus nonverbal behavior

The professional focuses on the language of the professional: diagnosis, labels, medication, and directives. The client focuses on nonverbal behavior: attitudes, attention, empathy, acceptance, and concern. The attitudes of some providers suggest distance from the client at best or, at worst, even blaming the client for the condition. Many clients report having been scolded. Perhaps the service provider is angry! Attitudes and feelings communicate directly to the client and often determine what the client will do about advice or even about returning for treatment. The client is the vulnerable one in health-related services and needs to feel safe in a caring, trusting relationship with the provider. Health care providers have not only been taught to keep a professional distance, but many are reluctant to become involved with the patient as a person. They fear that the emotions of empathy and caring will blind them to the objectivity needed for determining the health condition.

3. Controlling behavior

The professional focuses on the management of the client to follow procedures of the examination, and is especially concerned about compliance to recommendations and medications. In this scenario, the authority of the service provider is to be accepted without time for explanations. But the client wants to be seen as a participant in decision making and does not want to feel controlled. The client may accept the controlling behavior because of lack of an alternative, but the anger, the resentment, are there and may show up in a failure to take medication or keep appointments.

4. Medical versus everyday language

The professional uses medical language that has become as ordinary to her as regular conversation, without seeming to care that the specialized meaning is usually lost on the client and needs defining. Doctors don't always explain in everyday language what the medications do or what people need to know about them. Clients need everyday language to be used to explain the condition, the prognosis, and the path to restored health.

How many check marks did you make for the four conflicts listed above? What does this number tell you about the experiences with health-related services you have received? Pick one of your conflicts to examine in terms of RETHINK.

What happened?

What did you do?

How did you feel?

What did the provider do?

How do you think the provider felt?

How did the situation come out?

With the full description of the event in mind, what was the role of anger?

Did you feel it?

How did you express it?

Would you change your interaction with the health provider if that same situation occurred today? Could you use your anger more creatively?

Can learning new behaviors make a difference?

There is still much work to be done in increasing our understanding of the connection between anger and health. It is clear that there are certain prescription medications that can help some people maintain calmness in the face of anxiety producing situations. However, the likelihood of generalized medical inoculation against excessive anger appears remote, even if we as a society regarded it as desirable at all. Surely, anger management is needed to be part of any treatment plan as well as any attempt to manage our own health. The most practical and constructive avenue for real anger management remains learning and practicing the skills. RETHINK skills can be lifesaving as well as life enhancing.

How the mind influences the body, immune system, and potential for disease is extraordinarily helpful. But, as we know there is no magic to preventing disease nor is there one answer to healing. We caution against making judgments that people may be "ill" because they were not strong enough to manage their anger, or didn't have the will enough to live. Many patients feel guilty because they are sick. Guilt is the last thing a person needs when he is already vulnerable. As with any knowledge, use it in a balanced way. See this knowledge about the impact of anger on the body as providing an opportunity to be an active participant in preventing disease, and in managing your relationships with health providers. As we have stated throughout this chapter, anger can be an energy source that can be adaptive rather than destructive and can even help lead to a happier and healthier life.

CHAPTER 3

RETHINKing Anger Is Good for Your Relationships

Social interactions are a basic part of all human beings. And so is aggression. For personal, genetic, and survival reasons, animals and humans alike, aggression is biologically adaptive. How we become skilled at taming this aggression and use it in the service of relationships is enormously affected by learning, especially in childhood. The development of relationships is very dependent on our early interactions with significant others such as our parents, siblings, grandparents, extended family, community, culture, as well as our inborn temperament, genetics, and gender. These and other factors are associated with how we are socialized to express anger.

Erik Erikson proposed a developmental scheme that has greatly influenced our understanding of how children develop emotionally and become socialized. According to Erikson, all people go through a progression of important crises at somewhat predictable times in their lives. How conflicts (or psychosocial crises) are resolved will affect adult social relationships. (E. Erikson, *Identity and the Life Cycle*. New York: W.W. Norton & Co., 1980.)

Becoming Socialized

How you became socialized, how you learned to interact with other people, how you learned to behave in acceptable ways, and how anger became part of your reactions in social situations, is related to your development over the years. To understand the process, you will need to see the stages of development everyone goes through and the level of socialization reached at each stage. And you will need to see how anger reactions both continue and change through the developmental stages. As you read this, think of the characteristics of each stage of development that you recognize in yourself and what you might see as missing. And note how anger reactions are connected to each level of development, using Erikson's model. There are eight stages of development. They are:

1. Trust vs. Mistrust (0–1½ years).
2. Autonomy vs. Shame (1½– 3 years).
3. Initiative vs. Guilt (3–6 years).
4. Industry (Competence) vs. Inferiority (6–Puberty).
5. Identity vs. Role Confusion (Adolescence).
6. Intimacy vs. Isolation (Early Adulthood).
7. Generativity vs. Self-absorption (Middle Age).
8. Integrity vs. Despair (Later Years).

Trust: 0–1½ years

The developmental task of this stage is attachment to mother or parent, which lays the foundation for later trust in others. The psychosocial conflict is Trust versus Mistrust.

Trust began to develop during the first year of your life, and its development was promoted by one or two people, usually your parents or another caregiver. But trust in yourself was developing at the same time. You were learning to trust your ability to work out a rhythm of feeding. And you were learning to trust that your parents would provide what you needed, taking care of you when you were hungry, wet, needed love and comfort, or were afraid or angry. You were learning to trust your ability to calm yourself and increasingly manage your body. You were learning how to turn yourself over, sit up, crawl, pull yourself up, and walk, but with assistance. You also learned how to grasp, hold, and pull.

Think about how dependent you were on your parents or other caregiver when you were a baby. You certainly had to trust them. Your very survival depended on trusting others. Trusting and loving go hand in hand. At any age, good feelings—not necessarily love, but certainly caring or appreciation—accompany feelings of trust. If you could not trust your parents or another caregiver to meet your basic needs, then you might feel vulnerable to whatever harm came your way. You were helpless in the face of the neglect. This would form the basis of having no trust in your parents. But, because you were so helpless and could do little yourself to meet your needs, you would also lose trust in yourself. With such loss of trust in your parents and in yourself, it would take very little to finish the picture of mistrust to include everyone else in the world.

The Impact of Mistrust

The price of not learning to trust is great. Your present feelings of trust in others and in yourself are built on your early experiences. While you cannot recall those early experiences that shaped your feeling of trust and the accompanying love, you can begin to think about where you are today in terms of your feelings of trust in others and in yourself. And you can think about how these feelings about trust relate to your anger.

Trust and Anger

Barbara gave her classmate, Frank, a copy of a paper she had written for a class. He was supposed to read it and return it to her so she could give it to her teacher as a class assignment. A week later, her teacher asked her to stay after class, which was unusual and caused Barbara to feel tense. At the end of class the teacher asked Barbara where she got the paper she had written. And Barbara explained that she had written it at home. But the teacher looked skeptical and said she was not sure she believed Barbara; that someone else had written the paper and had turned it in to his teacher. Barbara immediately knew this was Frank. She was furious and shouted: "I let Frank see a copy of my paper when he asked if he could. He must have made a copy of it for himself and turned it in as his own! I can't believe this! You can't trust anyone. I have a brother I can't trust either and sometimes I can't even trust my parents! What a world." And Barbara began to cry. She thought about all the times her parents had let her down. They would promise to give her something, do something for her, and then not come through. You could not trust them when the chips were down. And here was Frank stealing her paper and claiming it as his. Whom can you trust? She was very angry and decided that she would be on guard all the time so that she would not need to trust others.

This scenario describes an incident where in fact, Frank did not keep his word and was not to be trusted. So when Barbara, who was raised in an unpredictable environment, experiences a person who was not trustworthy, she extrapolated that the whole world is deceitful and made a global decision never to trust again. On the other hand, a person who grew up in a trusting relationship with her parents and has the same experience with Frank, will make a different decision about relationships.

She will think to herself, "Frank is not to be trusted," but will continue to allow herself to develop trusting relationships with others who are in fact reliable and honest. As you can imagine, Barbara will be more quickly triggered to feel angry in relationships, always looking for the worst in the others.

If you have no trust in others, you may try to control them. You may reason that people who cannot be trusted are dangerous and potentially hostile, but if you can control them, they cannot harm you. Your anger from the distrust will provide the energy needed to try to control others.

Without trust you may withdraw from interaction with others. Perhaps withdrawing makes you feel safer and less threatened by the world. Your anger can turn inward and be suppressed and may well show up in migraine headaches, stomachaches, and high blood pressure.

Without trust in others, you may become overly self-reliant and independent, to the extent that you harden your heart and close down your emotions, even anger, and keep your distance if someone is nice to you. There is no room for anger, except at yourself for not being able to do everything by yourself. The anger energy is used to keep you going on your own, lonely way.

On the other hand, if you don't trust yourself, you may not fully develop your abilities. The reason for this is quite clear: if you cannot trust yourself to achieve, then you will protect yourself from what you perceive as inevitable failure. You will let others do things for you and will become dependent, often on people who are overly controlling. Perhaps you are easily manipulated because you are certain that other people are better than you or know more than you do. Your anger is suppressed to protect yourself, but the anger energy will find its way, possibly in your body and cause health problems or it may be passively acted out in relationships.

Trust and Accepting Limits

When a child can trust one or more persons, the child is more willing to accept their setting of limits to behavior. As you develop trust, you expect those you trust to have your own interests in mind, and trust them not to want to prevent you from doing things that are safe and appropriate. You can trust them to talk to you, to negotiate limits, and to explain why the limits are set. Or, when confidence is established, a child can even trust enough so that the parents do not need to give specific reasons. Here is a situation where that kind of trust became crucial:

A nine-year-old boy, Ben, wanted to play with a friend whose home was an unacceptable place to play, and was furious when he thought his mother did not trust his judgment to select his own friends.

Mother: I don't want you playing with Joey. I've told you that before, and it upsets me when you continue to play with him at his home.

Ben: Well, I like him. He's fun and I like to go to his house. He has his own room and we can play alone.

Mother: That's just it, honey. I don't want you in his home. There are some problems there, and I don't want you to be around those problems.

Ben: What kind of problems?

Mother: I'd rather not say. You'll have to trust me on this.

Ben: But I like Joey and I want to play with him.

Mother: Well, I guess it would be okay to let him come over here. You invite him over here and tell him your mother wants you at home.

If Ben did not trust his mother, he might have continued to play with Joey at his home, where his father was a heavy drinker and had been arrested for attacking his wife and Joey. Ben's mother was afraid her son might get caught in such an attack if the father came home drunk. She was reluctant to share this information with her son, because she believed he was too young for such a problem. In this exchange with his mother, in addition to asking him to trust her, Ben understood the rules, realized his mother showed her feelings of concern for his welfare, and saw that they could negotiate a solution to the problem. Each of these behaviors added to his sense of trust in her caring about him and his welfare.

Limits of Trust

Just because you are a trusting person does not mean you can trust everyone. Discretion is important. There are many people who cannot be trusted. One of the limits of trust is to recognize whom not to have confidence in. When you were very young, you relied on others to tell you who to stay away from, but as you developed more trust in yourself you also developed greater ability to assess other people. Perhaps you are now in the habit of comparing new people to people you already trust, or perhaps you know how to observe their behavior and question how trustworthy they are.

Think of an experience you had in which you were involved with someone who turned out not to be trustworthy. What was the experience?

Describe it in as much detail as possible. What was the role of anger? You can use these guiding questions:

What happened?
What did you do?
How did you feel?
What did the other person do?
How do you think the other person felt?
How did the situation turn out?

With that full description of the event in mind, you will now want to focus more on the implications of that event for your sense of trust in yourself and the resulting limits you feel in trusting others:

What did the person do that made you decide he or she was untrustworthy?
What did you do (what actions did you take and what decisions did you make) to prevent any damaging effects on you from what happened?
What did you do (what actions did you take and what decisions did you make) that may have aided and abetted the person in taking advantage of your trust?
What role did anger play in this situation and how did you deal with your anger?

Autonomy: 1½–3 years

The task in this stage is gaining some basic control of self and the environment. In the early stages, examples of this are toilet-training and exploration. The psychosocial crisis of the stage is *Autonomy versus Shame.*

Autonomy is the growing realization that you are separate from other people. You are distinct from your parents, brothers and sisters, and everyone else. This realization allows you to understand that what you do elicits responses from those around you and, in turn, they can get responses from you. You are a person. You are somebody. Although you recognize others, they are not as important as you. The self-absorbed, self-important ego is developing!

Your autonomy developed with a great deal of help and support from those around you. Your knowledge that you were a separate person and that you could influence and affect the behavior of those around you gave you a sense of control you did not have before. You could scream, "No!" and really get a response. With your new sense of autonomy, you also became aware of your independence—the two go together. You were learning about autonomy through walking, throwing, cause and effect behaviors (such as pulling things apart, and opening doors and drawers). Sometimes you wanted to feed yourself, dress yourself, and decide whether or not to be willing to be toilet-trained. You could use some words to assert your will and even your anger, declaring your autonomy and independence. At other times you did not want to do any of these things. Erikson calls this stage the "guerrilla war of the wills."

This is expected behavior from children at this age. They are developing strength in knowing who they are. However, shame can also develop during this time and can cause problems in later years with how you feel and act. Making mistakes can be a learning experience or a shameful experience. You had difficulty becoming autonomous and independent if you were not allowed to make mistakes or were criticized for trying to do things on your own. Perhaps your striving for independence triggered your parents' or your caregiver's anger, and that frightened you. If they were angry with you, if they scolded you and looked mad, would they still love you? So you would feel not only fear of loss of being cared for and loved, but fear and doubts about your abilities. Of course you probably do not recall those early experiences that shaped your feelings of autonomy and independence, but you can think about how your early experiences at this stage affect you today. And as you think about your current status, you may find it helpful to consider some of the reasons parents and family members do not encourage autonomy and independence, so necessary to development.

Why would any family member prevent a young child from becoming autonomous and independent? Are they afraid of the child? Are they afraid the child might get hurt? Don't they like the child? Some of the most common reasons parents give for not allowing independent actions or autonomy in their young children include:

a. Fatigue from chasing after the child.
b. Fear that the child will be injured.
c. Feeling incompetent as a parent.
d. Feeling embarrassed by the child's unruly behavior.
e. And/or, feeling a loss of freedom.

Other reasons are associated with the child's behavior:

a. Impatience and embarrassment with the child having temper tantrums (anger outbursts), sometimes in public.
b. Wanting order rather than chaos with knocking things over.

c. Annoyed with mess from throwing food and objects (anger outburst).
d. Irritated with crying, whining.
e. Fear of child running away from the parents or into the street.
f. Feeling powerless when child is yelling or screaming at the parents.
g. And/or frustration with refusing to talk or use the potty.

This phase of autonomy and independence can inevitably set up a power struggle between the child and the parents, which in turn began the life-long struggle you may be feeling right now concerning limits of behavior and freedom. This influences your relationships with all kinds of people whether it is with authority, with the law, or with people in your family or in your community. Such early experiences really do have far-reaching implications for your life. If you were given a great deal of freedom, you may find it hard to accept any limits to your behavior and become angry when someone or some law limits what you can do. If you were given only limited freedom, you may find it hard to make decisions on your own, relying on others, and becoming angry when that help is not forthcoming.

Think of an experience you had as a child, or even recently, in which your sense of autonomy and independence were affected:

What happened?
What did you do?
How did you feel?
What anger feelings did you have?
What did the other person do?
How did the other person feel?
What anger feelings did the other person express?
How did it come out?
Was the anger energy useful?

With a better understanding of the role of autonomy in life, the need for such autonomy, and the need for limits and rules, you can think about how you feel about rules and limits and how you feel about independence and freedom. Some people do not become autonomous, having no sense that they are separate from others or that they are responsible for their own behavior. They frequently blame others for whatever goes wrong. Men who engage in domestic violence almost always blame their female partner for making him so angry he had to hit her.

Where do you fall on the following continuum of blaming others for what you did?

1. It wasn't my fault, he did it.
2. It wasn't my fault, she started it.
3. It wasn't my fault, he made me do it.

Or

4. It was my fault. I'm sorry.
5. It was my fault. I won't do it again.
6. It was my fault. I take responsibility for my actions. I really learned a lesson from that!

When we blame, we lack insight and a feeling of control over our lives. Children who cannot resolve the conflict of autonomy versus shame move into adulthood feeling shame about who they are and carry anger into every relationship. It is, however, never too late to resolve the conflict and learn the skills and gain the awareness to do so.

Initiative: 3–6 years

The developmental task of this stage is becoming purposeful and directed. The psychosocial conflict is *Initiative versus Guilt.*

Again, the importance of your early experiences cannot be overestimated as you become socialized. Years three to six were transition years that prepared you for separation from your parents and entry into the "real world" of school. During these transition years, you developed an increasing ability to take care of yourself and manage your behavior. People around you were providing much help in how to behave but at that age you were beginning to have a say about what happened in your life. The role of initiative refers to the growing interest you had in starting new things, becoming involved in many activities, and reaching out to be part of the activities of others. You experienced a growing realization that the world is one great field of activities and you could be part of it. You wanted to explore everything! You did not look to your parents or others to stimulate your interest. You saw what was exciting, what appealed to you, and how you could create things. Your autonomy and independence joined to give you a sense of being ready to start things on your own. You were learning about symbols and asked endless questions about anything that tapped your interest. And you loved pretend play. You probably had some difficulty separating fantasy from reality, lies from truth. But fantasy is the beginning of creativity.

If you were not able to take the initiative to try things, or if you were rejected when you attempted to compete for the affection of one parent for the other parent, you would tend to feel guilty for doing something wrong. Or, you might have felt unworthy of love and attention. Or, you might have felt you were a naughty, even bad, person because you were scolded so much for being into everything and not accomplishing much. You even became angry with yourself.

You can probably remember experiences from the ages of three to six; many people have vivid memories of experiences during those years. But, even if you can't, you can think about where you are today. As you think about your current status, you may find it helpful to consider some reasons your parents might not have promoted as much initiative as you would have liked. Here are some reasons parents give for not promoting initiative in their children:

1. Tired of nagging the child to clean up.
2. Anxious about getting to work and keeping their job, no time to consider the child.
3. Not satisfied with their child care arrangements.
4. Fear for their child's safety in the neighborhood.
5. Problems with their spouse or close friend, which overwhelm the parent so there is no time to spend with the child.
6. Doubts about raising their child properly.
7. Angry about criticism of child rearing by relatives.
8. And/or a sense of facing endless problems with no solutions.

A child's typical behavior at this age that may hinder the parent's willingness to allow the child to initiate new behaviors or activities that include:

1. Shouting angry words, calling names, using "bathroom" talk.
2. Hitting, throwing objects, grabbing, biting, and spitting.
3. Teasing siblings.
4. Refusing to share, take turns, or play by the rules.
5. Arguing, lying to cover up actions.
6. Refusing to listen, tuning adults out.
7. Dawdling while eating, dressing, and/or going to bed.

Parents don't usually set out to inhibit their child's initiative; sometimes they do not understand the developmental milestones or they are simply too overwhelmed and preoccupied with their own problems. The child becomes one more burden and the child may interpret the parent's burden as his fault, thus guilt can develop. In reaction, some children withdraw from doing anything because they feel guilty for making the parents so unhappy. Some children feel they must be bad if they seem to need so much scolding. Some children feel they are unworthy of trying to be helpful—or take the initiative—no one wants help; it is rejected every time. These feelings can shape how you respond in relationships. Do you go out of your way to please others? Do you feel unworthy of respect and love? Do you feel guilty every time you feel angry? Do you feel you have no right to feel anger, certainly not show it, because you are a nuisance to others?

Think of an experience you can recall from your childhood or from something that happened recently that roused your anger but also roused your guilt:

What happened?
What did you do?
How did you feel?
What did another person do in response to what you did?
How did that person feel?
What was the role of anger?
How are things now?

There is a new power, beginning at three to six years of age, in your ability to express your feelings. Of course, your feelings have always been part of your development, starting with the feeling of trust and love that your parents provided and you shared. As language developed there were *words* that described how you felt. This made it easier to recognize your own and others' feelings. You even started to pick up body language that communicated feelings, and you were increasingly aware of what could hurt you and the feelings of other people. You also were learning how to express your thoughts about events and about what others were doing. All of these were steps in the socialization process that would become increasingly important in your life.

Learning to manage your behavior is not easy, especially if you tended to be disorganized and impatient. Whether you have accomplished all of the developmental tasks to this point, as well as recognizing your temperament, would be part of the problem or the solution. Examining a significant relationship you have now, ask yourself the following questions:

1. Did you want to take action before thinking through the consequences—do you still have that problem?
2. Are you easily roused to fight with words or fists?
3. Is your patience at the lowest possible tolerance level?
4. Have you learned how to prevent yourself from becoming destructive when your impulse is to attack?
5. Do you have these problems to face each time you become angry?

Here is where RETHINK skills can benefit you in establishing healthier relationships as well as be important to help you manage the destructive aspects of anger.

Think of an experience you can recall as a child, or even a more current experience, where you were impatient and angry because someone prevented you from doing what you wanted to do:

What happened?
What did you do?
How did you feel?
What was the role of anger?
What did the other person do in response?
How did that person feel?
What was the role of anger?
Where are things now in the relationship?

You will want to come back to the events you have described in this chapter after you have had time to master RETHINK.

Industry or competency: 6 years to puberty

The developmental tasks are developing social, physical, and school skills. The psychosocial crisis of this stage is *Industry or Competence versus Inferiority*.

Industry develops around the ages of six through eleven. Now you were taking on a larger society: school. You were responsible to and even dependent on teachers and the limits of the school setting. You were engaged in mastering two areas of your development: school subject matter and socialization within the school culture and with your peers. You strived to be successful and have a positive self-image as an achiever; you wanted approval from your teachers and probably tried hard to please them with your achievement. You wanted peer acceptance and approval, and close friends. This required mastery of social skill, including, of course, dealing with anger-generating situations.

Your focus on school and peers meant your parents were of less importance to your sense of achievement, acceptance, and approval. You became more interested in the school environment, where you were mastering academic skills. You were also learning a great deal about socializing with peers, sometimes in an organized, structured setting, and sometimes in a kind of free association. Your socialization outside the school also changed. You probably joined teams or scouts or church groups, or had a particular group of friends and had different socializing experiences. You probably depended on your parents to drive you to these groups and events, but you did not need them as much as you had previously.

One of the problems that can develop during this age period is a feeling of inferiority. If you were not successful in mastering academics or socialization with peers, you very likely felt inferior to others and became extremely sensitive to your limitations. Your parents, teachers, and/or friends might have made fun of you or communicated in a variety of ways that you were not much of an achiever. These feelings of inferiority can remain throughout life and rouse anger, as people can trigger the inferior feelings. Here is an example of how feelings of inferiority can get played out:

Justin, age twelve, threw a rock through the window, smashed the screen door, set off the security alarm, and was at home when the police arrived in response to the alarm. His father was supposed to pick him up in time for the ball game and it was his Dad's turn to have him for the weekend. His parents were divorced. His Mom had waited around with him but when his Dad was more than half an hour late, she left him waiting outside the house with his packed bag but no key. She had explained that she had to take the last ferry to the island where she and her boyfriend were planning to meet and spend the weekend.

When Dad hadn't shown up even an hour after the scheduled time, Justin was mad. Now they would certainly miss the game! Besides, he was getting cold as the sun went down. He was mad at his Mom for leaving him like that and he was disgusted and furious with his Dad, who just didn't seem to care. When his father did arrive, he was full of good spirits and funny stories. Justin was not amused. He could not be "jollied" out of his anger. He was a bit pleased that his Dad had some explaining to do to the police and had the expense of replacing the window. His anger had been destructive, but he wasn't sure he wouldn't do it again!

Let's replay the same scene using some of the RETHINK skills that could come in handy at a time like this. First is the Recognition. Notice how your body feels. Justin could try and calm his body by pulling out his iPod and sitting on the steps to listen to his favorite music. Or if he had paper and pencil in his backpack, he could even write his father an angry letter to be given to him when he arrived. Justin probably was saying to himself, "I hate my Dad. He doesn't care about me. He never is on time." This thinking fuels anger. He could re-Think by saying to himself, "I hate when my Dad is late. I know he will be here but I am really upset that we will miss the game. I am going to tell him how upsetting it is when he is late. And that if he wants to have a good relationship with me he will have to care more about me."

When Justin's father arrives, he still does not need to agree to be "jollied" or stuff his anger away, but rather Justin needs to be able to find a way to feel entitled enough to get what he deserves, a considerate father. If his father has a legitimate reason for being late (his car broke down, or he had no phone to call), and if Justin can listen with Empathy, this, too, will make a difference in the relationship. A different ending to the same facts. Nevertheless, as you read this story you can understand how important it is for Justin to feel competent or better about himself, and what he deserves. Then using the RETHINK skills to manage his anger would be a whole lot easier. This is how (and why) re-Thinking anger is good for relationships. Certainly, any member of this family (the Dad, the Mom) could use the Rethink skills and the outcome would be different and more constructive.

As parents, teachers, or adults in a child's life, we want to help the child resolve this stage of conflict and overcome the sense of inferiority. One way is by finding areas of activity where mastery happens. Computers have contributed an incredible sense of mastery with many children as well as adults. Or other talents that can be developed that you increasingly master: such as singing, dancing, painting, sports, playing a musical instrument, or making things. Many talents are not developed in the schools. Talents not consistent with the school curricula may or may not be developed in the home or supported by the family. But you as a youth or, more likely, an adult, can develop talents at any age. Remember the ideas that filled your mind during the years of Initiative. Go back to that thinking and take some action. It is never too late and you can manage your anger, even using the anger energy to do something or make something special.

Identity

Adolescence: The developmental task here is in making transition from childhood to adulthood: developing a sense of self. The psychosocial crisis of this stage is *Identity versus Role Confusion*.

Identity develops during the teen years. At that time, establishing your identity includes two very important new aspects of your life: becoming sexually mature, and developing your higher mental capabilities of analysis and reflection. This new status has important implications for analyzing and understanding what triggers your anger and for reflecting on what the consequences of actions will be. But, these years also include a great deal of confusion about who you are, a great deal of temptation to try things that are dangerous, and a great deal of anger about not being appreciated or recognized.

As a teenager, you were probably occupied with thoughts of who you are and how much you were appreciated by your family and, especially, by your friends. You wanted to be recognized as a unique individual with a clear and separate identity. You very likely wanted to appear competent and physically attractive. You wanted to be accepted and loved by those you loved, and you probably wanted to be considered popular and cool among your friends. The benefits of establishing a clear identity are many. They include greater skills in:

1. Comparing your behavior with accepted standards.
2. Being helpful and supportive of others.
3. Reflecting on values, emotions, truths, and ideals, and
4. Integrating sexual interests with responsible behavior.

However, if you were not successful in establishing your identity, you may have experienced role confusion. That means you were not sure of your true personality and switched from self-assured to self-doubting. You may have felt alienated and were certain no one understood you, including yourself. Being humiliated or laughed at by others not only reinforced the role confusion, but also generated a lot of anger in you. It is often common that when adolescents feel very misunderstood they also feel some depression. Think of an experience you had as a teenager that made you angry:

What happened?
What did you do?
How did you feel?
What was the role of anger?
What did other(s) do in response to what you did?
How did the other(s) feel?
What was the role of anger?
How did it come out?

As is true through each developmental stage and in the management of anger, temperament is a critical part of development. But it is particularly true when it comes to risk-taking for teens. Some teens simply need more excitement and stimulation than others. They easily get bored and indifferent to the consequences of their actions, believe themselves to be in less danger than others, and are more likely to try something most people would see as foolish. They also become angry more easily, especially if they are at the high end of a temperament scale, meaning they tend to react quickly. These adolescents need to be helped by others to calm down when feeling angry. But, they can also help themselves calm down with such simple acts as taking a breather—time out for some deep breathing—or going to a quiet place for a while, exercise, or talking to their friends. This is the time to learn to process what has happened to make the teen angry. And a teenager who knows enough to ask for "time-out" to analyze what had happened to make him or her angry, is well on the way to managing anger and developing mature, positive relationships.

Relationship Concerns Common to Teens

Adolescence is a time of transition from child to adult. This transitional period is notorious for its emotional turbulence and changes in body proportions, sexuality, and physical growth spurts. Of course, with all these changes, psychological upheavals are par for the course. There are at least three frequent issues that become a challenge for teens, each of which, when experienced, involve anger reactions:

1. Feeling unconnected to the family, the school, and the community. The importance of peer relationships as a way to be connected cannot be overstated. Gangs that form in some communities provide feelings of connectedness, so important to the socialization of youth. The fact that many of these gangs engage in acts of destruction, drop out or are pushed out of school, and often drink excessively, makes them a threat to many communities. Many gang members are angry with the world, believing that no one cares about them; no one respects them; they can't get a job; or you can't trust anyone. A sense of powerlessness pervades their worldview and through the gang they are able to achieve some sense of power. But of course, the majority of teens join other kinds of groups such as science fairs, acappella choirs, sports teams, and other constructive peer groups, and feel their sense of power and worth through constructive outlets.

   Some teens believe that they need to break from their family so that they can have more freedom and listen to their peers instead. What is important for teens is to be aware that they can maintain these important peer ties *and* make changes in their relationships with family members. Here are some things that teens can do to prevent anger reactions:
   a. Help the family understand their new need for more privacy.
   b. Talk with the family about their expectations that their ideas will be taken more seriously; and
   c. Express their desire to negotiate some of the house rules, particularly those in involving activities outside of the home, such as curfew, use of family car, etc.

2. Risk-taking.

If risk seems as much a hallmark of adolescence as headphones and jeans, it is! Research suggests that thrill-seeking behavior does a mountain climb during adolescence, then levels off in adulthood, and begins its descent in later years. Much—though hardly all—of this adolescent risk-taking is both necessary and healthy. Teens can't separate from their parents, affiliate more firmly with peers, flex their growing intellect, integrate new sexual and aggressive energies, or discover the colors of their true natures without it. In short, they can rarely forge an identity of their own without taking risks. How then can they avoid undue danger while still testing themselves, mastering inner fears and outer hazards?

The teens that are unable to stay connected to family, school, and community, who do not learn to manage emerging roller coaster emotions, and are overly eager to be accepted by their peers, are often challenged to jump a wide and deep ditch, frequently express anger, try drugs, see how much they can drink, and shoplift. And if they should pick friends that show disappointment and anger if the teen refuses to act in these damaging ways, he/she is more likely to engage in the self-destructive behavior. Girls' anger is often turned inward and is frequently played out by engaging in sexual activity with no protection, early pregnancy may result, and many take drugs and drink too much. As in all situations involving the growing child, adolescence is a time for parents and other adults in a child's life to help them grow. The goal isn't to avoid risks but to help the teen learn how to assess which risks are worth taking and which are not.

Teens need skills with which to make good choices. They are willing to take risks that they would not have taken before and experience a new and increasingly growing freedom, the awareness of greater autonomy, and the seductiveness of feeling invincible. These things, along with hormones kicking in and higher mental processes emerging, such as the ability to reason critically, all add to the joy of being young. Creativity, new ventures, and new solutions to old problems can emerge with few inhibitions. They can turn their anger into constructive solutions. For example, a fifteen-year-old boy, angry about the continuing accidents of children being thrown from their bus seats when the bus made sudden stops, led a campaign to have seat belts required in all school buses. An eighteen-year-old girl, angry about the terrible and dangerous condition of her old school building, led a campaign to rebuild the school. A seventeen-year-old youth organized community dances in a community where gangs threatened to draw youth into their ranks.

3. Resolving conflicts.

If teens do not learn social and problem-solving skills they are at a disadvantage. The shift from major attachment to the family and adults to peers is dramatic and often filled with conflict involving new demands and expectations.

Teens can learn more about social and problem-solving skills by:

a. Making friends who know how to challenge others constructively.

b. Learning how to listen.

c. Developing some effective analytical skills using higher mental processes.

The higher mental processes developed during the teen years go beyond observable cause and effect. They include inferring a past cause for something happening now. This is especially important when anger is involved. Something that made you angry many years ago can stay with you and still make you angry.

Sam was bullied in the Fifth Grade by an older boy. This bullying involved pushing, punching, teasing, scaring. Sam was sick with fear and anger and could do nothing. The bullying went on through the Sixth Grade as well. Then it ended. But, twenty years later, when Sam entered a restaurant and saw his bully as the host, all his fear and anger resurfaced as though it were a day back in school. The bully smiled and greeted Sam like a friend, suggesting they meet after work hours. Sam said, "Nothing doing! I remember like it was yesterday what you did to me. I'm out of here!"

An ancient Chinese proverb taught that "the fire you kindle for your enemy often burns you more than him." Keeping in a state of anger is not only physically unhealthy but also emotionally unhealthy. Sam ultimately understood his anger about being bullied and made a decision to become a teacher so he could help other children grow in a safer environment.

Reflective Thinking and Problem Solving

Reflective thinking, developed during the teen years, involves having a discussion in your head to examine the pros and cons of an action you are considering. Such thinking uses qualifiers such as, "It is true that Joe looks good as a candidate for class president, but is he more interested in the attention he would get than in taking strong positions on issues we are concerned about?" Reflective thinking about Joe as president would also include thinking about his behavior and predicting how he will behave when dealing with the problems the school faces, and inferring from his past and present behavior what alternative actions might be expected: How has he handled conflicts in the past? Does he get angry easily? Does he listen to people?

When people don't develop problem-solving skills or learn to use their higher mental processes, they fall victim to someone else's self-belief. They lose their autonomy/independence, they lose their initiative, they lose the skills of industry, and they lose trust in themselves and their own identity. They lose their ability to deal with situations that make them angry.

The Last Three Developmental Stages Concern Adult Development

Intimacy: Early adulthood ranges from approximately the twenties to thirties. The psychosocial crisis of this stage is *Intimacy versus Isolation.*

In this stage the developmental tasks are establishing intimate bonds of love and friendship. Many intimate relationships are forged at this time and result in marriage. A young adult's challenge at this stage is to be able to initiate and sustain adult relationships. Choosing a significant other who can assist the individual to develop his or her optimal potential is the main task at this point in time. The crisis of this stage is when the young adult is not able to find a partner or when he or she is not able to maintain the significant relationship and a divorce ensues. The potential for feeling alone and isolated is likely and the management of anger becomes crucial. The incidence of feeling alone has increased as the age at which intimate relationships are realized has moved some ten years later. It is not uncommon, however, for people in their twenties to remain unattached as they pursue higher education, have greater sexual freedom, and find satisfaction in a single's lifestyle.

The next stage of development is Generativity: Middle Age, from thirty years until retirement. The psychosocial crisis of this stage is *Productivity versus Stagnation.* And Erikson's final stage is called *Integrity:* the later years where the developmental tasks are looking back over one's life and finding and accepting meaning. The psychosocial crisis of this stage is *Integrity versus Despair.* If, when adults in retirement years review their life and can feel pleased and proud of how their years were spent, then they are filled with satisfaction and a sense of worth and integrity. "A sense of active mastery is the ego state most clearly associated with longevity," says David Guttman, researcher on aging at the University of Michigan. "Active mastery means having autonomy over one's life and circumstances, not power over others... the single most important factor (in aging) is that you make something creative from your experiences," wrote Deepak Chopra (*Ageless Body, Timeless Mind*, 1993).

Erikson writes about avoiding regrets about the past and instead building meaning into life by doing acts of kindness and giving back to family, community, and the society. Some examples of these activities are volunteering at the local school, or becoming a foster grandparent, or working at a Hospice Center. In this stage, adults RETHINK what is important and have a keener sense of the value of time.

However, if an individual nearing the end of her life feels a profound regret and disappointment and a loss of that which they have deeply desired but never fully experienced, she will experience despair. A sense of powerlessness can overcome the people who have spent a lifetime searching for an experience that has never happened. And with such a sense of dissatisfaction and despair, there is anger. Even at this stage of life, however, one can learn to manage anger. The RETHINK skills can be put into action to create more satisfying relationships.

"It is never too late to be what you might have been" (George Eliot).

Looking at all the developmental stages throughout the life cycle and how relationships are shaped by our ability to master each stage, it is understandable how trust in someone else or in yourself is important in developing relationships. When you question what is triggering your anger, you can ask yourself: Is it an issue of being treated as though you were not an autonomous individual to be respected? Is it an issue of having your initiatives scoffed at? Is it an issue of challenging your intellectual abilities? Or is it an issue of being ignored as a unique person?

While thinking about what triggers your anger, you will want to think about what, from each developmental level contributed to your becoming socialized in a satisfactory way and what detracted from or harmed that process. Parents can think of the process in their children. It helps in determining what contributes to feelings and expressions of anger over the life cycle.

CHAPTER 4

Recognize Anger in Yourself and in Others

Many things happen during the day to make you angry and many things require an anger response. Think about your most recent anger reaction. What happened that made you angry? What did you do to deal with your anger? What was the outcome? Did you lose a friend? Did you resolve the cause of the anger? These are questions that merit asking each time you feel anger. But, if you don't recognize your anger or understand why you are angry, you will have great difficulty in dealing with anger-provoking situations. These "things" that make you angry are better defined as "anger triggers." They are events that violate one or more of the basic human needs we all have in common. These anger triggers require a response, because you are in danger when your needs are not met. The anger trigger is a signal for action. In each situation that becomes an anger trigger, there is a point at which one or more basic human needs have been violated. It is at that point you will want to do something. So, it is important for you to recognize those points and link them to the basic need or needs being violated. Do you respond with anger or do you begin to diffuse the anger by a creative use of the anger energy?

It is important, however, to recognize the basic human needs. They include:

a. Security within trusting relationships: The most basic need for all human beings is security within a trusting relationship. You must be physically safe, emotionally bonded, and have food, shelter, and clothing.

b. Autonomy and Identity: You need to be aware of your individuality, being a separate person who has unique characteristics and a strong sense of self.

c. Visions of opportunities: You need to feel that there are opportunities for you and that you can form visions of what they will look like.

d. Hope and Confidence: You need to have a deep sense of hope that you can deal with life's challenges successfully, and the confidence to accept the challenges.

e. Achievements: You need to feel you are reaching some goals you set for yourself and that your achievements are not only appreciated by you, but also recognized by others.

f. Fairness and Justice: You need to feel you live in a family, a group of friends or colleagues, and a society that is fair and just. You trust your life to that belief.

g. Competent and in Control: You need to feel you are competent in what you do at work, with friends, in activities or in driving a car. You need to feel that your competence is related to your sense of control over what you do.

h. Responsible: You need to feel responsible for what you do and feel others will be responsible for what they do. You are willing to take the consequences of your behavior and expect others to do the same.

i. Connected: You need to feel connected to others so that you feel part of a group as small as a friend, or as large as a congregation, or a nation.

j. Respect for yourself and others: You need to feel respect for yourself and for others to respect you. You also need to respect others and to acknowledge their need for respect.

Violations of Human Needs

Knowing your basic human needs is especially important as you respond in anger when they are violated. It is important to recognize which human need has been violated so that the anger energy can be used creatively to respond. Here are some experiences that are anger triggers:

1. Labeled as selfish, lazy, or messy
   Being labeled in negative ways violates your need for Respect, your need to feel Competent and in Control, and your need for Fairness

and Justice. Labeling you is a put-down intended to humiliate you by violating those needs.

2. Not involved in rule-making

Being kept out of important activities violates the need to feel Connected with other people, the need to feel Competent, and the need for Respect. Keeping you out of making rules is an attempt to put you down as not important or necessary. This is often a problem in the workplace (see Chapter 10).

3. Lied to, cheated

Being lied to or cheated violates the need for Security within trusting relationships, the need for Fairness and Justice, and the need for Respect. When you are lied to or cheated, you are being insulted and manipulated for someone else's advantage.

4. Rejected

Being rejected violates the need to be Connected, to have Security within a trusting relationship, and to have Hope and Confidence. When you are rejected, the person is saying you are not important or loved anymore.

5. Poor

Being in poverty violates the need for Fairness and Justice, the need to have Visions of opportunity, and the need for Hope and Confidence. The grinding down of people in poverty suggests society is rejecting and humiliating a large group of humans with the same needs as everyone else.

6. Teased

Being teased violates the need for Respect, the need for Autonomy and Identity, and the need for Competence and Control. When you are teased, you are being treated as someone who does not merit recognition as a valued human being.

7. Yelled at

Being yelled at violates the need for Autonomy and Identity, the need for Competence and Control, the need for Fairness and Justice, and the need for Respect. When you are yelled at, someone is trying to control you so you lose your own powers.

8. Criticized

Being criticized violates the need for Competence and Control, Respect, the need for Security within a trusting relationship, and the need for Achievement. When you are criticized more than seems necessary, the person may be trying to control you, prevent you from achieving what you are capable of, and may even be jealous of your abilities.

9. Abused

Being abused violates most human needs. Its intent is to make the abused person feel totally unimportant and worthless. It debases the person for the abuser's needs.

10. Pitied

Being pitied violates the need for Competence and Control, the need for Hope and Confidence, the need for Respect, and the need for Autonomy and Identity. The intent of pity may be to make the person being pitied seem weak and helpless, and incapable of competence.

Certainly, there are individual differences in what triggers anger. And there are individual differences in how quickly an anger response is triggered. Those who have a temperament that responds quickly to stimuli are usually the ones who respond quickly to anger triggers. They have a special need to recognize their speed of response and to develop a pattern of stopping all action until the anger trigger is fully analyzed. This takes RETHINKing.

What triggers your anger? You can determine this by thinking about what others do that make you angry. Notice the point at which you feel the anger and then determine which needs have been violated. Did you notice more than one basic human need was violated by each anger trigger described above? You probably found more than one violated in experiences that became anger triggers for you. It would be useful for you to write down some experiences you have had where you were not quite sure why you were so angry:

What happened?
What basic human needs do you believe were violated?
What did you do with your anger energy?
What did the person do in response to what you did?
Would you do things differently if the same thing happened today? How?

Basic Responses to Anger Triggers

There are the basic ways to respond to anger triggers—the well known fight, flight, or submit choices. Children often choose one of these. You can watch it on the playground: Barbara takes a bicycle from Jenny. Jenny is angry but has nothing more that the primitive choices. She can fight

Barbara, knocking her off the bike and reclaiming it; she can choose flight and run crying to the teacher; or she can accept the incidence and do nothing but cry.

These primitive responses to anger are acceptable in young children, and most adults see them as opportunities to teach the children more acceptable, more effective, ways to deal with the anger trigger. The goal is to restore the relationship between the two girls. But when we see adult responses to anger limited to fight, flight, or submit, then we are seeing dangerous consequences. Here are two real life events, one that dramatically shows the consequences of the fight response, and the other that shows the consequences of the flight response to an anger trigger:

Road rage continues to be a primary factor in the fight response to an anger trigger. Road rage is anger out of control and in the fight posture, with an added ingredient of malice. The enraged driver wants revenge, retaliation, and inflicting harm, which may be fantasized or, indeed, acted out.

A man, driving a van, cut off a car in order to get in front of it. The driver of the car then sped up and passed the van, honking his horn and pulling in front of it. This dance continued and the anger was increasing, rapidly becoming rage. Each driver's need for Safety, for Respect, for Fairness, was violated. Finally, the driver of the van decided to ram the other car in retaliation, as there seemed no apparent end to the confrontation, or for the increasing shouting, rude gestures, horn-honking, flashing of lights, that goes along with road rage. He rammed the "enemy's" car, fired shots at the driver and his passenger, pistol-whipped the driver, and then drove off.

The violated needs caused such an explosion of anger that there were no Decision points that did not add to the escalation of the confrontation.

A young woman was out with her boyfriend; he was driving his own car. He wanted to go to a town about seventy-five miles away for some drinks and to look at the lake. She did not want to go. She had to be at work that evening at a restaurant, and felt she didn't have time for the trip. So she said "No" to him. He didn't like that and started to yell at her for not being a good sport, for spoiling all their fun, for being a bore. He finally said, "We're going there and I don't care what you say. You can tell your boss you were sick." She insisted she did not want to go and begged him to take her home. When they stopped for a light, she tried to open the door to get out. He was furious and hit her in the face, telling her that he would decide when she could get out of the car. She was crying now because of the pain, but also because she was no match for him. She could not fight him, nor could she use reason with him. Should she submit? No! She had to flee. He had not locked the doors of the car, so when he had to stop at a pedestrian crossing, she got out and ran. He could do nothing because there were too many witnesses. She knew he would retaliate so she told her father and he talked to a lawyer. Father knew how to "fight" in a civilized way!

Fight, flight, or submit responses to anger triggers occur daily. What is often missing, however, is recognizing the deeper causes of anger responses. It is clear: we all have basic human needs and violation of them can become anger triggers. There is a point in someone's behavior toward you at which you recognize one or more of your needs being violated. That is a critical point, because it is when you become angry. You want to take action of some kind to reestablish your sense of having your needs met. The sequence then becomes one of making decisions about how to react to the anger trigger. You now have the anger energy to work with. Here are some examples of the process:

A man was driving home from work when he was cut off by another car, scaring him with its abruptness and violating his need for security. It became an anger trigger, with a great deal of anger energy available. How dare the driver do that to him? This was the first decision point. What decision would he make: Ignore it as another driver wanting to get home and take a rest; dismiss it as something that is so common—there are those kinds of drivers; figure it wasn't worth retaliation? But, he thought, the guy probably cut him off in disrespect, violating his need for respect. So he began the road rage dance of cutting off the other car, while mouthing insults, with the other driver joining in the dance. The two cars were approaching a stoplight and the offended driver positioned himself in front of the other car at the light. Here was another decision point. He could wait for the light to change; after all, he was in front and could get away from the guy, or he could do something else. He was still angry and still thinking the guy had no business starting this. It was his fault and he should be taught a lesson. "Don't mess with me," was stating, "I am competent. You must respect me. I expect fairness."

So he got out of his car, walked back to the other car and yanked at the door in order to "beat him to a pulp." The door was locked and the anger energy increased; he now desired a physical exchange. But he could not get the door opened and that added even more energy to the anger. His need to feel competent was challenged. Here was another decision point. Should he get back in his car? He saw the light had changed. Why not just go home, share the experience with his wife, vent his anger energy by talking, and get on with the evening. NO! He couldn't get the door opened and he needed to teach this guy a lesson in driving behavior. So, what he did to vent his anger toward the man was to kick out the headlights. He did that and then went back to his own car. It was only when the anger energy was spent after telling his wife about the incident that he realized the man could have had a gun and shot him when he tried to open the car door. He was terrified in thinking about the possible consequences of the decisions he had made! "I lost it! I reacted in the wrong way. This should never have happened!"

A twenty-five-year-old woman was trying to exit the cul-de-sac where she lived. She was on her way to a church service and had some friends in the car with her. A group of teenage girls was standing at the exit and did not move. The woman felt this as an anger trigger—she could feel the anger energy. Her need for security, for respect, for fairness, for feeling competent and in control, were being violated. This was her first decision point. What should she do? Explain to the girls that she and her friends were trying to get to church and would appreciate it if the girls would let them through—using her need for hope and confidence to work here? Should she drive slowly toward them, wave to them and thank them for letting her through—showing respect for their behaving appropriately? No, she chose to get out of her car and confront the girls. She was angry and wanted to let them know they could not get away with this.

The confrontation escalated and the woman was fighting with the girls, accompanied by a lot of language from both sides. The woman was no match for the girls, as she soon learned. Here was another decision point. She could stop fighting and stop the insults and walk back to her car, but would she be safe? Anger had moved to physical exchanges and she saw no way out. She managed to hit one of the teenagers in the face. Now, anger was an exploding time bomb. The girl knocked the woman down to the road and banged her head repeatedly on the pavement. No more decision points. The woman died a few days later and the teenager got a two-and-one-half year sentence for contributing to the death of the woman. The time bomb exploded.

Think of an experience you had when your anger or the anger of someone else reached a dangerous level:

What was the event that triggered your anger?
What basic needs were being violated?
What did you do as a first response?
How did you feel?
What was the response of the other person?
How did that person feel?
What did you do to resolve the cause of the anger?
What did the other person do in response?
What was the outcome of the anger-producing situation?

Recognizing Anger in Others

It is indeed an achievement to recognize anger in yourself; how can you be expected to recognize anger in someone else! But, that is almost as important as recognizing your own anger. Most times you feel angry, you are angry with someone else, and you are learning to recognize those times and your anger responses. But, recognizing anger in the other person is certainly high on the list of what is important to RETHINKing anger. How do you Recognize anger in another person? There are a number of ways. One is to ask the other person you think is angry if that is the case. You can ask: "Are you angry about something? Has something happened to make you angry? Have I done anything to make you angry?" Or, if you don't want to go that far, you can say: "You seem a bit upset. Is anything wrong? Can I help with anything? I don't like to see you upset."

The signs you have noticed, which you may or may not refer to include:

a. Tension in the other person's body.
b. A flushed face.
c. The eyes squinting.
d. The voice rather shrill.

In short, the same signs you present when you are angry. Noticing these signs alerts you that anger is present, whether or not it is admitted. Obviously, you cannot say, "I know you are angry; I can see it in your behavior." That would only add to the anger. What you can say is: "If you want to talk about something that is bothering you, I am here for you."

From RECOGNIZE to RETHINK

Here is an example of using decision points in response to anger triggers and using RETHINK skills:

Bob was sitting in the aisle seat of the airplane. He liked it there because he could get out without climbing over other people and annoying them. He also liked to stretch his legs out in the aisle when it was free of flight attendants or passengers moving around. He was content in his space.

Then a number of things happened. First, the person sitting behind him kept kicking the back of his seat. He accepted this at first as part of the settling down process. But it continued. Bob could Recognize his initial annoyance escalating into anger. And he said to himself: "What on earth is going on! Can't that guy settle down? Here I am thoughtful of others and he is a klutz, banging away and really getting to me. He is showing me no respect. I Recognize I am angry and can feel myself getting hot. How do I deal with this? What do I Think is safe to say to a guy who obviously doesn't think of others?

"Let's see. I could say, 'Are you about through banging?' No, that is a little too provoking and suggests I am challenging his sense of Competence and Control, and Respect for him. I must show some Empathy for him so I won't violate his needs. Besides, he might just tell me to 'Go to hell!' I could turn around and look at him with a quizzical look, but he might resent that as not showing him Respect, and just stare at me as if to say, 'What's eating you?' But his banging around is really making me boil and I don't want to take this any more. I know what to say—it just came to me!"

Bob turned around, smiling. "You seem to be having a problem back there. Can I help you?" Bob was integrating Empathy and Respect as he managed his anger. The man was so absorbed in his problem—insufficient space under his seat for his TWO stowed bags, and failing to find a solution. To Bob's surprise and relief, the man was not responding with anger. Bob could Hear that. As a matter of fact, the man apologized! "Oh, I'm sorry! These bags are driving me nuts. I didn't realize I was bothering you." The man had some sensitivity about violating another's needs.

Bob, seeing the two bags, responded lightly, "Well, sometimes two are not better than one!" Then, he Thought about a helpful response. "There is room under the seat in front of me, if that would help, or we can call the flight attendant." The response was a light laugh at the humor and a thanks for the help. Bob could go back to his comfort, feeling especially good about himself. He Notices he had calmed down by "doing the right thing." He got his novel out, slid comfortably down a bit in his chair, crossed his legs, and began to read. He was into the third page when his knee got a whack that sent pain up and down his leg. "Ouch!" he shouted, not able to contain the pain. Nor could he contain his anger (Recognize) when he saw the cause of the pain was the fact the woman in front of him had pushed her seat back as far as it would go, as fast as it would go. Swoosh!

Now, a second aggravation. He thought, "What's happening to people that they can't be civilized? How hard is it to see what you're doing and where you're going?" What's happening to the airlines as they insist on giving airplane builders directives to design the cabins so seat rows are closer together—and with people getting bigger and fatter? It's enough to drive you stark raving mad!" (Recognizing the anger). These thoughts took only seconds and the person pushing the seat back heard the shout of pain. "Oh, excuse me," said the culprit. "I'm so sorry. I sure didn't think before I made that move. Are you OK? Can I do something?" The woman was using Empathy.

"Yeah," snapped Bob, "you can put your seat back up and get it out of my knee!" (He used a little humor that took a good deal of Thinking about how to respond without being offensive.)

The culprit laughed nervously, but appreciated the humor. "Well, would it be satisfactory if I push it back slowly and warn you each time?" (She felt some Empathy for the victim.)

Bob was still smarting and his knee hurt, but he realized his anger wouldn't add anything. Besides, he had made his point. He could cool down now and get back to his book. (He Noticed what was calming him down.)

And then there was the high school boy who had just been dropped from the gang he was in and he didn't know why. He liked the gang, but realized he was not included in plans and learned about them from someone else. Also, he was not called or e-mailed to share experiences and gossip. He felt hurt and angry. (He Recognized his anger and its cause.) He was at a Decision point. Should he walk up to the gang next time he saw them, and tell them what he thought of them? His need for Connectedness and for Respect were being violated. Should he form another gang and start a "war" with his old gang? Should he ask a member of the gang why he was being left out? He Thought about the importance of the gang to his life and realized that he wasn't as interested in what they were doing as he had thought. Maybe this was a good time to form his own gang with several guys he had been spending time with in a science class, and forget about the other gang. Who needs to waste time on a group that doesn't seem to care about you? (Think about what is important more than being angry and acting out on the anger.) He talked with the science classmates, found they were happy to do things together, and so the other gang was of no further value. When the two gangs saw each other, they greeted each other and that was that.

Styles of Anger Expression

Understanding the complexities of anger and the many styles of anger expression is not easy, but it certainly is worth the time. It helps you to be more comfortable with understanding anger in others and in yourself. It prepares you for being in charge of what happens as you use your anger energy creatively rather than being overwhelmed by it or using it in destructive ways.

There is actually a sequence in the anger experience and recognizing it will help you understand more about anger and how to manage it:

a. Anger is a response to threats against basic human needs.
b. There is a point at which you recognize the threat and that becomes the anger trigger.

c. In response to the anger trigger, you have many decision points where you choose the response you will make as the event develops. Do you decide to respond by Creative Anger, using the RETHINK skills, or do you decide to respond with increased anger? But, wait. There is something more to add and that is the anger styles you tend to develop.

Life seems easier when habits kick in. Who needs to think about how to dress every morning? Who needs to think about how to start a car? Who needs to think about how to respond to anger triggers? The most common styles people use as anger expressions are Exploders, Imploders, Chip-Stackers, Blamers, and Transformers. In which category do you fit, or do you fit in more than one? See if you recognize your style.

Exploders

You may find that sometimes you explode with anger. And you may, in fact, choose to Explode to make a point. It may be more like a simulated form of anger than an uncontrolled expression of anger. Banging the table loudly with your shoe may well get a group's attention. They sense the anger. An anger explosion, then, may be a calculated power play that succeeds more often than not. Other times an anger explosion may be a rare expression of unresolved anger that has never been put to rest. Or it may be an immature reaction of a person who has not yet mastered impulse control.

Most likely everyone explodes with anger some time or other, either to make a point or because a special vulnerable part of the person has been touched. It's the person who explodes all the time who is called an Exploder.

Mary-Beth is a talented and beautiful woman of forty. Her parents, her older sister, and her husband, or rather her former husband, would all agree that Mary-Beth has an explosive style of expressing anger. And, they would agree that it is easier to admire her from a distance—she lives abroad for months at a time—than to live *with* her or even to love her. Her style of "losing it" when she gets angry has cost her close relationships, and she has some insight to the fact she is more feared than loved. How did she get this way? It would be easy to say it is her artistic temperament and you just have to accept that she is more sensitive than others and has stronger feelings that need to be played out.

Mary-Beth was born with a congenital heart disease at a time when they were just developing surgical procedures to correct this disorder. She had many operations during her early childhood, both for her heart and for other malformations that were discovered and corrected. As an invalid or very fragile child, she learned that her power resided in her tantrums. People came running each time she exploded with anger or frustration. She never had the corrective give and take of peer relations in play and continued to be the "enfant terrible" even after her health was restored. Limited in strength and tolerance for frustration as a young child, she resorted to a strategy that worked well enough then, but persisted long beyond the time it had been effective.

Many chronic exploders feel weak and helpless even as they appear to rule as tyrants. Women who shout and slam doors when they are angry, drive people away from them, and don't really get to solve their problems. The futility of their outbursts raises the question: "What options do they have?" And it is Creative Anger, using the RETHINK skills that is the path out.

Imploders

People who deny they are ever angry, who consider it vulgar, unpleasant, not lady-like, or agree that gentlemen don't behave that way, can find that rage "boomerangs" for them. They find themselves the victims of their own anger.

Stuart had a heart attack and was rushed to the hospital. He was an Imploder. Everyone agreed that Stuart was a nice guy, a perfect gentleman, easy to get along with, never raised his voice, or used harsh words. He was a sales representative, very successful, with a friendly smile for everyone. His smile, his jovial manner, was his livelihood. Could a man like that feel anger, even rage?

After his heart attack and after learning something about the role of anger in more than a few heart attacks, he began to Recognize what he was angry about. He realized he was much more upset about his son Charlie's divorce than he had admitted. After all, he had reasoned, his son was a grown man who could decide whom he wanted to be married to. Stuart had no right to interfere, to object. That seems plausible, but he went a step further. He felt he had no right to feel angry, disappointed, deeply grieved by his son's divorce. He would not even acknowledge such feelings. Anything Charlie did was fine with him.

Yet, his former daughter-in-law, Judy, had provided some bright moments in his life. They had played tennis together and had enjoyed each other's company. Now Judy was the spurned wife who had not shown up at the club since their break-up. She was angry and one way she used that anger was to refuse letting the grandfather visit his grandchildren. Judy was the woman scorned and her anger was all too visible. Stuart had no skills for handling his own anger with his son for getting him into this predicament. He also had no way to deal with the anger that Judy was now unleashing in all directions. He was devastated to be the target of her anger. People were supposed to be civilized at all times. The stress he was experiencing in reaction nearly killed him.

If denying anger is a characteristic style of yours, if you insist that you never get angry, if you think you don't have the right to feel angry because you are so reasonable, such a nice person, you will certainly want to reconsider that description of yourself.

Chipstackers

Those people who carry around with them lists of injustices, hurts, insults, and grudges, are burdened to exhaustion. They also bore people as they ruminate about each incident. They can't seem to let go of their grievances. The more they think about each of the anger-provoking events, the more they build the case against the person who insulted them or wronged them. They can't let go and the price they pay is increased stress on their bodies as well as increased hostility toward people they feel have caused them problems.

Nancy hates to call her mother. She would love to speak to her mother if her mother could just skip the ritual of recounting her daughter's neglect, her not having called sooner, the times she had come to town and not visited her, etc. These ruminations, the review of the list of grudges, make Nancy hesitate to call even when she misses her so much. Nancy often wants to share some news about her life. Her mother's style of expressing her anger is so annoying to Nancy that the period between calls does get longer and her mother's complaints become more accurate. Nancy's mother needs to learn the K skill—KEEP to the present situation!

The question of how such a seemingly destructive style develops and persists is puzzling. The style clearly has protected the mother against some perceived threat and had some utility over time. It probably has also given her some control over her daughter by tapping guilt. But, the price paid is too high. The mother has limited her daughter's desire to have a closer relationship with her.

Blamers and Shamers

Blamers and Shamers are quick to respond to any perceived threat to their sense of self or to their basic human needs. And the response is too often to blame someone else for the threat. The use of words such as, "You always. . . " "You never. . . " tend to set the stage for the attack.

Those who can only project blame onto others when they are either angry, or more likely the target of someone else's anger, find themselves ill-equipped to manage the complexities of life. People in public life, those in positions of authority or leadership, are constantly blamed and must learn to react in varied ways, without a quick counterattack. One candidate who was recently attacked with blame and shame countered with the quip, "My opponent is better at insults than ideas." Blame can be used as a premeditated strategy for provoking anger, or it can be a rather simplistic response to anger. Other styles are needed and perhaps Empathy is a good one to start with.

When Mrs. Snow, teacher of sixth, seventh, and eighth grades at a rural two-room school, was confronted by a group of tough kids on the way to her car, she was frightened. The members of the group were angry, blaming her for the expulsion of one of their friends. She responded to their anger with an acceptance of their blame. She also realized they had some empathy for their friend. She said she did not like resorting to such a tough strategy. She explained to them that nothing she did seemed to make their friend stop hitting or teasing or destroying papers students had, so she told him to go home. Yes, she was angry with him; he seemed totally out of control. Then she asked them, "What would you have done if you were in my shoes?"

But, they had talked to their friend and had heard his side of the event. He said he was having trouble with the reading assignment and didn't want to tell the teacher that; so he just sat in his seat until he got bored and began bothering people. His friends felt some empathy for what he had experienced as well as empathy for what the teacher had experienced. They talked about a solution, and finally suggested a student review council that could intervene. The teacher could call on that council to intercede when things seemed unmanageable in the classroom.

And that is what happened. Even tough kids come up with some great ideas!

Transformers

Musicians and composers who can express their anger with thunderous chords, joined by the young rappers of the generation, can often find satisfying ways to transform their anger. Other art forms, including painting and sculpture, or dance and poetry, give people ways to sublimate their less acceptable emotions. Lawyers who argue cases, leaders of campaigns to protect the environment or to right some social injustice, are using their anger as a tool for change and so to transform society. A journalist who can write a column that expresses his anger, or a photojournalist who exposes something that she finds outrageous, has each found a way to transform anger to a more advanced social purpose. Scriptwriters, directors, actors, and producers—can all find channels for expressing anger?

Comedians and humorists can also teach us much about how to manage anger by transforming it. The story is told of Lucy, who was caught in traffic with a flooded carburetor. The driver of the huge truck behind her leaned on his horn unrelentingly. The elements of road rage were in place when Lucy got out of her car, her keys in hand. She offered the truck driver her keys, saying, "If you can start my car for me, I'll take over and lean on your horn for you." Humorists not only transform their own anger but they also help us do the same. If you can just remember a good joke at an anger-provoking incident, you can often dissipate the anger energy.

Begin Your Journey

You might as well begin now to use what you have been learning so far. Of course, there is much more to learn, but you are ready to use some of the information you are reading. Remember, there are anger triggers that occur when your basic human needs are not being met or are being violated. Remember, you want to Recognize at what point a need has been violated so you recognize what is making you angry. Remember, there are decision points you have as you respond to the anger trigger and interact with the person or persons who caused it. It is at these decisions points you will learn how to draw on the RETHINK skills to deal with the anger trigger rather than a habitual anger style.

Think of an experience you had recently that really made you angry:

What happened?
What did you do?
How did you feel?
What basic needs were violated?
What did other(s) do in response to what you did?
How did the other person(s) feel?
What basic needs of the other person(s) might have been violated?
Was anger involved?
How was it resolved?
What would you do differently now?

CHAPTER 5

Hear with Empathy

If you are so angry with a friend who failed to pick you up for work that you cannot HEAR what he is saying, you are, in fact, deaf to any resolution of the anger trigger. If you insist on verbally expressing your anger when your friend tries to explain why he didn't pick you up, there will be no resolution, except a lost friend.

Some days you are feeling particularly sensitive to what others do. You have just been told you will not get that much anticipated raise in pay you had so counted on. You are angry. So, this is the day you are not likely to HEAR what your friend is saying as he tries to explain his behavior. And, quite simply, if you don't attend to what another is saying, you will:

Misinterpret, hearing a slight or an attack where none was intended.
Miss important information that might change your feelings or point of view.
Smother empathy.
Alienate your friend.
Compromise the ability to resolve the anger feelings.
Increase the anger.

On the other hand, when you hear accurately, just the opposite happens. You:

Calm down as you concentrate on the other person.
Recognize the feelings your friend expresses as he responds to your anger with his own anger.
Create the opportunity to clear up misunderstandings.
Be sure the information you both have is accurate.
Work to find a solution to the problem so it doesn't happen again.

Hearing Is Not Surrender

Many people fear they have to give up their own opinions and feelings to HEAR and acknowledge someone else's. You do not have to surrender anything. You must simply listen, to HEAR what is being said. However, to HEAR someone else, you do need to temporarily hold back your own anger, opinions, or comments. You will want to curb the urge to interrupt, judge, or impose your own views.

Listening without becoming defensive or trying to "fix" the problem is not easy. It is natural to want to challenge an unfair accusation or to immediately correct a misunderstanding. This is especially true if you are under attack. For many people, retaliation during a verbal argument is almost reflexive. You want to protect yourself, not necessarily physically, but emotionally.

HEARing well gives you more power than insults or recriminations. By calming yourself enough to hear, you gain control over your own emotions. By HEARing, you help the other person calm down, too. You are then in a position to change the argument into a conversation, and the problem into a solution.

Think of a time you were very angry with your best friend:

What happened?
What did you do?
How did you feel?
How did your friend respond to what you did?
How did your friend feel?
How did it end?
How are things now between you and your friend?

Techniques for HEARING

Here are some techniques to help you master the skill of HEARING. Try them as you encounter situations that generate anger.

Reflective Listening

Goal: To HEAR accurately what the other person is saying

The primary tool of HEARING is *reflective listening*. With this technique, you mirror back what the other person is saying to make sure you have understood what was said. Reflective listening requires a set of behaviors you can think about and practice. The behaviors include:

1. Giving full attention to the other person. You signal that you are attending when you lean toward the speaker and make eye contact.
2. Manage the urge to interrupt, correct, or ask lots of questions. Patience is needed. You'll have your turn.
3. Wait until you are sure the other person has finished talking and to collect your own thoughts. Then reflect back what you have heard.

Here are some examples of how to phrase reflective listening statements:

If I heard you correctly, you're . . .
It sounds as if you're . . .
So what you're saying is . . .

Reflective listening is most powerful when used to detect the emotions behind the words. What is the person feeling? However, it also helps defuse arguments based on misunderstandings. The facts can be made clear and important information noted.

You can practice reflective listening in many situations. It is especially helpful when meeting your children's teacher. It is also helpful when brainstorming with colleagues, or even when you ask your partner how the day went. The more skilled you become in using reflective listening in situations that do not involve anger, the easier it will be to draw on during conflict.

For reflective listening to be effective, however, you must make every effort to HEAR. If you simply say the words: "I'm listening!" then sit in angry silence, with arms locked across your chest, you are unlikely to get someone who is in a state of anger to open up and tell you what he/she is angry about.

If you are too angry to listen, it is better to say so. Tell the other person that you need some time to calm down before you can talk things through.

HEARing is not a one-way process. As you listen to others, you have the right to expect the same in return. The fact that your listening may sometimes be enough to help the other person calm down does not mean that you are not entitled to the same treatment. As a matter of fact, N stands for NOTICE what calms you down. This allows you to build a kind of repertoire of ways to calm yourself down.

Reflective listening can happen just by watching the behavior of someone else. Their behavior can tell you as much about their feelings as what they say. Body language is especially important when you are listening to someone who wants your attention. It sets the stage for what may be called Active Listening, which refers to listening without giving advice, clarifying your understanding of what is being said or done, picking up the emotional content of the words, and labeling them, summarizing the situation, and helping in a plan of action.

As the listener, you need to pick up the emotional content of what a person is saying to you and what the body language is expressing. You can then ask if you have labeled the feelings correctly. Of course, you can be very wrong about what body language is saying about feelings. Here's an experience a mother had that exemplifies the challenge:

One evening, my children—five-year-old twins, boy and girl, and a seven-year-old girl—were watching the movie *Johnny Appleseed*. It was animated for children and beautifully produced. Johnny Appleseed's story is great. Here is a man who has found a mission in life, walking around the country and planting apple seeds with the faith that trees will grow. He dies, but even after death, finds he can do the same thing in heaven. He's a happy man. My children began to sob. Quietly, but they did not stop. I said, "He's fine. He's in heaven and is very happy." They continued to sob. I said, "Really, he is okay and is doing exactly what he wants." They continued to sob.

Now I was becoming worried. What was wrong? What was upsetting them so much? I thought I'd better find out. "Are you crying because he died?" All three heads shook no. "What is it then?" Finally, one of them said, "Because he had to walk so far!" The other two nodded in agreement. They had not said a word among themselves, yet each cried for the same reason. I tried to explain that he did the walking over many, many years and had lots of time to rest in-between. That still was not enough to stop their crying. And then I realized that my children connected emotionally with his walking. We lived out in the country and one of the problems was getting the three ready to drive into town for all kinds of appointments: shopping, church, and errands. Even school required being ready for the school bus. The common threat we used to get them moving was, "If you aren't ready in time, you will have to walk to town."

As soon as I realized the connection, I felt better, and after a few laughs over their interpretation of his walking, we all felt better. I also realized that the threat had roused too many unpleasant feelings. From then on I found different, less distressing, ways to get the kids ready.

HEARing with Your Heart

Goal: to HEAR the feelings behind the words

When we complain that someone is not listening, we rarely mean that they are not attending to our words. Rather, we are frustrated and angry because they don't recognize the feelings our words are meant to convey. HEARING and EMPATHY are closely linked. To be heard is to have our feelings recognized and understood. When they are, anger energy can begin to subside. Similarly, when we HEAR and validate the feelings behind someone else's angry words, we gain the power to release the anger energy.

When you listen with empathy, your objective is not to change the other person's point of view—although that may happen—your objective is to put yourself in her shoes. Only when you can do this will you have an opportunity to understand why others feel the way they do or why they experience a situation differently from you. But, this does not mean you give up your own perception of what happened. The other person may be completely linked in her understanding of what happened. Empathy can work both ways, but the angry people must come to some agreement on what really happened to rouse the anger in the first place.

Answering the following questions can help you HEAR with EMPATHY and defuse the anger:

What is the person upset or angry about?
Can you let the person know by words or gestures (or a combination of both) that you understand his feelings?
Can you use reflective listening statements to suggest that the other person might be frustrated, angry, upset, hurt, or frightened?

Reflective listening helps you HEAR with EMPATHY in two ways. First, it focuses your attention fully on the speaker. Once focused, you are ready to listen with your heart as well as your ears. You are better able to notice body language—stiff, clenched fists. Tone of voice often speaks louder than words.

When you HEAR with EMPATHY, you use gestures, such as a brief nod, and words, like "uh-huh" to communicate that you are listening and to encourage the speaker to continue. You avoid cutting in, even to ask clarifying questions. Asking questions in a cross-examination mode is the opposite of empathic listening.

The second aspect of reflective listening that enhances empathy is the act of reflecting back. Reflective listening statements that convey empathy name the feeling that the speaker seems to be experiencing:

It seems like you're feeling (misunderstood, unfairly treated, etc.).
I wonder if you are feeling (left out, ignored, or slighted).
I get the impression that you might be feeling (unhappy, very angry). Is that right?

Through statements like these, you communicate that you are trying to understand what the other is feeling. Sometimes an adult needs to intervene to help achieve these goals.

Two sixth-grade boys, Sid and Jack, were fighting in the cafeteria. Sid's homeroom teacher heard about it from another student, so he confronted Sid the next day.

Teacher: Hi, Sid. I heard about the fight in the cafeteria yesterday.

Sid: Oh, that.

Teacher: Now, I'm really upset by that information and am having trouble trying to understand why you fight with your friend Jack. Are you angry about something?

Sid: Oh, Jack is a jerk. He goes around the cafeteria and takes food off our trays. When he got to me today, I was ready for him. I let him have it. He won't do that again.

Teacher: That certainly was a bad scene, Jack behaving the way he did. Do you think there's another way you can stop Jack's behavior so you don't fight? You know, fighting is what little kids do because they don't know what else to do. Besides, fighting doesn't improve your feelings about Jack and what he does. It might not even stop him.

Sid: He deserved what he got, and I think I'd do it again.

Teacher: Where will that lead—fight after fight after fight? I'll bet you can think of something else to do. You know, maybe Jack is having troubles at home or with other friends. Maybe he doesn't know any other way to show his frustration and anger.

Sid: Well, he did say something about his parents divorcing. I wonder if that's what's bugging him. I really should talk to him.

Teacher: That's a good idea.

The teacher guided Sid away from his anger reactions toward empathy and hearing with his heart.

Often, an adult needs to become part of the process of resolving anger. Sometimes, a teenager, who is able to think about past behavior that is affecting what is happening now, determines the source of anger in a friend.

Judy doesn't talk to me anymore. What could be the reason? Let's see. Oh, I'll bet it's because I didn't like it when she criticized me for ignoring her when I saw her at the mall the other day. I can't think of anything else that happened. That must be it. I'll try to set things straight. We could talk about both versions of the event and resolve the conflict. I really want her for a friend.

Compassion

Compassion is a unique quality that combines the recognition of the pain of someone else or yourself with the desire to do something that shows your caring for the welfare of that person or yourself. RECOGNIZING and feeling the pain is an act of empathy. Being motivated to do something about the pain brings in altruism, and both define compassion. As you feel the pain of someone else facing serious problems that make the person very angry, you are in a position not only to help that person deal with the problems, but also to learn more about creative anger for yourself.

Compassionate people hold a basic set of values about others that guides the way they express their compassion. They care about what happens to you because they care about you as a human being. They see you as a worthwhile, even sacred individual, as is everyone. Their behavior reflects that belief in your worthiness. Their skills in interpersonal relationships express that belief.

Compassionate people are recognizable by the way they behave. You don't have to get to know them too well to determine they are compassionate—their behavior shouts it. You intuitively reach out for them, trust them, and know they will help you. The skills of compassion are recognizable. Perhaps you have some of these skills as you help others deal with situations fraught with anger.

1. Making friends easily.
   The compassionate person is friendly. He is not afraid of people and can reach out to them. He is open to becoming a friend if that seems

to be a good idea, and is not defensive or shy in the sense that he fears rejection by others. The compassionate person assumes acceptance.

2. Feeling empathy when something unpleasant happens to someone.
The compassionate person is empathic. He can feel, at least for an instant, the pain someone is going through when a serious problem that causes anger reactions occurs. He shows concern by saying some words of comfort or understanding and offers help, if it is desired.

3. Honest about reactions.
The compassionate person talks to others when they do something that upsets her. She does not hold a grudge or wait to get even. She can express what is bothering her about the other's behavior, with the intent of it changing so the relationship can continue.

4. Managing negative emotions.
The compassionate person knows that others are distressed by her anger, fear, or desire for revenge. She seeks discussion, negotiation, and resolution of problems causing strong negative emotions; especially anger.

5. Expecting fairness.
The compassionate person assumes fairness in relationships and is quite willing to address a perceived violation of fairness. Violations would include unfair rules and regulations, unfair grading, unfair promotions, unfair treatment of family members, and other acts that seem unfair when measured by concepts of equity and equality. The questioning would be done without rancor or accusation. Anger may, however, be expressed and explained.

6. Demonstrating affection.
The compassionate person is not afraid to show affection for others. He is quite willing to hug someone or tell the other person how he feels about them. Some people do not want physical contact, so they can be told in words and smiles that they are liked.

7. Listening.
The compassionate person listens to those who approach him. He gives attention, responses, and respect to the person being listened to. He does not try to tell the person what to do.

8. Accepting compliments and praise from others.
The compassionate person is able to accept approval from others without belittling it with comments such as, "Oh, I didn't do anything special," or "I don't deserve this praise. Others did much more." (For example: This when he helped the two directors resolve their anger toward each other by talking with them separately and then suggesting they get together. He would be willing to join the discussion. The future of the organization was at stake.)

9. Initiating conversations.

The compassionate person is willing to start a conversation with someone else or with a group in order to show a friendly recognition of others. How many times have you been in an elevator of your apartment building or your office where no one says a word? You can feel the tension or, worse, the indifference as the floors go by.

10. Asking for help.

The compassionate person trusts others enough to feel free to ask for help when she needs it. She has built a network of supports so that she does not feel alone or abandoned when trouble appears. She approaches others with respect and a clear need, and her attitude says she expects them to help because she knows others are good human beings, too.

Taking the Sting out of Trigger Words

Goal: to identify and defuse trigger words

Certain words undermine our ability to HEAR more easily than others. These *trigger words* are provocative statements designed, whether consciously or not, to hurt and inflame. They are often labels, put downs, or reminders of past failures. Bill's story will probably sound familiar.

Bill was trying really hard to listen to his wife, Carly, until she said: "You never help, no matter how many times I ask. You're such a lazy, self-centered bum!" An image of the preceding night flashed through Bill's mind. He was still at this desk at 8 P.M., feeling guilty about missing yet another family dinner but overwhelmed with work. It was that extra project he'd taken on. But how could he have said no? Half the department had already been downsized and the job market was not looking good. Didn't Carly understand? Didn't she know that he worked this hard for the family? That he'd like nothing better than to spend more time with the kids, to paint the trim, to build that shelf unit he'd promised her? But he was done in. Spent. Exhausted with work and worry. It wasn't fair? How dare she call him lazy! How dare she not recognize how hard he worked!

"Lazy? Self-centered?" he roared at his wife. "I'll show you lazy. I'll quit my job and let you worry about keeping a roof over our heads for a change!"

Each of us has certain words that trigger our anger just as *lazy* and *self-centered* did for Bill. By identifying our personal trigger words, we can often neutralize them. Forewarned may well be forearmed.

What words trigger your anger? Why? What are they connected to that makes you angry—experiences, labels given you? If you have some and are aware of them, you can be prepared for their impact.

Get Comfortable

Goal: to eliminate distractions so that you can concentrate on listening

Your back is aching. Your head is pounding. The TV is blaring. The phone is ringing. Your eleven-year-old storms into the kitchen, screaming that she's going to fail art because of you. *You* wouldn't buy her new markers. *You* made her use the old, disgusting dried-up ones. *You* never get her anything she needs. *You*. . . .

Your blood begins to boil. You are really angry. You want to calm down. You want to listen and talk. But instead you're getting more and more angry. No wonder. Few things drive us to distraction when we are trying to resolve an argument more than, well, distractions. You will need to tone down the environment to tune into your daughter.

First, make sure your body is comfortable. If you begin arguing as you turn from the kitchen counter, a plate of peanut butter sandwiches in hand, don't continue to stand there until your legs turn to jelly. Sit down. If the kitchen chair is uncomfortable, move to the sofa. If you are hungry, eat the sandwiches before you talk. You'll be better able to turn your energies outward once your body's needs are met.

Similarly, quiet your outer environment. Listening well requires tunnel vision and tunnel hearing. Your eyes and ears need to focus exclusively on the other person. Turn off the TV. Ask your eight-year-old to practice his violin later. A quiet environment makes it easier to HEAR.

Hearing Aids

Goal: to refocus attention on hearing the other person

If you find that you can hear with perfect attentiveness all the time, you are very special! For most people, this is an unachievable goal. Trigger words often catch us off guard, provoking our own habitual responses. Or we may grow impatient listening to a long and familiar litany of complaints and find ourselves cutting in. Even the sudden growl of hunger can break concentration and undermine efforts to HEAR.

At such moments, you will want to use a word, an image, or a sound to calm yourself and restore your focus. You will want to do this when your attention shifts from the other person to yourself—or to the task you have tomorrow. When you think of it, other mental activity momentarily pauses, giving you time to reestablish your hearing mode.

The Listening Perch

Goal: to create a mental safety zone from which to HEAR

It is particularly hard to HEAR if you don't feel safe, and it is hard to feel safe when someone is yelling at you, verbally abusing you. The natural desire to defend yourself can undermine your efforts.

A listening perch is a special kind of hearing aid designed to help you tolerate the other person's outburst without feeling threatened. It's a mental image you can call upon when you RECOGNIZE anger or anxiety building up inside. Rather than react, you can take refuge in your listening perch, using it to distance yourself emotionally so that you can continue to HEAR the other person. Keep calm. Sit where you feel safe or can get out quickly if necessary.

Think about an experience you had where an angry person seemed so out of control that you were frightened, yet angry, yourself:

What happened?
What did you do?
What did the angry person do in response to what you did?
How did the angry person feel, besides angry?
How did it come out?
What RETHINK skills did you use? (Especially HEAR.)
What RETHINK skills would have been more effective?

RETHINK in Action

Think about what it takes to HEAR what the other person is saying as you read the story below. Then answer the questions.

Maggie was already running late for work when her teenage daughter, Hannah, stumbled out of the bedroom, looking groggy and puffy-eyed. Maggie was furious. Hannah should have been showered, dressed, and finished with breakfast by now. Maggie had assumed Hannah was in her room getting her books together. She had just five minutes to catch the school bus.

"Mom, I . . . " began Hannah, but before she could say another word, Maggie cut her off. "Great, Hannah!" she exploded. "I can't believe you overslept again!" I am not going to drive you to school. I have a meeting this morning and I will not be late because you stayed up all night instant messaging or whatever it is you do. You'll walk to school and face the consequences!"

"Fine!" Hannah shot back, her lip beginning to tremble." "Be like that. Go to your stupid job. That's all you care about anyway. But you'll have consequences, too. Oh, yeah, lot of consequences," she continued, now barely holding back her tears. "You'll have to tell grandma why you let me get so sick I needed to go to the hospital!"

Taken aback by her daughter's tears, Maggie swallowed the retort she was about to shout. She looked closely at Hannah. She noticed her daughter's feverish cheeks and glassy eyes for the first time. She reached out to touch Hannah's brow. Hannah arched away but not before Maggie felt the heat.

"Oh, Hannah," Maggie said, all anger dissolved. "I'm so sorry. I just assumed you had overslept. That wasn't fair of me. Now, tell me what hurts."

But now Hannah was the furious one. She stormed into her room and slammed the door.

Here are some questions for you:

How do you think Hannah felt when her mother misjudged her?
How do you think Maggie felt when she realized her error?
How did Maggie's thoughts about why Hannah was late influence the way she felt?
How might HEARing have helped Maggie avoid the argument with Hannah?
What should Maggie do next?

Think of a recent time in your own life when, like Hannah, you felt angry and misunderstood. How would HEARing have been helpful to you and the other person? What would you have liked somebody to say to you that showed understanding? How do you imagine that you would have felt?

Now remember a time when you were more like Maggie, failing to HEAR. What happened? How did you feel? How did the other person feel? How might HEARing have changed the outcome?

Finally, think about a situation in which you used reflective listening. How did you feel after expressing empathy for the other? How did the recipient feel?

Putting the Skills Together

Here is a story about Martha and Jim, two strangers who ended up friends because of a narrowly averted argument. As you read their story, think about how they used the RETHINK skills you've learned so far to transform their anger. The RETHINK skills they used are:

RECOGNIZE what makes you angry and how you react.
EMPATHIZE with the other person.
THINK about the situation in a new way.
HEAR what the other person is saying.

Martha swung her car around into the Symphony Hall parking lot. She took the curve a little fast, but she knew what she was doing. She prided herself on handling her Mazda well and she knew this lot—after all, she'd been a trustee of the Symphony for the past ten years. As she pulled into her reserved space, she saw the parking attendant running toward her. "Hey, YOU!" he shouted. "Where do you think you are, the Indy 500? Wanna get us all killed?"

Martha tightened her grip on the steering wheel. She felt her cheeks flush. Who was he to talk to her like that? Didn't he know who she was? Besides, she had never so much as dented a fender in this garage—or anywhere else for that matter! Did he think she was some ditzy woman who didn't know how to drive? How dare he shout and preach at her! She should have him fired!

Fired? Martha suddenly felt ashamed of herself. She realized that the parking lot attendant wasn't the only one overreacting. Who knows? Maybe he had a bad day. His outburst wasn't appropriate, but really, neither was her bristling pride.

Martha took a deep breath, calmed herself, and rolled down the window. She looked at the man who was now leaning tensely against her car, panting. She saw not anger but panic in his eyes.

"I bet you've had a rough day today," she said, overcoming the urge to justify her driving or demand an apology.

"Rough? That's an understatement," replied Jim, He sighed and closed his eyes for a minute. The tension drained from his body. When he looked back at Martha, sadness had replaced panic in his eyes. "My boy was hit by a car as he was cycling to school this morning. Thank the Lord he had his helmet on and a hedge broke his fall. But his arm is in a cast and he can't play football for the rest of the season. Lady, I'm sorry I yelled but you gotta be careful. The guy who hit my son was coming around a curve, too. He never saw him."

Martha sat there and listened. This man had already had a terrible day and he needed to tell someone who could empathize and sympathize with him. His angry outburst had been inappropriate, but understandable, given his son's accident.

Now, Martha and Jim exchange warm greetings whenever she comes to Symphony Hall. They always take a few minutes to tell each other some news, like how the boy's arm is doing and how the team is getting on without him. Martha enjoys these chats and tries to get there early enough to share a few moments with Jim. And he is always helpful and courteous.

Imagine how differently Martha and Jim's situation might have turned out had Martha not:

RECOGNIZED her own mounting anger.

Depersonalized Jim's outburst by THINKing of what other than her driving might be making him mad.

EMPATHIZED with him by expressing concern that he'd had a rough day rather than giving vent to her own annoyance; and

HEARD what he had to say.

CHAPTER 6

Anger in Couples

There is probably no other relationship that benefits more from the creative use of anger than the relationship of couples. Anger can be experienced either as a slow burn in which there is a gradual escalation of feelings from bothered, interrupted, disturbed, annoyed, irritated, angry, to rage; or a wild rapid escalation that leads to an all-out war. With the level of wishes that frequently go unfulfilled in relationships, such as the longing for intimacy, dependability, time spent together, compassion, knowledge about each other's moods and behaviors, and shared love and experiences, couples are more vulnerable to deep feelings of disappointment. The use of RETHINK anger management skills has the potential to turn a full-blown outburst of anger into a creative problem solving moment. Anger can be used to improve relationships rather than destroy a hard-earned connection. Intervention into the destructive cycle of anger is possible anywhere along the cycle of bothered, interrupted, disturbed, annoyed, to explosion. Partners can begin a dialogue by telling the other what is bothersome and explaining why. Keeping the discussion at this level can prevent an all-out war. Skills and practice are essential. The RETHINK skills are intended to disrupt the cycle of destructive anger and initiate a rewarding conversation that enhances the relationship.

As you read this chapter, make note of where the anger is triggered, where it could have been avoided or managed when recognized as times to take action to prevent the stronger, potentially harmful expression of anger.

The Expectations of Intimacy

Many people want their partner to know magically what is on their mind without even having to say anything. ("If I have to tell her what I want, then it's not worth saying.") Couples have profound yearnings for closeness and trust ("If only someone could know me as well as I know myself"), while simultaneously carrying huge fears of dependency. ("If I let him know me too well he could take advantage of my vulnerabilities.") With these conflicting emotions, misinterpretations are bound to happen, resulting in antagonism and anger.

Partners who blame each other for not meeting their basic needs become bitter. They interpret the other's behavior in biased ways. ("You're never there for me," or "You always forget about what I need!") Frequently they distort the meaning of their partner's words and actions. ("You are giving me flowers because you want to quieten me.") As you can see in this comment, it is not necessarily the actions per se (giving flowers) that trigger the anger; rather it is the interpretation of the actions (you don't want to do what I want you to do) that determines whether someone experiences anger. Anger, and even rage, develops when we ascribe our own interpretations to our partner's behavior.

Early in our lives we build theories that help us make reasonable guesses regarding beliefs and intentions of other people. With couples in highly conflicted situations, one's guesses about the partner's intentions can become biased and negatively skewed.

Misunderstanding, misinterpreting, and attributing ugly motives to people close to us, all lead to the on-going anger in the relationship. Remarkably, misinterpretations can be so harmful to a relationship that even the person whom you once loved can be seen as evil or as the enemy out to hurt you. Many times the couple's interpretation is exaggerated. Because the imagined "Enemy" may *appear* dangerous, vicious, or evil, the supposed victim feels compelled to do something drastic. Although conflicts in couples can be dangerous physically, they are more often dangerous emotionally. The threat is to their pride, their self-image—particularly if they believe their adversary has the upper hand. The sense of vulnerability is generally out of proportion to the adversary's actual transgression.

Transforming a Relationship

Regina and Joseph have been married for fifteen years. They met in college and fell in love at first sight. Although their marriage has withstood the test of time, each has some dissatisfactions with the other that are more than pet peeves. These dissatisfactions periodically flare up into serious arguments followed by long periods of icy silence. Sometimes weeks can go by with Regina not speaking to Joseph. Regina understands that such silence is the product of unspoken anger and that the silence does no good for the relationship. Even more, she realizes that the enforced silence effectively eliminates any chance for reconciliation or the intimacy for which she longs. She feels empty and feels the beginnings of a depression. Her unexpressed anger drains her. Further, shutting herself off from her angry feelings has the unintended consequence of shutting herself off from her feelings generally, including her naturally warm and nurturing style toward her children.

Joe, of course, also hates silent periods, and survives them by avoidance—spending more time at work. Ultimately, these silent "fits," as he calls them, would blow over and the two of them would get back to business as usual. Since many of their fights centered on what Regina regards as Joe's inattentiveness, his retreat to his office only reinforces Regina's anger and makes matters worse.

One day Regina was angry when Joe did not come home from work early when he knew she had an important parent-teacher meeting at school. Furious, she said to herself: "Joe has time for everybody else but me! He never cares about me. I guess I'm not important enough to him." The phone rang and with anger and self-pity, Regina answered it. It was her sister, and without her usual reserve, she found herself pouring out all of her complaints about Joe.

Her sister responded: "Come on, Regina, you know Joe loves you. Why not tell him what is bothering you. He really cares about you and I know he will listen. Do it now before you run off to the meeting." Hanging up the phone, Regina decided to take the risk and try something different this time.

Instead of running out to the meeting the moment Joe came home, Regina asked him to sit with her for a minute and hear how angry, disappointed, and frustrated she felt with him for once again being late. She began by stating how important this parent-teacher meeting was and added that she was anxious about meeting the teacher and wanted Joe to go along to support her. She let Joe know how much she valued his strength and clear thinking and needed his support at this moment. And then she admitted that she was afraid to talk to the teacher without him being there because she worried that their son may have a learning problem.

Having entered the conversation prepared for a fight, Joe was stunned and softened by the words. In all the years of their marriage, this was the first time Regina ever said she was afraid and needed Joe's help. He hadn't realized how important the parent-teacher meeting was to her, and was truly sorry he was late. Joe asked if they could go together if he dressed quickly. Tears came to Regina's eyes. She now was deeply touched by his willingness to give her support and by his responsiveness. Joe got washed and dressed quickly and they were off to the meeting.

By their use of many of the RETHINK skills, a situation that easily could have ended in an argument and lengthy period of silence, ended instead with increased intimacy and feelings of appreciation. Regina Recognized her anger; both Regina and Joe showed Empathy toward their partner. Regina Integrated her respect (and love) for Joe into the conversation when she spoke to him about her concern, and KEPT in the here and now. All these actions provided the atmosphere for each to respond differently than usual, with a different outcome.

They became a team that could laugh together, play together, and make love together. The habitual script changed from ice to a more passionate loving relationship. Regina had used her anger creatively as a tool for change.

On the Road to Chinatown

Arlene and Janet made plans to go to Chinatown, New York, for dinner that evening, along with their husbands. Arlene drove to pick up her husband, Jack, from work. Jack obviously had a difficult day, and was in a visibly bad mood. It would take little to irritate him. Oblivious to the obvious warning signs, Arlene asked Jack to drive, which he did in a huff. Off they went in their cross-town journey in heavy rush-hour traffic to pick up Janet and Bob. By the time they had picked up the other couple, traffic was bumper-to-bumper and moving at a snail's pace. Janet kept giving directions from the backseat, but they sat in snarled traffic for close to forty-five minutes. Jack was furious, thinking, "How could Arlene put me into this situation?" He stewed until, fuming, he blurted out: "You know I had a lot of driving to do this week and you know how much I hate being stuck in a car. How could you do this to me?" Then he turned to Janet and screamed: "You give terrible directions. You have no idea how to get to the stupid restaurant!"

Janet, who was not used to being screamed at, said with much anger, "Don't you yell at me like that!" From there, things got worse. Now, heavy rains brought traffic to a stop. It looked like they would never get to the restaurant. An hour later they arrived at their destination, but couldn't find a parking space. Janet kept saying, "Park here. Park here!" or "It's not necessary to get so upset," trying desperately to help lighten the tense situation. Each of her comments only made matters worse. Janet also offered to drive. "No," Jack answered adamantly, "The damage has been done."

After a continuing series of problems, they finally got to the restaurant and throughout the entire dinner, Jack was coldly silent. The others continued to talk, acting as if they were not bothered by Jack's irritation—his anger. When dinner was finished, the couples returned to the car and their friends asked to be dropped off anywhere; they would take the subway home. They clearly had enough of the tension.

After dropping off Janet and Bob, Arlene and Jack continued home in silence. Jack refused to stop at a newsstand to let Arlene pick up a paper as she had requested. Arlene lost her temper, jumped out of the car, walked to get the newspaper, and walked home alone. By the time she arrived home, she had clearly had enough. The walk had not reduced her anger. "How could you act like that?" Jack was silent. Arlene stated, "I am so angry I could punch you!" "Go ahead," said Jack. Arlene started to punch Jack as hard as she could on his arm until she began to cry. Through her tears she bemoaned, "How can I be married to such a cold-hearted, insensitive man? I hate you!" It felt like the relationship was moving into a downward spiral, with increased bickering and fighting and she feared the collapse of the marriage.

In this event, very little went right and much went wrong. How could RETHINK skills have enabled the parties to have a different story? How could they use anger energy creatively for beneficial outcomes?

First, *R:* recognize. The whole scenario would have changed if either Jack recognized that he was in a "bad mood" when he entered the car, or if Arlene had been more focused on Jack and seen the warning signs. It was clear he was irritated and tense. One or both might have suggested that (1) Arlene drive, or (2) the dinner plans be abandoned or moved uptown to avoid a long drive. Or one of the other people in the car could have (*R*) recognized that Jack was angry, showed some (*E*) empathy for the guy who had the bad day, acknowledged the lousy situation, and (*I*) integrate respect for Jack's point of view by suggesting they eat somewhere else that didn't involve so much driving. Jack could have thought about his behavior, realizing his anger was mounting, by trying to talk to himself: "I am getting upset over something that is really in the scheme of things, very unimportant." And he could have (*N*) noticed his tension mounting in his body and then worked to calm himself down by deep breathing or turning on the radio and seeing if he could find some relaxing or distracting music. Or he could have given up driving, recognizing that he was very upset, and taken a backseat in order to recover his equilibrium.

Not only Jack, but the others in the car were also caught in a destructive cycle of anger. And some experiences of the past could have fueled more anger. Arlene's father was verbally abusive and consequently, Arlene shrank at the sound of angry words. (This was her ghost from the past). Jack's father died when he was only twelve years old, and he was prematurely cast in the role of the responsible man who had to persist in the face of extreme difficulty for his large family. He adopted an aggressive (sometimes even tyrannical) style of asserting his immature authority. In this situation, even though not really comparable, the same feelings were aroused and he went into autopilot, feeling like he was forced to endure the difficulties and became aggressive, tyrannical, and then silent and depressed. (This was his ghost from the past.)

Janet's mother had died when she was only seven years old; her father quickly remarried and she grew up with the prototypical Wicked Witch from the East stepmother. She was especially frightened by Jack's irritability and kept trying to make things better with unwanted advice. (This was her ghost from the past.) Bob, born in a repressive political culture, lived his childhood frozen in a silent fear. (This was his ghost from the past.) So when he experienced Jack's anger, he never uttered a word in the car. None of them understood the complex dynamics that were triggered in the car—either individually or as a group. Obviously, none of them knew or utilized any of the necessary anger management skills to forestall what each experienced as a disaster.

To continue the story:

Interrupting the Cycle

The next day Arlene, still upset, called her friend Janet to talk about the prior evening's events. Arlene tearfully blurted out: "I am caught in an abusive marriage and I don't know how to get out of it." Janet was very empathic, but, in the end, observed (correctly), "It sounds like everyone in the car was stuck in a bad place, not just Jack. Nobody was willing to stop the exchanges," Janet continued, "and nobody considered the other person." Janet pointed out that even Arlene was single-focused, and not particularly considerate of Jack and how upset he was becoming. Arlene began to see the part she played in the prior evening's fiasco. Jack had no right to be so out of control, but she too played a part in the destructive angry scene. Certainly Jack needed to recognize what was going on for him personally and manage his own behavior. But Arlene could have opened herself to Jack's situation, empathized with him, and, at the very least, done no more harm. The other couple, too, might have intervened more constructively with empathy, problem solving, and calming techniques.

There are lessons here. The first is that managing anger is not achieved by magic any more than winning the Derby. Skills and practice are crucial. RETHINK skills are designed to interrupt the angry sequence of events, and to lead to effective problem solving and improve a relationship. Another lesson is that it takes more than one person to create an anger situation. With few exceptions, in relationships there are no clear victims and among people who know each other, everyone usually plays some part. Intimates, especially, often share responsibility for creating, sustaining, and intensifying conflict. At any point in an angry exchange, the use of the RETHINK skills has the potential to turn a situation around. This is the effect of using the anger energy creatively. The foursome could have used empathy, for example, toward each other or even some humor and laughed at the many obstacles that surfaced. The night could have been reframed as a memorable war against the elements and closer relations might have evolved.

Here are some general RETHINK skills that a couple can use:

R = Recognize each other's cues that anger is being tapped. Am I or is the partner disturbed, interrupted, bothered, annoyed, irritated, or angry?

E = find Empathy for each other's feelings and points of view.

T = Think about what is being said and use listening skills to guide your own thinking. Can you reframe or rethink the situation?

H = Hear what your partner is *really* saying. Listen with your heart and determine what the underlying feelings are.

I = Integrate respect and love as you respond to your partner. When you speak, use "I" statements that include the following framework: I feel (state an emotion) when (state the situation) because (state what happens inside of you).

N = Notice what is happening in your body. Use relaxation skills to keep your blood pressure from rising and your thinking clear. Touching, stroking, and other ways of calming each other can be developed.

K = Keep in present time. If the argument reverts to past experiences that are then used as weapons, remember that this is not war. And keeping in the framework of a couple means building an alliance in which old hurts can be spoken about in caring and safe ways.

Destructive Anger in Couples

All couples experience anger in their relationships. How it is expressed, how frequently it occurs, and how capable couples are in resolving the anger, make a difference between a good, happy, and healthy relationship and a difficult, unhappy relationship. Frequent expressions of antagonism, lack of respect for each other's ideas, and continual conflict can obliterate the feelings of love that the couple felt when they were newlyweds. Constant criticism and negativity, and an inability to resolve even the smallest disagreement are signs that a relationship is in trouble. Ineffective communication such as we saw with Arlene and Jack, only leads to a desire to escape.

It is easy to fear your own anger, not only because it brings about disapproval from others, but also because it signals a need for change, and change generates its own fears. With our fear, we tell ourselves, "He will just blow up," or "It's not worth the trouble," or "If I say something it won't matter anyway," or "I better pick my battles and this is not the one— I don't know if I am right about the issue." We tell ourselves these things because it is a way of rationalizing, explaining our own fear, and avoiding going into unknown territory, even when everything is telling us change is necessary.

Many of us are inept at expressing anger or make all kinds of excuses to shy away from saying what is on our minds. Frequently we feel hurt and withdraw rather than address the person who has hurt us. We justify this behavior by telling ourselves that we need to protect the *other* person. We want to preserve harmony in our relationships, fearing that if we *really* state what is on our mind, the relationship will fall apart. With withdrawal and fear come a loss of self, our dreams, our own sense of competency, and our own sense of worth. Not wanting to risk our security (even if it is minimal, it's all that we know) we live with a kind of emotional paralysis. Women who are abused are particularly vulnerable to that kind of thinking.

But, there are other problems with this inhibition of feelings. The more we do not say what we need to say, the more we store up our anger (either consciously or unconsciously), the more these feelings can turn to rage. Rage always finds expression, either as an external explosion or as internal depression. Rage is often out-of-control anger. We talk about "blind-rage." Rage can bring about destructive consequences pushing people away rather than improving the things that need to be corrected. Or, people can easily discount a concern you have and not consider your complaint on its merits. Often, the more you "rant and rave" the easier it is for the other person to simply disregard you. Nothing changes, except that you feel worse about your relationship and the situation.

Anger to Rage

Angela and Jim have been married for ten years. They have four children. Jim declares that he has never really loved Angela. He has just stayed with her because of the children. He complains that the relationship is so bad he rarely talks to her. Night after night, she will plead with him for some communication. He refuses. He does not believe talking will do any good since "every time Angela speaks, she is critical, harsh, abrasive, and just ugly." However, every once in a while she pushes him "just a little too far" and then he explodes. He has been known to punch holes in the wall, throw whatever was in his hand, scream, and curse so forcefully that the children cry in fear. The relationship has remained turbulent for over seven years.

Rage can not only be destructive but it also creates stagnation in a relationship. Frequently, we only wish to change the partner. This approach hardly ever works, especially when the other person does not want to change! Angela would like Jim to go through a metamorphosis, to talk to her, to tell her what is on his mind, but to no avail. Jim would like Angela to be less critical and more accepting of him. Neither one has any plans to change their own behavior. Jim is convinced that there is only one way out of this terrible situation—divorce. Their patterns of reacting to each other have become predictable and ineffective. They do not see other possibilities. Each one blames the other for the problems in their marriage. They are stuck in a lose-lose battle.

Rewriting the Script

In order to resolve the chronic conflict in Angela and Jim's relationship (and many other similar relationships) one of the partners, let us say Angela, but the same applies to Jim, has to decide that she *wants* to solve the problem (above all else). She seeks to understand her own reactions by looking at her personal belief systems, automatic thoughts, and interpretations. Why does she constantly criticize Jim? What purpose do her verbal attacks on Jim have? What might she be afraid of? With introspection she discovers her own fears that she is unlovable and that she deserves the neglect and disrespect she is getting. By tuning into her automatic thoughts (although we recognize how difficult it is), she then is free to start giving up trying to change Jim, and is now willing to start changing her thinking and her verbal attacks of Jim. She, additionally, tries to consider alternative explanations by Hearing what her partner is saying from his perspective.

Jim and Angela had to do some serious RETHINKing. Angela had to come to understand that her profound feelings of loneliness, worthlessness, and despair were not Jim's fault. She sought psychotherapy and antidepressant medication, which helped control her feelings of helplessness and sadness. She found friends in a women's legal defense group with whom she could discuss the legal issues of those who could not afford health services, and what fertilizers and pesticides are least harmful to children. She realized that the concrete, reality-oriented topics were not subjects for gaining her husband's interest. Other women from her tennis club could be consulted about clothes for the children. The replacement for her washer-dryer was based on a recommendation from her brother. She could address each of these concrete problems without disturbing Jim. What she could expect from Jim was redefined.

As Angela begins to change what she expects from Jim, her disappointment and anger subside and she stops criticizing Jim. She Recognizes that she is angry (probably with good reason!) and then she turns her critical eye on herself, not in a self-hating manner but in a loving compassionate way. Notice "I will be conscious of my own overreaction and calm myself down before I respond to a perceived provocation. I will stop my negative thinking. I have to stop lashing out at Jim and lashing out at myself."

Jim, on the other hand, might focus on Recognizing his own anger and his belief system that fuels his anger; that is, "She will never be available to me emotionally. She will never be able to meet my expectations." In his belief system the reality of a relationship never measures up to his fantasy, over which he has complete control. Jim RETHINKs and with sadness, recognizes that he cannot expect Angela to enjoy and share his enthusiasm for the appreciation of abstract fields such as science, philosophy, abstract art, and modern music. He accepts that he needs to find other ways in which he can share his interests and not be angry with Angela who rejects the music he likes, but not him.

Jim's new insight leads him to have some Empathy for Angela. Jim might say to her, "You must feel very lonely in this relationship. I am sorry I cannot give you all that you want and need." Integrate respect by commenting on her strengths and helpful behaviors and tell her "I will try to be there for you, but I don't want to be a whipping post." Hear— "I know I have not listened to you in a loving way, but we can respect each other's differences and redefine how we engage." And when he feels himself becoming angry, he can become conscious of Noticing his body's response and calm himself down *before* he reacts.

As Jim and Angela learn to separate their expectations and interests they also can see places where they can come together. Vacations and meals with their children, visiting extended family and community events are perfect opportunities to be a couple. They have decided to separate their bedrooms with an adjoining door. Paradoxically, the less they expect from one another, the more frequently the adjoining door is opened in the middle of the night.

Before Angela and Jim learned to limit their expectations from one another, they attributed the worst characteristics to the other. Negative attributions have a destructive impact on relationships. But how is it that we can develop such negative frameworks when we used to see the same person in a positive, loving light? When partners regard each other in positive ways, things tend to go smoothly. They interpret (HEAR) their partner's words as loving, and experience kindness in their partner's actions. (He bought me these flowers because he knows I love roses.) During courtship and when the couples are newlyweds, they view each other through positive lenses. Once the couple starts to spend more time together, or live together, the reality of the daily disappointments sets in and the positive framework with which they began their relationship is challenged. The dreams and high expectations of the "greatest love ever lived" begin to be recognized as unattainable. Some couples adjust to the daily ups and downs of life and find delight in their partnership and satisfaction in their relationship. Love matures and the relationship grows. However, if the couple's frame of reference turns negative in response to the disappointments, a negative viewpoint can overwhelm them, frustration can upset them, and mistrust of all actions ("the flowers he brought me are meaningless"), resentment and disrespect will follow. Black and white or all or nothing thinking can set in. (He always . . . She never . . . He's evil . . . She's a liar . . .) and all deeds are seen through this negatively distorted way of thinking.

With expectations come unspoken desires that can crystallize into rules or "shoulds." If these rules are broken (she *should* be on time for our meetings) the partner can interpret the actions as a break in their contract (she promised she would be there for me). Naturally, the "rules" are not made explicit, so the offending party doesn't even know he or she is breaking a "rule" nor did they ever agree to the edict! Many couples live in a tyranny of the "shoulds." Once again we see the idea of "mind reading" being adopted ("my partner should know I don't like that") causing conflict resolution to become extremely difficult. Making matters worse, the unspoken "rule" becomes solidified and rigidity in thinking takes over. The partner feels violated ("I never thought she would stoop so low and try to buy me off by buying me stupid roses") and rejected ("she does not love me").

A vicious cycle is unknowingly created. Each partner believes that the very feelings yearned for, love and devotion, are being violated. Here is another example:

Mary and Rob were married four years ago. Rob had lost his first wife in a car crash and felt some responsibility for her death. When he met Mary, he fell in love with her and thought to himself he would take care of her completely. He asked her to give up her job and stay at home. She agreed. Rob treated her with respect and high regard. In return, she took care of the house, cooked, cleaned, and rubbed his back when he ached. When it was time to write their wills, Rob explained that although all his possessions were in his name, when he died she would receive all that he owned. Mary however, was worried about her financial security and asked if her name could be joined on the ownership of the property. A fight ensued. Didn't she trust him? (Rob's hidden expectation was that Mary would never question his ability to take care of her.) She responded, of course, that she trusted him but wanted some personal security. (Mary's unspoken agreement was that Rob would *want* to make her feel secure, especially financially). How could he even question her love, she wondered? A break in the unspoken contract appeared.

Mary threatened to return to work in order to secure her financial well-being. She was flooded with fears of insecurity that reminded her of her past. Rob once again felt that things were out of control and he held some responsibility. He not only lost the trust he had with Mary, he could also lose Mary. Was she thinking of a divorce?

When the unspoken expectations are violated, anger ensues. In Rob and Mary's story, they were following traditional ways of thinking about male (husband) and female (wife) roles in marriages. Each partner planned to take care of the other in, what they assumed, were fair and equitable ways. They came to the marriage with these beliefs that formed the bedrock of their marriage. Both Mary and Rob came from traditional families who also believed in conventional male-female roles. When one of these beliefs was challenged, the security of their relationship was threatened and they did not know how to respond to each other.

In counseling, Mary and Rob learned the importance of making the unspoken contracts explicit. They didn't love each other less; they just had not articulated their specific needs. The RETHINK skills can be employed here to help the couple openly and frankly communicate. Certainly, "I" messages are very important. Mary can make a clear, nonaccusatory, nonblaming statement to Rob. ("I feel very worried when my name is not on legal documents because I fear being financially vulnerable.") At the same time she can understand and be EMPATHIC to Rob. ("I know your intentions are admirable and my asking for my name to go on legal documents comes as a surprise to you. I never mentioned this before and it might sound like I distrust you.") Rob also can make an "I" statement without defensiveness and blaming. ("I feel threatened when legal contracts are changed because it feels like things are slipping away from me.") Becoming aware of Mary's hidden fears would lead Rob to express his concern for her. ("I understand your need for financial security, especially if something should happen to me and I can't be there for you.") With open and truthful communication, love can grow. The admiration that the couple had for each other when they first met can continue, but now in a more mature and significant way.

This same example demonstrates the balance of power in a relationship. Anger flourishes in a relationship where there is an imbalance of power. Seeing oneself, unconsciously or consciously, as weaker, that is, needier and more dependent, generates resentment and disdain. For a relationship to stay healthy, the power needs to be equalized. That is not to say that at different points in a relationship one partner will not "give in" or compromise with the other. Sacrifices are always made for the one you love. But when the power is consistently uneven, the disparity causes problems.

Of course, imbalance is in the eyes of the beholder. Mary and Rob were both from very traditional and patriarchal families and cultures. When they married, they both tacitly agreed to recreate a patriarchal arrangement in their marriage. Only after a few years of marriage, did Mary, who had always been a strong, independent woman, begin to feel that she wanted more personal power in the relationship. She recognized that she entered the marriage with a basic belief that a wife should take care of her husband by keeping the house and making sure he is well nurtured. In exchange, he would take care of her financially. Her belief was consistent with Rob's belief system and influenced the way she behaved in the relationship. After being in the marriage for a number of years, and the women's movement ascending, Mary's basic belief system began to change. She thought, "I need to be an equal partner in this relationship. That would mean that I know, understand, and have some control over *our* not *his* financial situation. This would balance the power and I would feel more secure." But she never expressed this change to Rob. Thus he was shocked and upset when she wouldn't agree to sign the legal documents.

It is risky to want to change the thinking of another person, especially a spouse. Certain traits are accepted as part of the person, but when changes are made that are unfamiliar, these can be seen as threats. The submissive wife begins to assert herself. The calm husband begins to show anger on a regular basis. As these changes are noted, the resistance to discussing or arguing about the changes emerges from the fear of a loss (divorce) or fear of the impact on the children. Others need their partner both financially and socially. And fear of physical retaliation is also a reason for not wanting to change the major terms of the basic agreement.

John saw Marilyn as the most beautiful woman in the world. He couldn't believe that she was even interested in him. After all he was old enough to be her father. But, there she was, professing her love. They decided to move in together. She gave up her apartment, sold her furniture, and decided to quit work and return to school to get her college degree. Her parents asked her to think about her decision. No, she didn't need to think twice about it. She knew it was right.

It didn't take long, however, for things to change. At times, John was the most loving man in the world. Nobody ever loved her like this, so intensely, with such devotion. But there were other times when he just lost it. He was insanely jealous. It seemed to Marilyn that he was extremely possessive. When she would come home late at night from school he would grill her. When he didn't like her answers, he started to shove her, even began slapping her harshly across her face. She was angry, would insist he not be physical with her, but to no avail. Sometimes he would just lose it. He couldn't help it. He loved her so much.

She lived this way for five years. Marilyn needed John both financially as well as emotionally. When he was not in his fits of rage, John was kind, gentle, and understanding. He was older and wiser. He understood the finer things of life. He taught Marilyn how to act sophisticated and how to live the mature good life. His colleagues respected him and he had a way with words that impressed everyone.

Marilyn never stopped loving John. But she did finally RECOGNIZE her anger at the situation and that as she THOUGHT about it, she decided she could not stay in an intolerable relationship. Each time she spoke to him with EMPATHY and respect, he promised he would stop, but he did not stop. Even though financially she did not know how she would survive, she decided to leave John, get a small room in a rooming house, find a job, and postpone her education for just a year, until she got back on her feet. The decision to leave strengthened Marilyn. She was reclaiming her own sense of personal power and even though she loved John, she could not continue to sacrifice herself. John acknowledged she was right. She didn't deserve to live in a relationship of fear. To this day they remain friends, just not lovers.

Why would anyone agree to be in a relationship with a bully? Many people live with a bully because bullies are not tyrannical all the time. Some of the time they might be considerate caretakers. Some people have said they can handle the bully. Others have felt trapped and totally dependent. They figure out how to sneak around the "tyrannical" person and out-smart the despot! Although there are those in relationships with tyrants who figure out how to adapt to their partner, developing their own inner strengths, today there is much less tolerance for bullying behavior. In this story, the power started to equalize once Marilyn expressed herself and took action that was right for her. Her calm clarity, using the skills, didn't save the relationship, but did save her self-respect. However, in order to balance the power, a partner does not have to threaten the ultimate—to leave or end the relationship. Resolution can often be achieved much less drastically. Expression of thoughts and wishes in a clear, strong, thoughtful voice, will improve the chance of ultimately improving relationships and balancing the power. The desire to equalize power in a relationship does cause ripples, sometimes even domestic wars. The road is occasionally long and difficult.

Sara and Steven were as different as night and day. Everyone thought they would never be able to make it as a couple. He was a staunch Republican, she a Democrat. He was nonreligious and she was religious. She had a very powerful personality. He was often described as being a "push over." He was convinced he never wanted children, but knew she wanted children.

Nevertheless, they fell in love in spite of all their differences. They were married and lived together for ten years, having their difficulties. Steven frequently said to himself, "It's not worth the fight," and he would go along with Sara's wishes. As a matter of fact, Steven would even convince himself that what he originally thought he wanted no longer sounded as enticing, and persuaded himself that Sara's idea was really what he wanted all along. For no obvious reason, Steven started to feel more and more dissatisfied with the marriage. He found himself moody and had frequent anger outbursts. Then he began to realize that by becoming angry, it seemed to give him the extra boost to say "no" to Sara's "continual, selfish demands." Their relationship started to deteriorate. His "no" rigidly became more filled with accusations and refusals to listen to her point of view. Steven knew he needed another way to express himself, but was at a loss for words.

What would you suggest for Steven? What Creative Anger would help in this situation? You can see how complex lives of couples become. But, there is always a way to bring about the needed changes so that love can triumph. Remember, Steven entered this relationship knowing Sara had a very strong personality and liking, no, *loving* her that way. He also knew that he was more easygoing. He would even joke about how he liked being taken care of by such a strong woman. But after five years, their old way of being together was grating on him and he knew something needed to be different. What he didn't know was how she would feel about his new need to assert himself and have more of a voice in their relationship.

So if Steven takes the risk and uses the RETHINK skills in an attempt to express his point of view without a war resulting—although there is no guarantee—the scene might turn out something like this: Steven Recognizes he is feeling angry. The immediate concern is about their plans for Saturday night and how he never gets to choose what they do. He feels his heart beating fast and his palms sweating. He knows before he says anything to Sara about what he would like to do. He Notices his physical cues and calms himself down by taking deep breaths and saying to himself—I know I can do this, I know I can do this. Then he is ready to Think about the situation. ("I don't want to go to the movies tonight. I would prefer to stay home and watch a movie on our VCR. Perhaps I could give her a choice of which movie we watch.") He could also Empathize ("I know how hard she works all week and going out to a movie feels more special than staying home.") Integrate love and respect ("I'd like to talk about plans for Saturday night. I know how much you look forward to going out on Saturday night, but this week has been exhausting for me. I would really like to stay home together, watch a movie that you choose, and just relax.") Then he would listen to her response and really Hear what she says. As he listens with Empathy he can hear her request, understand that she has different needs, wants, and desires, and still state his desire to stay home. He can struggle to remember to stay open, be flexible, come up with a couple of options and keep to the point by not bringing up old grudges like, "You always get your way!"

The first time you try the skills it will feel awkward and you may not be successful. What if Steven used RETHINK skills but Sara responded with aggression, name-calling, and disdain. Learning to say, "You hurt me," in an offended roar, and not a whimper, is also important for Steven. Rather than feeling defenseless, using his emotions in a powerful way can give him energy. The first few times Steven practices the RETHINK skills, it may feel awkward and his form may be rough, even if he wants things to change. Most of the time, it is worth the struggle. Steven is trying to find some safety and balance in the relationship so they can have intimate exchanges as well as satisfying resolutions of conflicts. Relationships can improve if both want something to change. But it does take time, practice, and patience.

At one level you may be saying to yourself or to a close friend that you really want things to change. Couples fight for many reasons, some realistic and some not. Struggling to discover the true meaning of our arguments can be difficult. Many times the issues are camouflaged. Sometimes when we argue with our partner the hostility originates from our past. You or your partner may have unconscious reasons for *not* wanting things to change. These reasons could be connected to a belief system that developed in your family of origin. For example, you might have been given the message that men are not to be trusted; or that women are fickle, scatterbrained, and undependable; or that children "need to be taught a lesson" every now and then, or, don't expect too much from a marriage, or don't rock the boat, you will end up alone and poor, etc. We carry these messages into our adult relationships like keepsakes that were hung around our necks in childhood. These keepsakes, these ghosts from the past, can have a dreadful effect on our relationships as we attempt to negotiate conflicts and balance the power in our relationships. Here is an example:

Jake and Nancy met at college and married after they graduated. Both were architects and loved their profession. Nancy gave birth to three children. The third child was born with cerebral palsy (CP). Nancy decided to quit work and stay home with the children. She became extremely conscientious about the third child and dedicated her life to parenting. Jake, on the other hand increased his work hours. His days were long and Nancy complained that he was not attentive to the children, especially to the third-born child. He complained about Nancy's inability to keep the house clean. Their fights permeated their relationship. They became so out-of-control that they sought marriage counseling in order to try to avoid a divorce.

What became clear in the counseling sessions was how frightened the couple was about their ability to parent, especially concerning their disabled child. Their fighting served to divert them from their overwhelming fear and what felt like unbearable sadness. Jake remembered his father calling him incompetent and that he (his father) hoped nothing bad ever befell him. Nancy was told by her father that she was disorganized and couldn't handle large amounts of information at one time. They both believed the messages their different parents gave to them as children and carried these messages into their marriage, only to have their old beliefs exacerbated when they had a child with CP. Their anger covered up their real emotions that they were unable to express. The counselor helped them RETHINK their behaviors, show Empathy for each other and learn how to Hear each other in order to help one another.By Recognizing and articulating the formerly inexpressible, the couple becomes free to think about their real problems and work to resolve them. Each person has to discover his and her own hidden feelings. As with anything else, neither partner can do the work of the other. Each has to be willing to express the underlying feelings. Frequently, couples get stuck. The anger does not get resolved because it is difficult to speak the necessary words. Or a partner is oblivious to the belief system that is provoking their feelings. Discussions remain circular, stagnant, or even worse, meanspirited. But the arguments keep going, serving as protection from the truly "unbearable" feelings. Couples can feel detached and at the same time hold on to their anger.

Why do couples hold on to anger? Because anger can protect them from doing something necessary, but scary. If Joel holds onto his anger, he doesn't have to be intimate with the women he dates. Joel explains the reason he can't be intimate is not because he doesn't want to be intimate, but because women are so bossy, or he just can't find the right woman.

When couples hold on to their anger, they often identify the reason as a personal sense of virtue or principles. By holding on to their anger, couples believe that they are protecting their values; enabling them to stay in the right, "virtuous" place. A husband can justify his endless anger at his wife for taking a part-time job (and being less available to *him*) on the basis of his "principle" that a mother's place is in the home.

Nick was a very strong, dominant person. He ran a large company and his employees were grateful for the opportunity he provided them to gain such prominence and success. But he wanted things his way. And when he went home, he also wanted things his way: the neatness of the house, the children's behavior, his wife's cooking, and the type of friends with whom the couple *should* associate. All people who came in contact with him needed to do it his way. After a couple of years the people closest to him started to drop out of his life. Even his wife threatened divorce.

If you live with a tyrant, can you use the RETHINK skills to attempt to improve the relationship? Finding the Empathy for the tyrant might help you recognize that there is a sad loneliness that they experience. Often times they will feel bewildered. They have very little insight into their behavior's impact on others. People who may act like this seldom know how else to live. Their only role models acted the same way. They lack skills to do anything else.

It is not imperative or realistic to use the RETHINK skills in every single anger exchange. Clearly, there will be times when you feel angry, you will lose it, say something tyrannical or overly aggressive. Sometimes your partner will just let it pass. We all have those moments when such exchanges occur, but are not devastating. We don't always need a long conversation.

Madge is planning a fiftieth birthday party for her husband, Paul. Madge is lovingly spending an enormous amount of time on the project. She even proudly exclaims how the planning process has reawakened her love for her husband. In her excitement, she continually drops hints about the program and the party and what will actually happen. Her husband has asked her to leave some parts of the party as a surprise. Madge, because of her excitement, is unable to hold anything back. Paul becomes angry when Madge tells another detail about the party. He quickly RETHINKS and says to himself, "Let it go and accept that she is being loving in her way. Enjoy her enthusiasm." Then he gave himself credit for *not* blowing his stack! He sat back and enjoyed the party and the love his wife was able to shower on him.

Being in a relationship is hard work. It takes skills, patience, determination, and the ability to know when to be flexible, let go and forgive. Perhaps that is what is meant by saying that people are mature when they are able to articulate responsibly what they want, be empathic, and set boundaries when necessary and can enjoy life to the fullest without harming anyone.

Your Story

Think of an experience you had with someone you loved very much that involved anger.

1. What happened?
2. What level had you and/or the other person reached on the scale of: bothered, interrupted, disturbed, annoyed, irritated, or angry?
3. What did you do to deal with the feeling of the other person?
4. How did you feel?
5. What did the other person do in reaction to you?
6. How did that person feel?
7. How did it come out?
8. What would you do differently with the knowledge you have now about the Creative Use of Anger?

CHAPTER 7

Anger in the Family

The Paradox of Families

It is a paradox that in the setting of the family, where we expect to feel the safest, we are also at risk to experience the most destructive and painful feelings of anger. These feelings begin with infancy. An infant feels hungry and until he is fed, cries out angrily. With his feeding, he experiences comfort, and his anger subsides. We expect that within the family we can trust our needs will be met. And in the family we learn to feel we belong, and that we are loveable; we begin to develop our sense of worth, our sense of hope, and our sense of personal strength.

However, it is also within the family that we experience the greatest disappointments, especially when our basic needs or expectations are not met. Longing for someone to anticipate our needs and to fulfill our wishes, even before they are expressed, leads to feelings of being let down or neglected, resulting in distrust and in anger. Many problems can develop in this intense environment when anger goes awry. Confusion can occur when certain feelings are not permitted to be expressed. If open displays of sadness, fear, despair, uncertainty, and even sexual curiosity are taboo, children can learn to cover up many of these forbidden feelings with anger. The anger is more for the prohibition than any deep concern about the emotion. Such was the case with Sarah and her mother, who was struggling to ward off depression.

When Sarah was five years old, her Dad laced the small pair of red leather boxing gloves on her little hands and started giving her a few pointers. He bent down to her level and they were laughing and sparring in the front hallway when her Mom walked by. "She's a girl, you idiot!" she stated with utter disgust, and left them with their sport. Sarah knew she was a girl, and she knew her dad adored her. She also knew that the "boy" in her family, her brother, died very suddenly last year. Her mother had been sad ever since; but in this family, the difficulty with expressing sorrow was translated into hurtful, angry jibes. It did not help the family deal with the tragedy, and Sarah was growing up with a continuing confusion about anger and feelings of loss. She would have problems later in life separating these two feelings.

It is also in the family that children of all ages can become the targets of ugly tirades as they disappoint their parents, siblings, or other relatives. And children's behavior can elicit great fear in their relatives, who, in turn, can cover up their fear with hurtful, belittling, angry expressions toward the children. Here is an example:

Jack, a sixteen-year-old, is at a party and has a midnight curfew. At two in the morning he comes home to find his parents almost in a state of panic. They had been imagining something terrible had happened, and yet they felt great anger toward their son for putting them in this position. By the time he got home, they were furious; he had not even made a phone call to let them know where he was. They yelled: "You are irresponsible; we can't trust you! That's it, no more car privileges and no more allowance." Jack feels he is old enough to set his own hours and states: "I am not irresponsible! Stop treating me like an infant!" Anger is in everyone! But once the anger energy has been used up, they will have a better chance to discuss some new rules.

Jack's parents may ask themselves why they became so furious and ultimately so punitive. They begin to recognize that their anger was a cover-up for their fear. They need to find a way to communicate to Jack that they are really frightened and, most of all, they are concerned about his welfare. Jack, on the other hand, questions whether his parents can let go, give him some space. He feels the need for more freedom. Instead of staying angry at one another, they are now ready to work out a solution to solve the problem. Will Jack get more freedom? Maybe and maybe not.

Some family anger becomes so ingrained over time that it is more like a family feud. And there seems no resolution as the intense feelings of love and concern are juxtaposed with disappointment and rage. When anger reaches the level of rage, things can become very complex. Here is one account:

Mr. Stacy, a middle-aged businessman longed to make-up with his estranged father. The two had once been partners in a clothing company until the younger Mr. Stacy stormed off several years ago, after an argument over money. The two had not spoken since. But time passed and Mr. Stacy's son now had his own successful business. So, during the holiday season he went to see his father, bearing gifts, only to have the presents thrown down and the door slammed in his face. He was desperate for reconciliation. It did not happen. However, his anger now turned to a kind of pity for his father, who would never know the kind of love he could receive from his son.

Almost every family has a story about some relative who has done something to make them so angry they do not want any kind of contact. That is, of course, a tragedy. And learning to RETHINK such experiences may well be the way to reconcile. Can the son write a letter to his father, showing some Empathy for his father's rigid stance, trying to use words to soften that stance? Can the son focus on the issue that caused the break-up—the money, describing his role in the conflict, apologizing where appropriate, and asking for suggestions of how to resolve the feelings about the event? Can the son express his love for his father and his sadness at the loss of sharing some time with him?

Anger can often result from unmet expectations. And a common source of unmet expectations is the blended family. When a blended family is formed as a result of divorce, adoption, or death and remarriage, many expectations are unmet. This situation can cause reactions of strong anger. Even the joy of having a reconstructed family may not allow for the expression of sadness, frustration, and anger that will be part of the adjustment. Judy and Sally exemplify this conflict:

Judy, Sally's fourteen-year-old adopted daughter, lately began calling her mother "stepmother." Sally has loved and cared for Judy since she was six years old, when Sally married Judy's father. She feels hurt, pushed aside, and angry. Her first thoughts are: "How can she do that to me after all I have done for her?" And she feels some rage, leading her to get ready to lash out against Judy. Instead, she draws on RETHINK skills. "Judy is a teenager going through a lot of changes. Perhaps she is angry about something and I need to listen to her." When Sally regains control and sees Judy has calmed down a bit, she says: "Calling me stepmother sounds like you are feeling angry. But I feel hurt when you call me that. What is going on?" Judy responds, "You are like a stepmother. You won't let me go to Barb's party. You never let me go anywhere or do anything!" Sally is stunned, but keeps calm and states: "Well, I am glad you are telling me what's on your mind. I guess you see me as so mean and unreasonable. Now, we can do something about what's bothering you. Let's talk!"

Judy would love to avoid having to set limits for her daughter and avoid the confrontation. But she realizes that a fourteen-year-old needs to be guided by some rules and restrictions. As she accepts the momentary hostile feelings, she moves on to building an alliance with her daughter and jointly solving the problem.

Your Family

Think of a recent experience you had in the family that made you angry.

1. What happened?
2. Who started it?
3. What did you do as part of the experience?
4. How do you THINK the anger was expressed?
5. Was the word anger ever used?
6. What other feelings do you THINK were expressed besides anger?
7. How do you THINK it came out?
8. Was the cause of the anger resolved?
9. Do you THINK anyone, everyone, was satisfied?
10. What was learned or accomplished by the anger episode?
    a. By the family members?
    b. By the children?
    c. By the parents?
    d. By the family as a whole?
11. What would you do differently if the same anger episode reoccurred?

Children's Anger

Like adults, all children experience anger. And their expression of anger can cause many problems, such as school failure, truancy, discipline problems, emotional disorders, drug abuse, runaway behaviors, as well as acts of violence. Children can learn many different strategies to react to anger rousing situations, often by example. They watch their parents, people in their extended family, adults in the community and school, as well as characters in film and television. When children have many possible responses to anger in their repertoire, they can react quickly and appropriately. Good anger management can lead to higher self-esteem and an increase in children's ability to handle their environment. However, when children are ill-equipped to manage their anger and frustrations, they may end up acting out destructively.

Becoming more familiar with the RETHINK skills, you are very likely aware of the importance of how you THINK about an experience involving anger in determining what you will do. And it is in RETHINKing an experience involving anger that brings about change in the way you manage your anger and deal with the anger of others. Teaching children these skills as the occasions arise will provide them with a lifelong sense of inner strength.

Teaching RETHINK

The Very Young

An infant expresses her anger by crying. The crying is to let you know you have not met her needs immediately. The feeling is there. You can hear the tinge of anger in the crying voice. There is no other way to communicate annoyance, frustration, and fear of not being cared for. But, the flip side is that crying, especially the crying that doesn't stop, can easily rouse anger in parents and other family members. The frustration of not being able to meet the needs of the infant, and the continuing reminder of that fact, becomes too much. Now, everyone is angry and nothing good will come out of this.

Most family members have trouble dealing with angry, crying babies. These distraught babies require time to calm down. There is no room to communicate that it takes time to get the food ready, the diaper changed, and the discomfort removed. So, here the family is, faced with an angry baby and annoyed by the way the baby expresses anger—through persistent, annoying crying. What to do?

What the family does about this early expression of anger will determine to a large degree how the family will deal with future expressions of anger. Here are the major ways parents respond to expressions of anger in their children:

Anger can be ignored

Many families do just that. No one is much bothered by expressions of anger. They seem to be expected, and as long as no one is hurt in an angry outburst, they are accepted. The downside of ignoring anger is that no one learns how to deal with it: how to use it to clarify problems family members are having with each other. The anger is not understood so that it can act as a guide for determining what is going on that is distressful to the person feeling the anger. There is no resolution of the problem or of the anger. It is just there, growing with frustration or perhaps converting into health and emotional problems: maybe, just a feeling of anxiety.

Anger can be punished

"How dare you show anger to me, your father!" is not an uncommon thing to hear. Anger is seen as a challenge to power and when a parent cannot accept such a challenge, no matter what the age of the child, the parent must assert greater power, even punish the challenger. Fear of loss of power over children, even over other members of the family, can easily trigger anger. However, anger that is punished does not go away. It can be held in, taken out on other members of the family, on a friend, or on a pet. Anger that is punished can be expressed in self-punishment, like cutting one's wrists.

Anger can be encouraged

Parents and other family members may express pleasure at the "spunk" of the child. "No one will take advantage of her, you can bet your life. This girl will hold her own!" Parents and other family members may encourage the angry child to act out on the anger, confusing such acting out with being assertive, that is, stating what one is or is not willing to do, or where the lines are drawn. Many fights are the result of encouraging expressions of anger. And when these are also accepted by bystanders who offer no objection, rather seeming to enjoy the encounter, the process continues and grows.

Anger can be repressed or denied

If the family believes anger is an unacceptable emotion to express, because it may lead to undesired behavior, then the family members work very hard not to express anger; better yet, don't even feel it. But anger exists. Everyone feels it. It cannot be ignored. The energy remains and must go somewhere. And many times it shows up as feelings of depression; feelings of unworthiness and guilt—how can I even feel annoyed at Mom when she works so hard for us! Then there are the health reactions from denial and repression. These include high blood pressure, physical illnesses with no known diagnosis, headaches (migraines), and stomachaches. And when repressed anger is rewarded by statements like, "What a nice, quiet boy; he never gets upset or mad at anyone. How lucky we are to have such a son!" permanent damage may well be in the process of happening.

Anger can be recognized, respected, managed, and expressed effectively in the family. The family can become the training ground for learning how to develop the RETHINK skills. When parents help children recognize their anger feelings; when they help children label them; when they help children express them in ways not damaging to others; when they help children resolve the situation causing the anger; when they help children use anger constructively, then anger is not threatening. Rather, anger is an important emotion that helps bring about needed change in relationships.

Anger for the Ages

Anger in Infants

Parents can draw on the RETHINK skills to use with their infant. They need to recognize that crying is the main way the infant can indicate anger at being uncomfortable, hungry, in pain, or some other discomfort. The challenge is to find the cause of the crying. But, in the meantime, the parent can rock the baby, make eye contact and speak softly, or hold and cuddle him. The parent wants to help the baby learn how to calm himself. A pacifier is often a solution.

Seven-month-old Roger is being put into his baby car seat by his father, Tom. Tom has just put the straps over Roger's shoulders and is trying to fasten the ends into the lock. Roger screams and yells and tries to free himself. He is flushed with anger.

Now, Tom must draw on his knowledge of child development. What is going on with a seven-month-old baby that needs to be noted if the screams are going to stop! Roger is angry when he is:

1. Prevented from exploring.
2. Physically restrained from moving, crawling.
3. Physically uncomfortable.
4. Scolded for his behavior.
5. Not provided with comfort responses from his parents.

Developmentally, Roger is learning about himself and the world by:

1. Exploration and curiosity about his environment.
2. Testing cause and effect.

3. Doing things independently.
4. Getting comfort and safety responses.
5. Gaining some control over his body and learning to calm himself.

What can Tom teach Roger about managing anger, even at this very young age? He can calm Roger down with words, touching, and understanding Roger's distress. He can say something like, "OK, OK, Roger. I know you're angry. You sure don't like this car seat, do you? You think it's outrageous, but it's for your safety, and soon you'll be snug as a bug in a rug!" He can distract Roger: "Look, Roger, here's your rattle—let's shake it and make noise." He can check to see whether anything is hurting or pinching Roger. Or, he can put Roger's pacifier in his mouth. Sucking is an almost foolproof calmer.

Anger in the Second and Third Years of Life

Parents of these young children feel anger when their children engage in these age-related behaviors:

a. Having temper tantrums, sometimes in public.
b. Knocking things over, or throwing food and objects.
c. Crying, whining.
d. Kicking, hitting, biting, pinching, and grabbing.
e. Running away from a parent or into the street.
f. Yelling and screaming at a parent.
g. Withdrawing, hiding, or refusing to talk.
h. Refusing to use the potty.

When parents THINK these behaviors are deliberate and are intended to annoy them, possible signs that they are weak or powerless, they respond in anger. However, when they understand these behaviors in terms of the normal development of children, they have an opportunity to respond more positively. They can use the situation as a time to teach their child about managing emotions.

Brenda, age three, is resisting her mother's attempts to get her ready for their excursion. They are going to Grandma's house. Brenda will not let her mother dress her. She jerks her arms away, kicks her foot, and becomes rigid. She yells: "No! No! You are hurting me! Help!"

What is going on with Brenda that is consistent with her age? Brenda is angry when:

1. She is restrained:
   a. From independent movement, play, or space.
   b. From demanding everything is "mine."
2. She is frustrated by her own limits while trying to do something—like putting on her dress.
3. Her bid for attention is ignored or misunderstood.
4. She hears "No!" and "Stop that!" commands.

Brenda is learning about herself and the world by:

   a. Exercising her will.
   b. Struggling against the will of others.
   c. Gaining experience with words and recognizing her power.
   d. Learning that there are rules and limits.
   e. Combining thoughts, feelings, and behavior to achieve goals.
   f. Learning that what she does has consequences.

Here are some things Brenda's mother can do to help her child learn about managing anger.

> She can calm Brenda by holding her gently and talking to her: "My, my, you are a wiggle-worm today. Come on, honey, we need to put this arm through this sleeve. And the other arm in the other sleeve."
>
> She could offer her a reward; "If we are finished in five minutes, you can have a cracker to eat before we get into the car."
>
> Or she can play a game: "Are you upset because you want to play first? Then let's play a game. Where's Brenda's hand? There it is! Where does it go? Right here!"

School Age Children

School age children, who are learning to master skills of reading, problem solving, and interpersonal relations with peers, are also learning about cause and effect. It is this last bit of knowledge that can help them understand how their behavior can affect another person. They can also accept responsibility for the consequences of their actions. But, they are developing a sense of fairness and begin to recoil with anger at disciplinary measures that seem overly punitive, arbitrary, and mean, rather than logical and inspired by kindness. These same children can trigger anger in their parents with a string of behaviors that include:

a. Refusing to share, take turns, or play by the rules.
b. Arguing, lying.
c. Refusing to listen, tuning parents out.
d. Dawdling in eating, dressing, or going to bed.
e. Making and leaving messes where working or playing.
f. Teasing siblings.
g. Hitting and grabbing.
h. Shouting at others and at their parents.

Here is the Smith family. Ruth is ten years old and Lloyd is eight. They come home from school, have a snack, and begin watching television. Their sitter is a teenager and watches television with them. Their mother, Pam, comes home after a long day at work. The first things she sees are a pool of melted ice cream on the kitchen counter, a stream of grape juice leading from the refrigerator to Lloyd's place on the seat, and crushed pretzels all over the rug. She shouts with disgust, "What is the matter with you kids? You haven't cleaned up the kitchen and I gave you strict orders to do so! I can't trust you at all! You are lazy slobs!" Lloyd, who is angry with his mother for shouting and making him feel guilty, says, "Well, you're never home to give us anything we need!" And Ruth says, in anger, "Be quiet! I can't hear the TV!" Mom angrily turns off the set.

What's going on with eight-year-old Lloyd and ten-year-old Ruth? They are angry when they are:

1. Confronted by the fact they have not done as they were told.
2. Controlled by adults.
3. Made to feel inferior or lacking in competence.

But, in general, children of this age are beginning to learn about themselves and the world by:

Understanding themselves better.
Acquiring competence and confidence in themselves.
Being very industrious and hardworking.
Recognizing differences among people.

Being more aware of the views of others.
Learning more about how the world works.

These are complex skills and require time, attention, and with many set-backs. Being on the receiving end of anger because the skills are still developing, is hard to take. But, what can Pam do about her own anger? What RETHINK skills will work?

R: Recognize her anger
Pam: I just feel sick when the kids don't do as they are told... I don't usually turn off the TV so abruptly. I sure was angry!

E: Empathize with Lloyd and Ruth
Pam: I am gone much of the day and it must be hard to have me come home and yell at them. I bet they are starving and exhausted from school. I know expecting them to do all those jobs is a lot to ask.

T: Think of another way of looking at the situation
Pam thought: Those kids don't appreciate how hard I work.... They don't do their part. I really blew it. Maybe they would not have seemed so disobedient if I had greeted them before bringing up the mess in the kitchen and realized that the sitter needs better instructions. I guess I was also angry with the sitter for not supervising the children. The more I think about it, I was already angry. I walked in with tremendous frustration because my boss gave me an assignment at the last minute and kept me way beyond closing time. Maybe my expectations for an eight-year-old and a ten-year-old are unrealistic.

H: Hear what they are saying with their behavior
Lloyd: I feel neglected. I am not going to do your job for you.

I: Integrate love and respect with the anger
Pam: I don't want to come home and yell at you. I miss you during the day and want to appreciate the time we have together.

N: Notice what calms both herself and the children
Pam decides to go into her bedroom, change from her work clothes into something comfortable, splash her face with warm water, put some cream on her hands, and then return to her children, somewhat calmer.

K: Keep her attention on this particular situation
When talking with Lloyd and Ruth, focus only on the present situation. They can talk about what happened while they get dinner on the table, agreeing on who is responsible for what until the mother gets home. And if any previous event of anger is brought up, Pam can declare that "off limits!" Then, she realizes she must talk with the sitter about her expectations.

Pam can also teach her children about managing their own anger. She can help them calm down with, "O.K. We're all angry. Let's talk about what's going on." She can talk about the anger: "Let's see if each one of us can tell exactly why we are angry. Whatever it is, it's OK to say."

She can model RETHINK skills. If Pam can take the opportunity to respond in a positive way, she will see the situation as a time to teach her children about managing emotions, especially anger.

Eleven- and Twelve-Year-Olds

Eleven- and twelve-year-olds trigger anger in their parents with a different set of behaviors that the parents THINK are unnecessary, unacceptable, or done deliberately to annoy. These include:

a. Arguing and verbally attacking.
b. Defying directives and refusing to do chores.
c. Failing to do homework.
d. Fighting with siblings and roughhousing.
e. Not being ready on time and dawdling.
f. Having unacceptable friends.
g. Failing a subject in school.
h. Lying about why they are late getting home from school.

Twelve-year-old Alice came home feeling very depressed about the "D" she got on a paper handed back in school that day. When she got home and found her two younger brothers wrestling in the house, she became very angry and shouted: "Stop that! I'm sick of watching you two roughhousing indoors! Just get out of here!" They scrambled out of her way. Alice then went to her room and flopped onto her bed to sulk. When her father, Hank, came home and didn't see any of the family around, he called out but received no answer. Then he saw Alice's bedroom door ajar, and spotted her lying on the bed, looking miserable.

What is going on with twelve-year-old Alice? She is angry when she is:

a. Confused about who she is—her identity.
b. Unable to express or manage her anger.
c. Fighting and arguing with siblings.
d. Feeling inferior to classmates, siblings, and friends.
e. Humiliated or embarrassed in front of friends.

f. Prevented from participating in rule making.
g. Labeled as messy, selfish, inconsiderate, or lazy.
h. Teased or talked about by friends.
i. Feels inadequate or treated like a "baby."

But, Alice is at a stage of development that often determines what makes her angry. She is learning about herself and the world by:

a. Modifying her behavior to conform to more grownup standards and values.
b. Gaining insight into her own identity and personality.
c. Increasing attachments and commitments to peers.
d. Using fantasy and idealism in her thinking and planning.
e. Gaining increased knowledge about the world.

What can her father, Hank, do to help Alice learn to manage her anger? He can help Alice express her feelings and talk about what made her angry.

Hank: You seem very unhappy, Alice. Can you tell me what is upsetting you?
Alice talks about her brothers' roughhousing.
Hank: But they did go out, Alice. Yet, you are still upset. Is there something else?
Alice tells him about her "D" grade.
Hank can help Alice by saying:
Do you know why your grade was a "D"? What are some of the ways that you can improve your work so you get better grades? What can I do to help?
And, labeling feelings for her benefit, he says: "I remember how angry and ashamed I felt when I got a "D" once. But then I decided that "D" can stand for "determined" to do better! I decided to keep up with the class, even get ahead once in awhile."

Adolescence

During these years, usually from thirteen to nineteen, the adolescent craves more independence. Now they can think more abstractly and they can also become critical of their parents and the standards of society. Their idealism is high and they are often angry about the way so many people seem to be cynical—nothing is going to be all right, people only care about themselves.

Parents experience many clashes with their teenagers, and parents face the difficult challenge of meeting the adolescent's need for guidance that is neither too strict nor too permissive—but reasonable, fair, and respectful of the needs of the youth.

Adolescents can trigger anger in their parents when engaged in behaviors that their parents believe are unnecessary, unacceptable, or done deliberately to annoy. These include:

a. Arguing about limits on time and actions.
b. Blaming others for causing their own anger.
c. Withdrawing into a room or going out when a parent is trying to talk.
d. Borrowing things without permission.
e. Fighting or acting out.
f. Expecting privileges in spite of poor performance.
g. Taking unnecessary risks.
h. Violating curfews parents set.

Alan, fifteen-years-old, is playing his drums. Joe, his twelve-year-old brother, has just turned on his boom box in the next room. Alan screams at Joe, "Stop that racket! I have to practice!"
Joe retorts: "You are not my boss! You can't tell me what to do!"
"Oh Yeah? Watch me!" says Alan.
Their parents, Stephanie and Horace, hear this commotion and both become angry at the bickering.
Horace shouts, "Be quiet, kids! Or I'll really give you something to yell about!"
Stephanie says, "Don't be so hard on them, Horace. They're only kids."
Horace answers: "Great, that's all I need. When do you want them to start acting their age?"

What is going on with fifteen-year-old Alan and twelve-year-old Joe? Their anger is triggered by many of the same things as triggered Alice's. They are learning about themselves and the world just as described in the Alice event. What can Stephanie and Horace do about their *own* anger? What RETHINK skills will work?

R: Recognize their anger
Stephanie: I get so angry with Horace I can see red.
Horace: My stomach really twists when Stephanie defends the kids.

E: Empathize with each other

Stephanie: I know we both want them to become fine young men, and I want to help.

Horace: I may be expecting too much from them and I blame you.

T: Think of another way of looking at the situation

Horace and Stephanie agree that they need to think about what was really going on between the two of them and between Alan and Joe. Maybe they need to talk about what to expect from the boys. They could sit down and discuss in-house behavior. The boys were not trying to upset their parents; they were trying to establish their own turf.

H: Hear what the boys are saying

Alan is really threatening Joe and Joe is just ignoring Alan's request. They are being competitive and interfering in each other's "musical" space. Parents need to be watchful not to interfere in their children's struggles when the children can work it out themselves. Horace and Stephanie may decide, "We must listen to each other to see why we are at odds about the behavior of the boys. Maybe we don't discuss our expectations with each other enough."

I: Integrate love and respect with the anger

"It makes us angry when you kids don't get along. We love you and want you to be happy. Let's talk about what we can do so there is more harmony and less tumult, and we can hear the music in the house."

N: Notice what calms you down and what calms the youth down

Horace: "Can we go to the porch where it is comfortable and calm down before we talk about this?"

K: Keep the attention on this particular situation

There is no need to bring up old issues. This one is enough!

What can Stephanie and Horace teach Alan and Joe about managing their own anger? They can help the boys calm down while they all sit on the porch.

Stephanie: "Why don't we all take a deep breath and let it out slowly to cool off a bit?"

Horace: "Let's hear what is making both of you so angry. We know that playful competition is part of the game, even with music. How can we stop it from getting to be too much? Who wants to go first? Joe, Okay. Now, let's listen."

There are some common ways families deal with anger in their children as well as their own anger. And it is only when these ways don't work or are causing more serious problems that RETHINKing needs to take place. Here are some examples.

A family of four was sitting around the breakfast table and they were talking about a trip the two daughters of the family were going to take to Europe. It was a graduation present, as they were both graduating from college. The father was asking very detailed questions about the plans and began to be critical of each answer. The girls tried to explain why the plans were as they were, and their mother, who had made the plans with the girls, agreed. The father, apparently feeling that his views were not reflected, continued to criticize what was being said, and clearly was angry that he had not been involved earlier. His voice was getting louder and the tension grew. Finally, one of the daughters said, "Perhaps we shouldn't go." She was angry about the way her father kept criticizing their decisions, but understood why her father was angry and decided it was better to cancel the trip than to cause such anger. He should have been involved in the planning, and it seemed too late for that.

The father's reaction was one of shock. Clearly, he realized he had gone too far in expressing his anger. Whether he knew why he was angry was not as important as his desire for the girls to have the trip. He calmed down and they began to talk to resolve differences in the planning.

Parents or other relatives may exploit their position of authority by tyrannizing the children and the children are not able to defuse the tension.

Audrey received a Christmas gift from her grandparents that she found very disappointing. She showed her disappointment and her grandfather was furious, telling her she was a very ungrateful child. Audrey started to cry and her grandfather told her to stop or to go to her room. The grandfather became tyrannical because he was angry by her rejection of their Christmas present. Audrey still remembers the Christmas she spent alone in her room—the punishment made a long-lasting impact.

Changing Family Scripts

The Family As a Training Ground

Through RETHINK skills, anger can be recognized, respected, managed, and expressed effectively in the family. The family becomes the training ground for developing the skills. Parents can model real life behavior; that is, constructively resolve conflicts that will make the difference in how their children manage their anger. Parents can help their children RECOGNIZE their angry feelings; accept the feelings as a natural human emotion; label them; express them with clear communication that does not damage others; help children resolve the situation causing the anger; in short, use the anger energy constructively and creatively. Then anger need not be threatening; but, instead, a necessary emotion that helps bring about needed change in relationships.

Recognizing that anger episodes can be resolved and that anger is temporary are two important lessons that can be learned in the home. Then, in their interactions with their parents, children can learn that expressions of anger do not need to destroy relationships.

Anger in effective families

Effective families refer to those families that have acquired or promoted characteristics and behaviors that enrich and enhance each member. And it is within these characteristics and behaviors that anger is expressed and managed. These families are:

1. Caring and compassionate
   A family made up of caring members believes or shows that love and compassion are the bases of interactions. The basic love is expressed by taking care of new members, ill members, old members, in fact, all members of the family. Caring is aimed or directed to both physical and emotional needs. But the dominant expression of the love is *trust*. Family members who trust each other are not afraid to express negative feelings, including anger. They know it is safe. Parents appreciate and help children understand that there is a difference between thoughts and actions. All children as well as adults have negative, sometimes hate-filled feelings, and even gruesome fantasies. Parents teach their children to accept what is a normal part of every human being. The children can feel assured they will get help when they are not able to talk about the angry feelings directly. They expect compassion: that wonderful expression of empathy and helping; feelings are recognized and respected and they are not alone in dealing with the anger-rousing incident.
2. Using communication skills
   There have been clever ads on TV that show a father and son, a mother and daughter, sisters, or a husband and wife, who miss opportunities to communicate with each other. So critical moments for sharing thoughts and feelings are lost. It is important to note that

communication comes in three forms: words, body language, and attitude.

Words are a very difficult way to communicate. Giving directions or instructions can leave you totally frustrated because they are not understood or carried out. And you don't know what is not understood because the listener thinks he or she understood what you said. You miss meeting each other, you have the wrong time—was that to arrive or start from home? You buy the wrong things, mix the wrong ingredients, or copy the wrong page. All because words are not understood, or have different meanings to different people.

Now, words that involve anger in the family are a special case. The words chosen to talk about anger, communicate how much love and trust and compassion are part of the interaction. However, it is important to help children use words and learn that talking about an anger-provoking event is key to communicating strong emotions in constructive ways. Resolving anger usually requires being able to put feelings into words, spoken or written, with the goal of improving an anger producing situation.

3. Being together and doing things together
   When members of a family see each other at meals, when they plan vacations together, when they share chores and activities, and enjoy holidays together, they are making a commitment to each other. They are building lasting connections and memories. These connections help each member know the others as they move through the years. This sense of belonging encourages an intimacy, and even privacy, for feelings and expressions of anger, and is a safe place to talk about experiences involving anger outside the family.

4. Dealing with crises together
   Crises challenge the strength of families in ways nothing else can. When a member has caused or been in an accident, experimented with drugs, or become chronically ill, the family faces a crisis. And one inevitable reaction at some point is anger. How dare sister even try drugs! How dumb of father to wreck the car! Why does brother choose now to get diabetes! Why does mother choose now to decide she wants to take a new, more demanding job!

These seeming irrational responses of anger are not just annoyances that can trigger anger; they reflect the ambivalence of feelings that are common in crises affecting every member. The mixed feelings involve empathy versus inconvenience of the event; concern versus interruption of one's own life; and resentment toward another versus shame about one's own reactions. In other words, anger insinuates itself into crisis situations regardless of the cause or sequel of the crisis. Within the time of the crisis, stress is inevitable—high arousal of any emotion will often stimulate anger. And with the crisis it is important to recognize the feelings, accept the situation, and when appropriate, talk about the feelings of anger, trusting they will be accepted, understood, and resolved. Some family members will understand.

A Case in Point

Ray, Cindy, and Barbara (siblings aged five, seven, and nine) are watching a favorite TV show after school. Their mother is sitting in the same room, writing out checks to pay the family bills. Ray punches Barbara on the upper arm.

Barbara: Ray, stop hitting me!
Their mother looks up and sees that things seem to be settled.

Ray: (Now punches Cindy) Get out of my way, you're blocking my view!

Cindy: I am not and you stop hitting me.

Ray: (Punches Barbara again) Move over, you're taking all the room!

Barbara: You're crazy. You have plenty of room.

Mother: Stop that, Ray. I don't want to see any more fighting.
(Ray continues punching his sisters.)

Mother: Let's go in your room, Ray.
(They go in his room and the mother closes the door for privacy.)

Mother: What is wrong, Ray?

Ray: Nothing.

Mother: You don't usually hit your sisters and they really were doing nothing to make you angry. So what is wrong?

Ray: Nothing.

Mother: Did something happen at school today to make you angry?

Ray: No.

Mother: Well, something upset you. Did something happen in your classroom?

Ray: No, not in my classroom.

Mother: Where did it happen?

Ray: At the bus stop after school.

Mother: What happened?

Ray: I was standing in line waiting for the bus door to open and this big sixth grader always likes to go in first, but I was first. He told me to move back and I said I was going to stay there. Then he grabbed me by my shirt and bounced me up and down in front of all the kids. I was so mad!

Mother: How awful! You must have felt terrible to have your friends see that, let alone being mad at the sixth grader.

Ray: (Shaking his head and beginning to sob). Yeah, it was awful.

Mother: I can see why you are still angry. That was a terrible experience.

Ray: (Continuing to cry and shake his head). Yeah, it was awful. He's a rat and I hate him!

Mother: Well, your feelings make a lot of sense. But he's not worth your getting so angry. Stay out of his way or tell the bus driver if you have more trouble.

Ray: (Begins to calm down). OK.

Mother: Let's go back to the family room. I know now why you were hitting your sisters. But, really, you can't do that anymore. OK?

Ray: OK. I'm sorry.

When Ray's father came home, his wife told him about the situation with Ray and how she handled it. The father listened carefully and felt a great deal of anger at the boy who treated his son so badly. He would like to talk to the father of that boy and tell him what a rotten job he was doing in raising his son. But, he knew that such actions would only lead to trouble, and, come to think of it, his son was quite courageous to stand up to the boy. His wife was right to tell their son to tell the bus driver or just stay away if such a thing ever happened again. When he saw his son, he said, "Hi, Ray. I hear you had a bummer today. But I am proud of you standing up for your right to get on the bus first!"

CHAPTER 8

Anger in the Workplace

The Challenge

Of all settings, the workplace poses the greatest challenge to managing anger effectively. At least three factors contribute to this problem:

- Stringent limits exist on the ways anger can be expressed. At home, at school, at the ball field, or at the neighborhood bar, occasional outbursts of temper may be forgiven. However, in the workplace, only if you were a world-renowned star would such a display of anger be tolerated. Constraints are placed on whether any anger can be displayed at all or on how this emotion may be expressed. Only a courtroom, where a judge can cite you for contempt, imposes greater limitations on the expression of anger than most work settings.

- The many stressors reported by employees contribute to the lowering of the threshold of anger. A stressed person responds more readily to an anger trigger than one in a calm state. This increased vulnerability to threats in the work environment makes for more complexity in managing anger.

- Dependence on work for major life satisfactions as well as for providing a living further complicates anger expression in the workplace. This dependence may conflict with the needs that are being violated and lead to anger. Hostile dependence is uncomfortable and may be dangerous.

When people were asked what gave meaning to their lives, their work was identified by 72 percent of both men and women. Obviously, work is extremely important in a person's value system. People are very dependent on their job to bring satisfaction and pleasure. We are also sensitive to interactions with colleagues. Thus, work relationships are very important to all of us, giving each a sense of belonging, a daily dose of intellectual stimulation, and camaraderie. However, these very same relationships are periodically threatened by the inevitable competition that comes with climbing the ladder of a hierarchy. Additionally, finances and economic security are of crucial importance. Providing for our families and ourselves is one of the most central things we can do for our loved ones. Fear of losing our job and thus our security can play a substantial part in our becoming angry. Given our dependency on work, we can expect to be extremely sensitive to events or actions that threaten this meaningful and essential part of life. Anger is inevitable at times. These difficulties beset people at all levels of the hierarchy. As we examine these obstacles to creative anger management, we will draw on some cases and see how RETHINK skills may be applied.

Stressors and Anger Triggers

The problem of stress on the job is so widespread that many studies have been undertaken to examine its effects. The studies tend to agree that: one-fourth of the employees in the United States identify their job as the number one stressor in their lives; three-fourths of employees believe that they experience more job stress now than workers did a generation ago; and health complaints are more strongly associated with stress on the job than with financial or family problems. The major reaction to unfavorable working conditions is the sort of stress often expressed as:

"I am so worried, I can't think straight."
"I am so stressed out, I could attack anyone who comes near me."
"I feel so harried, I snap at anyone who asks for help."

These are common complaints from people on the job who are struggling to figure out how to manage their stress. Occasional stress is constructive, of course. It energizes you. The major reaction to unfavorable situations at work is the need for action. But there is a point when stress is too much, when you can't figure out how to turn it around, and it begins to interfere with your thinking, your emotional reactions, and even your physical health.

Some Specific Stressors

Assault on sense of control

An Example: When Roland Briggs crossed the threshold into his new office suite, was politely greeted by his new immediate staff of twenty people, and was handed his day's schedule by his administrative assistant, his heart sank. Life would never be the same. Would he ever again enjoy freedom? He had accepted this Presidential appointment, with all the "power and prestige" it involved, as an honor and a privilege to do the public service that he respected. Now, he found that his day was planned out for him in twenty-minute intervals; there were even little notations about times it would be convenient for him to go to the "john." When Roland gave up his academic appointment, he knew he would no longer be able to think about his garden as he went through his next lecture. He understood that he would no longer be able to walk his dog as he calmed down from the day's stresses. He had not realized, however, how much of his autonomy he was truly ceding as he stepped into his new role. With these new constraints, including exercising power only within federal "regs" the joke of his power became clearer to him each day. His anger was building. The first blowup came when Roland was told that he had been shielded from a call from his mother's nursing home. His secretary told him that since it wasn't an emergency, he could call back at a more convenient time. He erupted again when someone decided that he could not be interrupted for a call from his dog's vet. The poor secretary who bore the brunt of Roland's anger was hardly responsible for his heavy schedule, or for the general instructions that had been issued to her. However, he had to do some RETHINKing before he understood that. For all his new power in making policy decisions for the nation, former Prof. Roland Briggs felt he was being personally controlled, and his irritability and angry outbursts rose to a dangerous level.

Not many people in this country are named to a Presidential appointment, but many feel the same assault to their personal sense of autonomy when they enter their place of work each day. The struggle to maintain one's personal sense of control, while at the same time submitting to the requirements of an organization, sets the groundwork for vulnerability to anger. Thoughts of being injured, exploited, pushed around, or disregarded can create inner turmoil, stirring up old conflicts between needing to be free and needing to be part of an organization. The necessity to submit to rules, regulations, evaluations, and criticisms can lead to feelings of being undervalued, disregarded, and angry. Adding to the ferment are stereotypes that we all carry about gender differences, race, ethnic class, and age differences and who is entitled to "boss me around." RETHINKing these distortions in our perceptions and understanding that a high public officer is not being pushed around, exploited, and undervalued is not an easy task. Getting another perspective may often involve help from close friends or relatives to be able to laugh off these misconceptions and enjoy the power and prestige associated with the position.

More Specific Stressors

One's sense of control is threatened by unreasonable expectations, heavy workloads, long hours, unsafe working conditions, and no chance to participate in decision-making. What is meant by unreasonable expectations? There is a difference between high expectations of you as an employee: that is, when your supervisor respects both your intelligence and ability and encourages you to succeed versus abusive practices. High expectations can bring out the best in people. "May your dreams always exceed your grasp" is advice that many mentors have given their students. Athletes who are training for the Olympics, or those simply trying to make the team of their choice, work long hours, sometimes to absolute exhaustion. Everyone realizes that high expectations and long hours of work are ingredients for achievement and success. Future physicians, who during their training in medical school, are requested to work long hours, accept this as part of the training. Although they might rightfully complain, it is their choice to become doctors and they can think to themselves: "This will one day pay off. I will be proud to be a physician." Workplace anger is triggered when expectations or requests seem blatantly unfair, triggering feelings of lack of control. Are you expected to work more then anyone could possibly work and feel sane but you have no choice in the matter? Since the quality of your work cannot be maintained if you are seriously deprived of sleep and if you can think of no gain, resentment builds within. This resentment can affect your sense of who you are and how you would like to be treated. The apparent unfairness of the request or demand may very likely trigger your anger. Your need for autonomy, and for control over your life and the use of your time, can feel violated. Anger was transformed in the following story as reported on a television news channel: Telephone workers who were being forced to work overtime had no choice afforded to them. Some of these workers had children to go home to, sick parents to take care of, and were in need of their own quiet time and space. They decided to strike in order to create a fair workplace. This action gave them a sense of control over their lives. Even when there is no actual demand or specific threat from one's employer, workers who try to limit their workday to eight hours often feel pressured by their coworkers or bosses to stay late. The pressure is in the work culture. Even though an employee may like his job, the expectation of long hours on the job conflicts with his desire to go home, spend time with his family, and relax. Indeed, even if a worker is willing to put in long hours, conflicts with a spouse may arise, with more anger being triggered.

Other situations where feelings of lack of control can trigger anger include unbearably unpleasant or dangerous physical conditions. People often complain about crowding, noise, air pollution, toxic fumes, unsanitary washrooms, and nonergonomic work patterns. The latter condition can be injurious to your health. Employees often suffer from back pain, muscle cramps, and carpal tunnel syndrome as a result. When health is negatively affected on the job, or safety is threatened, the pleasure of the job is diminished. Resentment for such conditions builds, and anger is a likely response when a person feels trapped or helpless to change his environment.

Along this same line, a lack of participation in decision-making can also trigger anger. Do you need to get approval for every change you feel is important to speed the completion of your tasks? Do you feel you receive no respect from your supervisors, or are you ignored when you make suggestions? How can you make some sense out of the situation and change it? The need for some autonomy within the framework of an organization is critical to job satisfaction and the reduction of stress.

One's Sense of Worth

Another source of stress is encountered in the workplace when one's sense of worth is threatened. When the unique needs and talents of each worker are not appreciated, which can be exhibited by infrequent breaks, lack of family friendly policies, routine tasks with little inherent meaning, and nonuse of skills, stress builds up. When management does not recognize the need for sufficient employee breaks, it appears disinterested in the physical or mental welfare of its workers. Even though there are laws about breaks, they are not flexible enough to meet the demands of many jobs. If employees want to take time off for such occasions as maternity leave or family emergencies and they find they are treated with resentment or viewed as a nuisance, even though the Federal Family Leave

Act provides for such leave, they may quite rightfully feel annoyed. If you needed such leave and experienced such resentment, you might well feel anger at your employer's lack of empathy. Or, when your job fails to challenge you, teach you, or enlighten you; if your work becomes mechanical and suffocating and you feel ineffective or like a machine, then anger can be triggered. Such a situation can lead to the recognition that your skills are not being utilized. When a job is mismatched with a worker's skills, and it is of little concern to his employer, something needs to be done. Otherwise you run the risk of feeling demoralized because your talents are not recognized or used. Resentment builds and your anger is triggered.

Threats to Relationships: Poor Communications

One's need for *interpersonal relationships* is threatened by, among other things, poor communication. Many offices are physically organized in a way to discourage workers from interacting with one another. This separation of office space is an obstacle to productive communication and inhibits a sense of group identity. If your job satisfaction is related to interactions with colleagues, this kind of physical separation can trigger not only job dissatisfaction, but also anger. Recent reports in the press describe how open spaces, easy access to work machines and to each other, along with comfortable furniture and clothes, make for more productivity and creativity. Frequently companies are not aware of how important interpersonal relationships are to workers, especially when the job tasks aren't very attractive. Many employers fear that socializing on the job will decrease production; but, to the contrary, people frequently work harder when they feel camaraderie with one another.

Jeff, Todd, and David have been working on a project together. David was very upset about the course of the project but couldn't find a way to talk directly to Jeff, whom he found defensive. Rather than talking directly to Jeff, David had been criticizing him, behind his back, to others in the company. When Jeff found out, he was angry and hurt. He felt powerless to change the situation because he feared that he would lose any confrontation with David who had a much more aggressive personality. Jeff worried that confronting David would only make the situation worse. As a result Jeff became depressed. Neither of them was talking directly to the other. Jeff's work efficiency began to decline. He became angrily defensive to even routine supervision, and testy at home.

Backbiting and deceit on the job will interfere with camaraderie and can lead to anger and poor performance. Other examples of poor communication can lead to a destructive cycle. When an employee is unable to articulate his needs, either because he feels so powerless or because he doesn't believe asking for what he wants will make a difference, he can carry (unbeknown to the employer) resentment. Or the employer doesn't articulate her dissatisfaction with the employee's work and takes out her dissatisfaction in nonverbal ways—this can be a cause for a destructive cycle in interpersonal relationships.

Loyalty

One's loyalty is threatened by conflict, such as dealing with an angry customer or when a company is reorganizing or planning on going out of business or downsizing. Many workers, and this is particularly true of employees who interact with the public, are caught in situations where they must deal with the rightful expectations of the customer as well as the limits set by the organization for which they work. What does a worker do when he knows the quality of an item is not as high as it could be, yet he must respond to an angry customer without incriminating his employer?

Need for Certainty

Need for certainty during change is threatened by lack of information: Perhaps you've been with a company that has decided to reorganize its entire structure without letting its employees know either where they will be, or what their status will be, after the changes are made. This is a fairly common occurrence, as are mergers and the downsizing that often follows. Anxiety, stemming from a sense of insecurity and incompetence, is sure to be aroused in these situations, and anger is not far behind. When workers are not adequately prepared for change, they recognize their vulnerability to being replaced. These feelings of uncertainty can lead to an atmosphere of fear and hostility, with lots of anger.

Dealing with Anger on the Job

You may feel handicapped when you try to express anger on the job. You recognize that you do not have the freedom to shout, swear, tell others what you think about them, or challenge the boss. You may think to yourself that you can do those things at home, maybe, but not at work. There are clear limits to expressing anger on the job and these limits require a lot of anger management.

Exercise: How do you express your anger about the causes of stress on the job? What would you like to happen? What does happen? Here are some suggestions. Why don't you explore some ways to deal with the others?

What to do and when

Your *sense of control* is threatened by a heavy workload, long hours, unsafe work conditions, and a lack of participation in decision-making. For example: You are caught in a real conflict. The boss is making you work a ten-hour day. Although you enjoy your job, you do not want to stay such long hours. In addition, you believe that your boss is evil and doesn't care about his employees; you feel powerless to negotiate a fair compromise. Since you do not want to lose the job, but know you have to do something about this untenable situation, you decide to try to use the RETHINK anger management skills to see if you can talk to the boss and negotiate a more reasonable workload in terms of home and job. You Recognize your feelings of anger by the tightness in your stomach, the headache, and the overall feeling of stress and frustration. You want to do something about this without letting your anger get out of control. You look around to see how others feel about their workloads and hours, and share horror stories. At the same time, you begin to get some other perspective about the boss and his position on the workload, and you find you actually have some Empathy and understanding about his situation. After sharing your feelings with coworkers you begin to Think about ways to deal with your anger toward your supervisor. Earlier, you might have thought the supervisor was doing this on purpose to assert his authority. Now, you begin to re-Think and consider that perhaps he didn't know how you feel. Has anyone ever bothered to ask him or tell him? When you Hear him tell about the emergency and the deadline he must face, you begin to understand where he is coming from. Then, you decide to Integrate respect for your supervisor as you and some of your colleagues talk to him about your concerns. You struggle to make "I" statements such as, "I find I am feeling very stressed when I am expected to work such long hours. I would really like to talk about this." You will Notice how you feel as you express yourself, and focus on deep breathing and a sense of calmness, saying to yourself, "I need to do this. I can't hold off any longer. I can do this. I feel good about this." And, of course, you will want to Keep the focus on the subject and not bring up all kinds of other complaints, such as: the microwave didn't work last week; the drinking water was tepid last month. Hope for the best. This method of using RETHINK skills is not 100 percent fail proof, but you definitely have a better chance of negotiating a fair deal for yourself than not saying anything and fuming inside. Perhaps a compromise can be worked out where for the duration of the temporary emergency, you all pitch in, but later the boss will be able to accommodate your needs.

Exercise: If you had infrequent breaks—how would you manage your anger? If you must do routine tasks with little inherent meaning—how would you manage your anger? One's *sense of control is also threatened* when anger is triggered because of the uncertainty we feel about what one can do, and when. You may feel victimized by the system. You may believe you are being treated like a lackey or an incompetent person. You may feel your sense of identity is threatened and your respect as an individual has been violated. Actually, more stress, more job dissatisfaction, more job-related illnesses, especially those resulting in depression and anxiety, are caused by a feeling of no control over what you do, when you do it, or how you do it. A company team such as bowling or softball can alleviate some of the stress from feeling a loss of control or identity. You can become known as the pitcher who got the boss to strike out, or gain respect as a team player. Kidding about the last night's game can bring humor and camaraderie to a workplace that would otherwise be stressful.

Here is another example of a conflict in which feelings of lack of control trigger anger:

A manager was very concerned about the new startup division of his large technology firm. He had hired three new employees, each with excellent resumes and references. One of the new hires was made director of the new division. But, everything was not going well. The manager, John Chu, wasn't getting the kind of results he was expecting.

The new director, Stan Snead, had been given complete control of his work, but was neither producing nor managing his staff very well. Employees were coming and going as they desired, and were not being held accountable to the organization. The database had not been set up, there was little organization, and the filing system was inefficient. All of this was unacceptable to Mr. Chu.

Feeling angry, Chu attempted to organize the division by developing flowcharts, office responsibilities, and an overall management outline. He tried to bring the division under some control. He surmised that he had given too much freedom to the new director and attempted to take back some of the responsibilities. But, the lack of organization and production continued.

Finally, in justifiable anger and anxiety, Chu entered the director's office and began to berate him. Snead was furious with the way the manager spoke. He was a senior director; he was a professional, and he would not tolerate being spoken to in such a demeaning, disrespectful way. When originally accepting this assignment, he thought he would be in charge of the division; now he was being asked to report to this manager, and in an offensive way! Snead had thought they were colleagues and this was certainly no way to speak to a colleague! The manager and the director each had a legitimate right to feel anger. Fear and frustration were mounting for each of them. Chu was afraid that this new division, his idea (he put the team together, and by doing so put himself on the line), was not going to work. He worried that all his time, energy, and enthusiasm—as well as his ego—were going to be shattered. The director, on the other hand, was worried that he had made the wrong decision by taking on this new position. He had left a position he had loved and was now fearful that although he would have all the responsibility, he would have none of the power, the control he felt he needed to make the division successful. Because neither the manager nor the director communicated with each other, each lacked Empathy or understanding for the other's fears and concerns. When the manager Recognized he was feeling angry, he decided to do something about it but he neglected to let the director know what he was planning. Thus both manager and director didn't Hear what the other was saying. In order for the new division to function efficiently, the director and the manager each had to utilize some of the RETHINK skills. They had to take some time to re-Think the problem, agree to clarify what the problems were, and suggest ways to resolve them together. They could agree to be pragmatic, not ballistic, and Hear what each was trying to say. They had to learn how to Integrate respect with their anger. If they Keep in the here and now, without bringing up old grudges, some problem solving could be effected, and the new division could start to function smoothly.

Exercise: Think about a situation in your work life where you are experiencing a lack of participation in decision-making. How do you express your feelings? What would you like to happen? What does happen?

A Continuing State of Anger

There is occasionally a person in the workplace who seems to be in a continuous state of anger. Such a person is difficult to work with and more difficult to manage. Is it fear of criticism, fear of rejection that generates so much anger, or is it a serious mental health problem? And what is a manager to do when such a person is in her office? Here is one case where the manager was more or less successful in dealing with an employee who had, what is labeled, attitude.

An African-American woman was a secretary. She was a very angry young woman who repeatedly reported she was being discriminated against. There would be hearings and her cases were always dismissed. But that wasn't enough to quell her anger. She began carrying a tape recorder around with her, turning it on any time she interacted with someone who had authority over her. She was determined to have a case of discrimination against her made. Her entire body was attitude. It was rigid. The head shifted from left to right, back and forth as she talked.

She was criticized frequently for sloppy work and making unacceptable mistakes in her typing. She denied the criticisms and again said she was being discriminated against. Her supervisor decided that, indeed, real proof of errors was needed and so took the time to read everything the young woman typed, circling the errors, even in addresses on envelopes. Nothing was said but the supervisor built a file of papers and envelopes with the mistakes and placed the file on the woman's desk. The hidden message was clear—these kinds of mistakes are unacceptable and could lead to loss of job. The message was understood. What happened to the anger? Perhaps she saw it did not bring the results she wanted. Letting go of anger is not easy. She had the courage to do just that and became a working member of the organization.

The supervisor did not show her anger. Instead she Integrated respect and Empathy, as well as the fact no direct way would work!

What to do and when

Your *sense of worth* is threatened. Your anger may be triggered when bosses or supervisors do not adequately utilize your skills, thereby violating your need to be respected and seen as a competent person who contributes to the value of the organization. To turn this type of situation around, use your RETHINK skills. First, Recognize your anger and feelings of resentment. You may begin to feel flushed, and have a strong desire to speak your mind. You are ready to do something. You may want to then Think about a clever way to make your point. You might ask for a meeting to discuss your CV, or you might bring in some of your creative work to discuss with the head of the organization. As you make your "I" statement ("I feel disappointed when you do not use all of my skills because I know I can make a valuable contribution to this organization") you will be demonstrating respect for your supervisor. Integrate that respect into your choice of words and your body language. You may feel some Empathy for how busy your supervisor is, and remember to Hear what she is saying, while at the same time keeping your courage up so you can talk to her! You will monitor yourself as you talk, and Notice how you are staying calm and under control. Of course, you will also Keep the focus on the issue; no need to muddy the waters with other complaints!

Again, what to do and when

Your need for interpersonal relationships is threatened by poor workplace communication. There are many ways to communicate. Every time you reach out for help at work, you engage in communication. Every time someone has triggered your anger, upset you, or you have done something to trigger his or her anger, you need to communicate. Here is where "I" statements are critical. But "I" statements are only effective if the other person truly listens to what is being said. It is important to know how to listen as well as how to communicate effectively.

Reading *body language* is important. Is the body rigid or relaxed? Do the eyes make contact as an indication of listening or do they wander? Do both participants seem to be taking the discussion seriously, or do they have smirks on their faces? How do they stand or sit in relation to one another? How close do they stand? Do they touch? Cultural differences influence these behaviors and must be taken into consideration. Body language can set the stage for active listening, which is a more complex skill. Active listening includes:

Listening without criticism (Integrating respect with feelings of anger).
Clarifying and understanding what is being said.
Keeping attention on the specific situation being discussed.
Picking up the emotional content of the words and, perhaps, labeling them.
Empathizing with the feelings behind the anger.
Summarizing the situation, indicating Hearing has, indeed, occurred.

Verbal communication is incredibly difficult and becomes additionally frustrating when anger has been added to the pot. The words you use in communication not only express the way you think and the way you feel, but also the values you hold and the expectations you have from communication.

Emotional literacy, an increasingly recognized part of communication, involves the ability to name your emotions; for example, "I feel sad, concerned, angry, frightened, belittled, ignored, controlled, encouraged, criticized, protected, manipulated, rejected, approved, accepted, loved, good, bad, etc." When you can label your feelings, your challenge is to be able to communicate with those at your workplace who might trigger your anger. When you know your emotions, have words for them, and can recognize when you are feeling them, you are able to Think about them and learn how to manage them. Then, the next step is to Think of a number of solutions and discuss them with your colleagues in order to try to agree on a plan of action. For example, you know that one colleague annoys you by constantly chewing gum. This annoyance often builds up and triggers your anger. By Recognizing this, you will Notice what can calm you before you talk to the person. Think about what you will say, making sure your words express your feelings. It is amazing how deeply people tune in on genuine feelings, especially when they are not attacks on the other person. The difference between, "Good Heavens, would you stop with the noisy mouth. Didn't your mother ever tell you how to chew? Why are you so involved with your mouth during working hours, anyway!" and "Do you have a minute to talk? I need to tell you that I am having trouble with hearing you chewing things. I get distracted by the noise. I hope we can work out a way to deal with this." A more playful approach might be to offer a special reward for three days of silent chewing. A drink after work, or a box of lollipops for the children after a full week of silent chewing, might be the rewards, or even an award badge for soundless chewing! Humor like this only works where there isn't too much enmity among the employees.

Here is another example of poor communication and not using your emotions to guide your thinking and how it can trigger anger:

A CEO of a large company has been asked to leave. He has been very successful in his work and has done wonders for the company. But, he engaged in tyrannical behavior toward subordinates. Fellow workers claimed his management style contributed to a climate of tension and anxiety. They were afraid to disagree with him because he could verbally attack them in front of others and humiliate them. He scolded and shamed people in public to the point that observers felt grown people were being treated like children. He managed by fear, and that is what "did him in."

The CEO's kind of interpersonal relationships and manner of communication are not accepted any more. Today we know that people increase their productivity if they feel involved in decision-making, are consulted with for opinions and ideas, and are treated with respect. New management techniques focus on increasingly democratic interpersonal relationships as well as communication styles in which each person is seen as a valuable part of the functioning of the business, the workplace, and the job.

Special Issues

Office Bullies

There has recently been added a group of people in many offices who, in fact, bully other workers. A recent issue of the *Monitor*, a publication of the American Psychological Association, included a series of reports about the growing awareness of office bullies. (Office Bullies, *Monitor on Psychology* (July/August 2006) 37(7): 68–78.) Even though there is not total agreement on what characterizes office bullies, there seems to be agreement that office bullies:

1. Intend to harm the target and violate the norms of respect.
2. Are verbally abusive.
3. Threaten or intimidate the target so as to interfere with work and undermine the legitimate business interests.
4. Exclude the target from meetings.
5. Withhold information or leave the target off of an important e-mail.
6. Yell, call names, make threatening statements, micromanage, or undermine someone's reputation.
7. Engage in repetitive or patterned behavior.
8. Exploit position of power.

According to the *Monitor* report, some 24 percent of workers claim to be the victims of office bullying:

> Bullying is a form of aggression that needs to be met with aggression. Combining some of the RETHINK skills with aggressive maneuvers is what is called for here. For example, begin with Recognizing your anger, talk to colleagues about what is going on to see if re-Thinking the situation is helpful, stay in present tense with the situation, then if you need to, call in supervisors, heads of company, board members, unions, anyone who has some power over the bully. Work with whomever you need to stop the bullying.

Extreme Stress or Danger

Police officers are faced with daily, and frequently extreme, stress. Here is a personal account of one police officer and his experience with stress and what triggers his anger.

> Cops sometimes have a John Wayne complex. It's like cowboys and Indians or cops and robbers, the good guys always get the crooks. You always get your man, just like the Mounties. In a chase, the siren alone raises your blood pressure, raises your adrenaline. It causes your brain to go into overdrive and you get tunnel vision. Hey, he didn't pull over; that's contempt of cop. That's what it's called, "contempt of cop." It's a cop phrase. You tell someone to do

something and they don't do it, and you get pissed off. You can lose control. It's caused by the stress of the job, the stress of the moment. When it's one on one, there's a lot of fear; when the troops get there, you can forget your training, you can get this gang mentality. We're the biggest and baddest gang. We have permission to shoot you if we want to. I worked undercover drugs, and maybe I look at things differently; when you get away from that mentality of them and us, it opens your eyes, you look at the world in a wider way instead of that tunnel vision. You see things that are wrong that are done every day by cops. It only takes one person to get out of control, one hothead taking offense at "contempt of cop." It's very troubling, even for me. You should prevent a situation like that, not escalate it. Cops are there to protect people, not to beat them up.

Mostly what keeps a cop in line is his own integrity. But his view of the world can get skewed. Violence can escalate from the way the job goes over days and years. It's like a time bomb. This violence builds up, and it's got to blow. With some people you can see it building up; they don't have masks where they can hide emotions. You can see them get angrier and angrier with each passing day and each passing year. But it could happen to anybody. There is more fear today. You've got ten-year olds carrying guns. Cops say they'd rather be "tried by twelve than carried by six." They want to go home at night (Story by the Officer, Doug Martin, *The Washington Post*, July 23, 2000).

How can Doug Martin learn to manage his anger under such extreme stress? He can begin by Recognizing his body's responses to anger—his blood pressure, his adrenaline rush, and his tunnel vision. Next, he could Recognize what he calls "contempt of cop," that is, the behavior of the source of his anger, the "bad guy." He can tell himself not to escalate the situation. If he has the time and is not in extreme danger, the cop should take time to respond in a measured way. Listen to the other person if possible rather then just reacting. Ultimately he could also Think that he should know how to prevent a situation where a hotheaded cop takes offense and escalates the situation into violence; this thought is right on target. However, it is not the moment to start thinking about prevention.

Police need to be provided, in advance of such crises, periodic workshops where roleplaying can help them regulate their responses to hostility and danger. Police should be trained and given time to practice such skills as regulating breathing, practicing self-talk and rethinking their anger. Recognizing the enormous amount of tension in daily police work, we suggest that police have available to them reminders of anger-management techniques at morning roll call, audiotapes in the car, and recreational facilities to let off steam. Police officers, especially those who experience a lot of fear in their daily activities, would benefit from learning another way to think about facing danger and managing their emotions, especially their anger.

These recommendations may raise a lot of skepticism among police officers. For example, a law enforcement instructor, Donald Bassett, who taught the use of force to other officers, had this to say when participating in a RETHINK program:

> How do we teach law enforcement officers to keep their emotions, their anger, under control? That's the $64,000 question, whether you can teach officers to preempt their human instincts when confronted with extreme danger or provocation.

To what extent can law enforcement officers be taught to manage their emotions and keep their anger under control? Can they be trained to understand the physiological and psychological effects of fear and stress? He continued:

> I wish I was smart enough to answer that question. There are certain things you cannot train officers to do under extreme stress. We used to try to teach agents in the tactical unit to keep track of the number of rounds they fired, until we found that it's impossible for most people in an actual gunfight. That's because of the effects of stress, physiological and psychological. It's the "fight or flight" response. The body mobilizes for action, strength increases, fine motor control diminishes. Things happen to your mind, too. In police shooting cases, we hear, "I had tunnel vision. My peripheral vision was lost; I was so focused on the threat." There's also auditory exclusion, where you don't hear things. I've talked to officers who fired eight or nine rounds and didn't even hear the shots go off. We're not talking here about policies or doctrines or ethical standards on using force. We're talking about our limits in molding human behavior through training. I have to believe we can do it, or else we've lost the battle. But I have a question in the back of my mind as to what extent we can do it. We are advocating teaching skills early on, and repeatedly, in police training. Prevention of unnecessarily violent outbursts is necessary, but in a timely way. When a fire breaks out we don't look for the oily rags that were left behind. Rather we just put out the fire. For prevention we need to teach skills beforehand and expect mastery of these skills.

Another police participant in a RETHINK program found that being always reactive to dangerous situations, where so much anger is expressed, is not as effective as being proactive. He illustrated:

That's what I like to do. We have to be more proactive, not always reactive. On my last foot patrol, a neighborhood with several issues, including an open-air drug market, I worked with local residents and business owners. I got abandoned vehicles off the street. I did not just arrest people but educated and assisted them. This prevented criminal activity. In disadvantaged neighborhoods, some people don't trust the police because family members have had negative experiences. To them, most police are crooked, and the black cops are working for the white man. I'm sympathetic to a point. I was raised in the inner city, and I've had my own negative encounters with police. But now I'm a little older and a little more experienced, and I don't have a lot of room for people's excuses. I don't see any good reason why anybody should sell drugs. There are legal ways to make money. I like working with people. Most of the time, I get really positive responses. I understand that not everything is going to be effective. But if you talk to ten people and one of them hears you, you've made a difference. I want to make that difference because I am a product of DC and its public school system. I love my job, except for the money. The money stinks.

Women at Work

It is no news that women are gaining ground on the job. The daughters and granddaughters of Rosie the Riveter now make up 46 percent of the workforce. Everyday many women prove that the glass ceiling isn't shatterproof after all. As a result, more women now collect the wages of increased self-confidence, financial security, social support, and personal success that jobs and careers have long paid men. Many others, however, even those with a better education than that afforded previous generations, are having a more difficult time advancing their careers than do their male colleagues. Women still earn only three-fourths of what men do; they are overrepresented in word processing positions, and underrepresented in corner offices. The frustrations and injustice of such a situation often generate anger, and many women are feeling the strain.

Ambivalence about Change and Tradition

Even in an era when Astronaut Barbie has displaced Homemaker Barbie in many a young girl's fantasy play, women can feel ambivalent about giving full reign to their ambitions. Some claim that women who earn more money, assert more authority, or put their needs before those of men, violate the patriarchal model. A woman's place may not be exclusively in the home, but some seem to accept that it is a step or two behind a man's. However, even women who, of their own accord, turn away from the possibilities of their own talent and intelligence rather than risk challenging traditional expectations and the vilification that may follow, still harbor anger and resentment toward the men for whom they were making way. A woman who has had her father's support in her ambitions, and earned his praise for her achievements, has grown up with the message that you can be competitive and successful and still be Daddy's pride and joy.

Such was the case of Laurel Ayers, portrayed by Whoopi Goldberg in *The Associates*. Laurel was furious when she was passed over for a promotion at the investment-banking firm where she worked because she not only had seniority, but superior skills as well. The promotion went to a "young Turk" whom she had trained. After she re-Thought her anger, Laurel moved on to solve her problem. She decided to quit her Wall Street job, borrow money for a new business (using some property her father had left her as collateral), and take some risks by setting out on her own. When a banker warned her of the risk she was taking, Laurel answered with a combination of courage and bravado that her father would have approved. Not many women have either Laurel's resources or the inner strength she had from her father's encouragement; nor do they have the financial support she enjoyed for starting out on their own. Others in Laurel's circumstances are left angry and disappointed when faced with such discriminatory practices.

Confronting Discrimination

Whether a woman is a line worker or a lawyer, on-the-job discrimination can undermine her success and satisfaction, leaving her feeling hurt and angry. The discrimination she faces can be as subtle as not having her comments recorded in the minutes of a meeting, or as blatant as sexual harassment. It can arise from a coworker's base need to exert power; or from stereotypical assumptions, such as a male manager supposing that a working mother would not be interested in assignments that require long hours. It can be especially pernicious for people of color, who may confront the double wrongs of racism and sexism.

When women confront discrimination, they are likely to go through a predictable set of responses. They may not, at first, be sure what is happening. Initial approaches by a harasser are rarely direct, for example, or behavior might be interpreted as "horseplay." A woman might laugh it off even though she feels some anger and discomfort. As her awareness dawns, however, confusion and self-blame may set in. The woman may begin to wonder what she is doing to cause the problem. If the harassment and/or discrimination continue, she will begin to feel afraid. She may dread contact with the harasser, or feel anxious about confronting the colleague who has been taking credit for her work. As anger overtakes her, she must find a way to resolve her situation. Her health, her ability to perform on the job or care for her kids, and her relationship with her husband or boyfriend—all may suffer.

How a woman responds to being "sweetie-pie'd" or pawed depends, in part, on how much power she has relative to the offender. The less power, the more likely she is to try to avoid him or change jobs. Changing jobs can be a way of ending the immediate problem, but it is likely to cost her seniority. And, she must still resolve her anger, finding a way to use it as a tool for change; for example, her energy could be directed to seeking an organization with the same concerns, or to think of legislation to end harassment and discrimination. She could even form a women's support group at her new job, before she experiences any difficulty.

There are, of course, other effective responses to discrimination and harassment. Reframing the experience by changing the way she thinks about it, from "I'm to blame," to "How can I handle this problem? I am not to blame," can help a woman feel more creative and able to take control. Or, she may learn how to nip harassment in the bud and practice with friends, ways to deflect unwanted advances or demeaning asides with a joke, or a friendly but firm "no." The trick is to find a way to stop the behavior before it escalates. Another method is to talk to the offender. It takes a lot of courage to call the offender to task, firmly but pleasantly, at the first hint of a problem. A woman who was attending a board meeting saw her new boss walk in. He looked around, saw she was the only woman, and asked her to get him some coffee. "Yes, I'll get you coffee if you'll Xerox these papers for me," she quipped. He laughed and, one assumes, got his own coffee. The incident was never repeated.

Another avenue to changing a corporate culture, for women who have experienced discrimination, is to enlist the help of colleagues. Filing an official complaint and/or seeking emotional support are both paths available to such a woman, so that she does not feel trapped in her anger.

Creative Anger Management at Work

The paradox of work is that the very place we find meaning and security in our lives is also the place where we encounter so many anger-provoking incidents. The office, the factory, the stage, or any other work setting, provides significant challenges to our creativity in managing our anger. Women, facing harassment and discrimination, are learning to handle their anger with humor, understanding, and creativity. Those who face extraordinary stress, such as police, need special training and mastery of anger management skills. More generally, the ability to recognize, to avoid, or to reduce the stresses and triggers of anger can be a worthy goal for management and employees. Creative approaches to anger will be as varied and as numerous as the people who invent them.

CHAPTER 9

Friends and Anger, and Anger in the Community

Some people fear that expressions of anger toward a friend may cost them the relationship. Rarely does that actually happen. Instead, experience indicates that as anger is expressed, warmer and more meaningful ways of relating follow. Explanations and understanding tend to resolve the conflict.

Other people indicate that people who express their anger report the outcomes have been beneficial more often than not. And many targets of the expressed anger said their relationship with the angry person had been strengthened rather than weakened. Targets more often gained rather than lost respect for the angry friend. As the poet William Blake intuited more than a century ago in his poem, "A Poison Tree:"

> I was angry with my friend,
> I told my wrath, my wrath did end;
> I was angry with my foe,
> I told it not, my wrath did grow.

On what grounds do friends get angry with one another? Arguments or hurt feelings about money are a common cause, and keeping someone waiting or worse, forgetting an appointment, can cause bruised feelings that generate anger. It is, of course, the meanings associated with each of these anger triggers that bring some automatic thoughts to mind. "She has no respect for me or she wouldn't keep me waiting," is one interpretation, whereas the person who is late may have a chronic problem with managing her time.

"He thinks I'm a cheapskate," may be the thought when one friend wants to treat another to dinner. The possibilities are endless, as friends interpret each other's behaviors as reflecting on their own perceived shortcomings. When two people are sharing space, as in the case of roommates or office partners, both extreme neatness and untidiness can become another frequent contributor to anger. Talking it over, as indicated by reports and Blake's poem tell us, can resolve anger and reestablish important relationships.

Some friends may be more difficult, especially when they place great emphasis on protecting their right to do and say what they please. They feel they have these entitlements:

I have the right to do exactly what I want to do.
I have the right to criticize when I think my friend is doing something unreasonable.
No one has the right to tell me what to do.
I expect friends to do what I consider proper.

You may well know someone like this. The interesting fact is that these are the beliefs of a very, very, young child! A two-year-old, who is just learning that she is a separate person, assumes she has the right to do as she pleases. But for adults, it is important to talk about the conflict so that each can become aware of presumed entitlements. It is also important to recognize that the vulnerabilities of the other person must be respected or protected. For example, if a friend tells you something and assumes you will keep his confidence, that friend is very angry when he learns you, indeed, have told someone else. He assumed you knew his vulnerability to having what he tells you passed along to someone else. He didn't think he needed to state this fact.

Friends are frequently the targets of our anger, but they may also play a number of roles when we experience anger at others. These roles can range from inciting undesirable action to providing insights. How anger may be safely expressed depends on the norms in which we find ourselves. Here are some "rules" of anger among friends, including how friends sometimes play a dangerous role inciting conflict and even violence; and on the other hand, sometimes how friends can be helpful with transforming anger with humor and distraction. How can friends, by listening with understanding and empathy, help each other gain mastery over an unpleasant emotion? And can friends help other friends recognize their automatic thoughts that cause so much pain and may, upon reflection, seem absurd? From incite to insight, our friends can play an important role in the way we manage our anger.

Know the Rules

Katharine Graham, the former owner of the Washington Post newspaper, describes in her autobiography, a scene in her home where her late husband, Philip Graham, was sitting around the table with his friends, all former or current Supreme Court clerks under Justice Felix Frankfurter. The Judge was there as well. She watched, with some envy and some amazement, as they debated all the issues of the time so passionately and so irreverently. When one of the friends, who had remained silent, was asked why he was so quiet, he responded that he was just sitting there and counting the nonsequiturs. No one was offended; everyone just laughed. Katharine Graham, brought up by nannies to be polite and respectful at all times, had never learned this kind of banter.

The rules of what constitutes playful teasing and what is construed as insufferable provocation of anger vary from one part of the culture to another. With a gang that views others as the enemy, much less confrontation might lead to anger and violence. The Supreme Court clerks' banter might be construed as fighting words. But generally, a friend, or a group of friends, provide a safe place to try out ideas and use terms like, "ridiculous," "nonsense," and "you're off the mark," without causing undue offense. One might even question the veracity of a friend's facts with "what a distortion!" without causing any harm to the relationship. In another situation, making this last comment might lead to being grabbed by your lapels and having a face in your face demand, "Are you calling me a liar?" In some groups, this verbal parrying can resemble trading friendly pokes in the ribs or punches on the arm. The rules for such roughhouse must be well understood. Usually, a strong basis of respect for one another must be firmly established before insults are interpreted as playful. In the case of the Supreme Court clerks, they had all been chosen as members of a small elite group and none had fears about his own adequacy. In another context, such behavior would be provocative and lead to serious consequences.

With a group of friends, an easy expression of disagreement may be permissible and rewarding. Friends are often able to discuss anger that was generated outside the group and the friends might be able to give some insights that would lead to resolving the anger.

A hazardous role that friends can sometimes play involves goading the angry person on and escalating the anger to rage or violence. The comforting role friends can play, and this is the expected and most important role, requires listening as a valued confidante. When friends go beyond being confidantes to help one another resolve the anger by gaining new perspectives, and even laughing at the once troubling situation, they are treasures. Here are different roles friends can play.

Goaders: Friends as Hazards

A schoolyard fight breaks out during recess and some spectators GOADED the two students to really get tough. A knife appears, is used, and one of the fighters is down. The crowd that had been cheering and GOADING, now waits solemnly for the ambulance to arrive. Friends sometimes have their own agendas and are not committed to maintaining behavior friends have a right to expect. The slogan, "Friends for life: Friends don't let friends fight," was developed as a public service campaign in an attempt to alert students and adults that they can help to create a safer environment.

In the schoolyard fight that ends in violence, the "friends" seemingly enjoyed inciting one boy's jealousy by reporting what his girlfriend had been heard to say or what someone else had reported having seen:

"Then Frank put his arms around Jane and she looked up at him and she smiled."

"She seems really hooked on this new guy!"

"Jane was your girl until Frank stole her away!"

"Yeah, I'd give him what he deserves, what he has coming to him!"

The inflammatory comments, rumors, and dares, raise the level of vicarious excitement among the peer group. The dynamics are not very different from the so-called "friends'" incitement in a barroom brawl. Anger builds up to the rage level and the violence that ensues is interpreted as an act of defense by the violent person. He probably sees himself as a victim and must fight to even the score. The inciters experience a moment of power as they let the energy build and erupt. But "Friends for life: Don't let friends fight," is a message to be taken seriously. It is not just teenagers or men in bars who play this destructive game.

Peg is the next door neighbor of Ann, and when they have coffee together, having dropped off the children in school, Ann often unburdens herself:

Joe was late getting home again last night. I had fussed for hours to get everything just right for dinner. I had this new cookbook and bought all the ingredients for a gourmet meal. By nine o'clock, when he hadn't showed up or called, I was furious. Every last morsel went down the disposal. I got a high just dumping it all down there. That guy doesn't deserve such good treatment."

Peg responded: "You bet he doesn't! I'd have thrown the food in his face, not down the disposal. He is mean and inconsiderate. How long have you been with that guy? Maybe it's time to dump him!"

Peg got her friend more agitated and less able to resolve her problem with her husband.

Neither of them would ever find out how beaten and bullied the husband had felt when compelled to work late by a tyrant of a boss. With friends like Peg, who needs enemies?

Confidantes and Hooters

Friends can play the opposite role when they listen with respect and empathy.

Bob, a fifteen-year-old, is sounding off to his friend, expressing his anger at his parents for having unreasonable restrictions on what he can do. His friend joins in by reporting on the restrictions his parents also set. The suggestions of how to deal with this situation range from "Let's run away from home" to "let's defy our parents by engaging in substance abuse or sex." But, a good gripe together about how mean parents can be can quickly be transformed to a comic imitation of the "tyrant parent" and a good laugh. Parents are rarely as awful as they seemed before such a good talk with friends. It's all reframed as: "Parents are soooo . . . terribly old-fashioned and simply do not understand what is going on with kids," or similar rethinking. The rigid parent or rule can be addressed after a good laugh has diffused the intense anger of the youth. A friend helps a friend see the humor in a seemingly terrible situation. A friend helps a friend RETHINK.

Friends are often in danger of becoming the object upon which we project unpleasant feelings about ourselves. We read their minds as if we know exactly what they are thinking. Then we get mad at them for thinking such disparaging thoughts about us. Here is such a situation:

Fred was mowing his lawn on a hot Sunday afternoon when the blade snapped. He was frustrated as he started over to his neighbor's house to borrow his mower. But, he thought enroute, "Hank will think I am such an idiot. Another stone on the lawn, another snapped blade! Why can't I be more careful? Besides he'll remind me that I never returned his hedge clippers. Well, I never finished clipping my row of yews. They do look messy and uneven. An eyesore on the block!"

By the time he got to Hank's doorbell, he was perspiring and furious with his neighbor for being so critical of him! Hank probably thought of himself as so superior, so high and mighty! When Hank opened the door for Fred and was about to invite him in for a drink, Fred had decided that he would not allow himself to be put down by this arrogant neighbor. Never mind the lawn mower. A good offense is always better than a defense, so Fred heard himself say: "You better keep that mutt of yours on your own property. I am tired of cleaning up after him." Hank was startled by his neighbor's accusation as well as his angry tone. "Sure, sure, Fred. I am sorry about that. I try to keep him on a leash, but things get out of hand sometimes, you know."

Fortunately for Fred, his friends at the office were good listeners at lunch the next day. They were convulsed with laughter when they heard about the neighbor's dog and the profuse apology Fred managed to get. He was surrounded by friends who really had high regard for him, and, as a matter of fact, thought he was quite brilliant. He was able to drop his distorted premise that he was such a slob and a problem in the neighborhood. Not only was he OK, he realized, but one of the guys, Marty, got him to think differently about his partly clipped hedge and other imperfect features of his garden.

"Seedy is cool, in my neighborhood," Marty explained. "No one would want to be considered a compulsive, manicurist of lawns." There would be some explaining to do to Marty's neighborhood association if things were too precise on his property. Fred was helped by this group of office friends to gain some new perspectives and some mastery of automatic thoughts that popped into his head and got him angry when that emotion served no useful purpose. One friend from the drafting department at Fred's workplace even printed up a banner that read: "Keep that mutt off my property!" They always laughed when they remembered that story. It became the symbol for imagined insults and angry responses. Also, they all recognized something of themselves in that absurd situation. And everyone could agree with Puck's "What fools we mortals be."

Insights from Friends

Dorrie's story was different in that it was colleagues at the office whom she chose as the target of her anger. Dorrie was fed up with her job and ready to quit. She asked her trusted friend Jennifer to meet her for lunch:

"I'm thinking about quitting my job. I am fed up!" Dorrie told her friend. Jen was amazed. "Didn't they come through with the raise you told me about?" she asked. "It's not about money," Dorrie answered. "I'm probably the highest paid executive secretary in any think tank in the region, maybe even the country. I am just up to here!" she said, indicating her throat.

"But you can't be bored, going from one interesting topic to another every few months," Jennifer persisted. "What's getting to you?"

"I am tired of being everyone's mother. Everyone comes to me with their problems, with their hurts, and expects me to make it 'all better.' I am not in the mood for mothering a sixty-year-old man who is having troubles with his wife's children, or even with a twenty-six-year old guy who is feeling rejected by his latest love. I do not want to be everyone's mother!"

Jen was puzzled at the intensity of her friend's complaint. "It would be different if it were a cute bouncing baby of your own?" she ventured. Apparently she was right on the mark, because Dorrie's eyes welled up with tears.

"Yesterday I bumped into Peter, the guy I spent a lot of time with until a couple of years ago. Well, he and his wife were strolling down the street pushing their baby along in a carriage, the cutest newborn I have ever seen. You're right, Jen! I really want to be a mother so much, a baby's mother. I'm thirty-five and I wonder whether I ever will have a kid of my own."

"What went wrong with you and Peter? It seemed like you were great together for awhile?"

"Yeah, it was great for awhile. But then I blew up at him and it got worse and worse, until I finally broke it up. It's not the first time, you know. Remember I was married at eighteen, divorced at nineteen, and in and out of relationships for the last sixteen years. It gets stormy and I get out. And I end up mothering a bunch of old men at work."

Jennifer was empathic and helped Dorrie understand that she was angry about her situation. Her colleagues at the office were not the cause of her distress. They were as innocent as Fred's neighbor's dog. Dorrie needed help finding a new love and maintaining a relationship, not finding a new job. She was able to recognize how anxious she was getting about her age.

"Jennifer, you are a gem of a friend!" she said as the waiter brought the check. "I'm paying, and no arguments."

Beyond playing the role of confidante and helping to think about the situation in a different way, a friend can help with solving a problem so that the discomfort dissolves. Here are Lillian and her friend Shirley who share an apartment.

Lillian was in a master's program in anthropology at a major university. Always an "A" student, Lillian excelled at everything she tried: academics, violin, cooking, and athletics—everything. But she was petrified of public speaking and never took a course that would require more than the perfunctory oral presentation. When her professor informed her that in order to get her master's degree, she had to defend her dissertation in front a panel of distinguished faculty members, she became furious. She wasn't afraid of content, but she got hives at the mere thought of making a major oral presentation. It wasn't fair, she thought. Perhaps they just didn't want to see her graduate. Maybe they were sexist. She locked herself into her room with a quart of Rocky Road ice cream and began to cry, paralyzed with anger and fear. It was in this condition that Shirley found her.

Lillian trusted Shirley and spoke of her unendurable stress. Lillian had to face her demon or fail to achieve for the first time in her life. Shirley, who was at the School of Communication, suggested, "Let's get you hooked up with the best speech tutor in my department. You can train for the big day and be a smash hit when you have to speak!"

Lillian followed up on her friend's lead. She used her exceptional ability to do hard work to overcome her major deficit, fear of public speaking. She realized that as she coped with her fear, her anger started to subside. This probably wasn't a plot to show off her incompetence. After three weeks of training, when the day came, she got through it. No Gettysburg Address, mind you, but good enough to pass and get her degree. Shirley had helped her get through her anger and paralyzing fear in order to move on to solve her problem.

Beyond Reason

Friends can play another set of roles beyond listening, reframing, and problem solving. Distraction, like humor, can often go a long way in dissipating anger. Singing together, jamming some music, painting, shooting baskets, all sports, recreational, and art activities can be ways to gain distance from the anger-producing event until, in a calmer moment, it doesn't seem as bad as earlier. Even a shopping spree can be therapeutic for some people. Knowing how to distract a friend who is overwhelmed with angry feelings is a special way to help, a role a friend can play more readily than family can. This playful approach does not involve analyzing, rethinking, or directly solving any problems. The antithesis of this helpful role involves destructive activities to distract: drowning one's sorrow with alcohol or drugs, or other dangerous activities, such as fast driving. But friends for life don't let friends speed or fight. The cure that good friends can bring to a troubled friend is constructive play. Joy can override angry feelings in many situations.

Anger in the Community

Situations that arouse anger in the community often involve acquaintances, strangers, or the impersonal forces of bureaucracy. The relative anonymity of these conflicts differentiates them from the highly personal nature of those within the family, among our friends, and of many at work. Standing in a long line at the Post Office; trying to get a human being when phoning a bank, a publishing house, public services, or cable companies. The menus presented by the recorded voice seldom contain what service is needed, and, often, especially where computers are involved, the help is coming from another country.

The frustrations of many of these encounters certainly can erupt into anger. It is the sense of helplessness, of seeming to be a victim, and of not having your needs met that is so infuriating. There is really no one to express your anger to, but sometimes it is worth a try. For example:

Janice is a professor of some repute and she is often asked to write a letter of recommendation for a student, a colleague, or someone she met in her professional work. She was asked by a young man she knew to write letters of recommendation for him as he applied to five universities for admission into their graduate schools. She was more than happy to do this, as he was outstanding in his work and in his promise as a very successful professional.

Then the stress began. She got on the various Web sites for the different universities and went through the sequence of steps to provide the requested information. At one Web site, she had only good luck. She had written a letter of recommendation as part of the information requested, attached it, sent it, and the job was done. She felt very good about the whole experience.

But, hold on, that was the exception. The other four universities had different requests and it turned out there was no way to deal with them all. She kept getting notices that she had not completed the questions or followed the directions correctly. After trying to comply, it became clear nothing she was doing was going to solve the problem. And hitting the "help" button got no response, none! The anger from the frustration began. "What am I supposed to do?" Janice asked herself. "Here I am trying to help this young man and all I get is trouble. Why can't they use a system that isn't so full of obstacles?"

By not being able to fill out and send the recommendations, she kept getting repeat requests—time was running out. Even the young man was e-mailing her, expressing his concern. She had mixed feelings about his contacting her. Was he spying on her? Did he have a right to monitor her? She felt anger toward him, but dismissed it quickly as she realized he was so anxious to have the help he needed.

Janice would go back and try again. She had a second success when there was an opportunity to use her file containing the recommendation and attaching it to the form. So, now there were two successes and still three failures. The requests kept coming and Janice decided to write to two of the remaining universities—she was familiar with faculty in each—to tell them her problem and to include the letter of recommendation. She made clear how frustrating the process was and how unfair for the young man and other applicants. Her anger did subside. She was doing all she could to help the young man and hoped the universities would do something about this peculiar, frustrating system. She thought, "They have made clear they don't want the Admissions Office to be bothered with receiving letters of recommendation—better to do it by Web site. That is fine, but the system is not working!

Two of the universities receiving the letters from Janice, accepted them to finalize the application! So, now Janice was down to one. The anger was diminishing. She received another request from this last university to fill out the on-line form. And she went through it, seeing it had, in fact been made clearer and simpler to complete. But, NO! There was a trick in this one, too! They asked for an electronic signature. Now that was a first. All the hope Janice felt that this would work was shattered. She had no way to comply. Now the anger really was roused. "What is this? A game? Why is something new added that wasn't in any of the others? I can't believe these people! Don't they want students? I give up!" But, there was also something on the form that was different: an emergency phone number. That was new. That was great! She would call immediately. Would she express her anger? How would they react to that? She thought about the negative consequences of expressing anger over the phone to a stranger, but she would do her best to curb it. She phoned and the answer came after one ring. A soft male voice identified himself and Janice felt comfortable enough to say this: "Good morning. I'm Janice Smith, and I have just filled out a recommendation for Ronald Silver, and I have run into a problem. But first, may I express to you the complete frustration I have experienced with most of the requests to make recommendations online. There are so many obstacles that can't seem to be overcome. There is no response to hitting the "Help" button, and the experience is very stressful. Now, I am trying to fill out the form for Ronald and everything is fine except now they ask for an electronic signature. That is a new request and I cannot fill it." His response was calm as he asked, "Do you have the form in front of you?" And with her "Yes" response, he said, all you have to do is type in your name." Janice did not understand that and said, "I thought you had to sign it as requested." He responded, "Your recommendation has been accepted. Thank you." And he hung up!

Now, Janice was really surprised. This made no sense. But she wasn't going to argue! Job done! Now she was amused by the system. The stress was gone, she had no idea what had worked, and she wasn't going to be bothered by it any longer. She had helped the young man and that was the goal!

It is interesting how anger can ebb and flow during interactions. Now you're angry. Now you're seeing the humor in the situation. Now you're frustrated. Now you're relaxed. It is this flexibility not only in our emotions but also in our responses that make it possible for us to RETHINK situations as they are happening. No emotion needs to take over. No thought needs to dominate. It is the flexibility of our reactions to the situation that gives RETHINKing the possibility to work and adapt to the changes.

Describe an experience you had where your anger was roused and calmed at least several times during an interaction with someone in the community:

Where did the experience occur?
Who were the people involved?
What happened? Describe the experience in total, with all the facts you
    remember.
When did you feel angry?
How did you express it?
When did something happen that broke the tension and you might even
    have laughed?
Was your anger roused again?
How did you express it?

You can go through the experience and note how many times your anger was roused and how it was dispelled? You may find you were using RETHINK skills even if you might not have encountered them before. But, you can be consciously using them now as you deal with situations in the community that alternately trigger your anger and can also set off your humor, or even provide a resolution.

Anger, Fear, and Terror in the Community

The Journalist

David Rosenbaum, sixty-three, was taking a stroll on his street near his home in January 2006, when he was mugged and robbed. He was pounded on his head with a metal pipe by robbers. When help came, he was treated as a drunk by DC firefighters, and other emergency workers, none of whom noticed the head wound. He was taken to a hospital farther away than the nearest because one of the ambulance workers had some business nearby that hospital. When they arrived, the victim was kept in a hallway, again with no one noticing his head wound. Rosenbaum, who had recently retired after some four decades at the *New York Times*, died of brain injury two days later.

The DC inspector general's office gave a critical report faulting firefighters, emergency workers, police, and hospital personnel for the "unacceptable chain of failure." And the new Mayor, Adrian M. Fenty, vowed to correct the system that led to the death of Mr. Rosenbaum.

But, there is more to the story. The family of Mr. Rosenbaum has sued the DC Government for up to twenty million dollars for the unnecessary tragedy resulting from the incompetence of the system. The family has taken its anger energy and is using it to bring about change so no one else needs to suffer from such incompetence. The family wants reform, not money. And it has agreed to withdraw the lawsuit in exchange for an overhaul of the emergency medical response system. The family has given the city only one year to make these changes. Mr. Rosenbaum's brother, Marcus, stated it quite clearly: "As details of the case started to come out, we decided among ourselves to do something for all the citizens so that things would be improved."

The newly elected Mayor, Adrian M. Fenty, has gone into action. A task force has been formed and David Rosenbaum's son-in-law, Toby Halliday, will serve as the family's representative. He stated: "Our goal is to look beyond the individual errors in this case to bigger issues of emergency medical services. The results must be meaningful and measurable, with changes and results that can be tracked over time to see if they are effective." They have until March of 2008 to make the changes.

The Snipers

The Metropolitan area of Washington, DC, was victim not only of the 9/11 assault on the United States, with the Pentagon being one target of the attacks, but just over a year later, the area was the victim of a series of shootings and killings by the so-called Snipers.

Between October 2 and 4, 2002, seven people were killed in DC, Maryland, and Spotsylvania County, Virginia. An assumption was made that these killings came from the same person, a sniper. On October 7, not only was the sniper continuing to shoot people, killing some, and injuring others, but in the ninth attack, the sniper shot a thirteen-year-old boy in the chest as he was getting out of his aunt's car to go into school. The entire region reacted. Parents rushed to the middle school to get their children. They were in a state of shock, fear, and anger.

The response to the shooting came from the whole region. Chief of Police, Charles A. Moose, expressed his anger, and urged parents to talk to their children, calm them, show them love, and do what was necessary to make them feel safe. He assured people the police and all related security services were being used.

On Wednesday, October 9, two days after the boy was shot, a man was shot in Virginia, while he was filling his car at a gas station. The incident had the same pattern as the previous shootings and was assumed to be another act of the sniper. Anger can be contagious and can spread. Fear, anger, and lack of control became generalized and endemic.

On October 14, a woman was shot. By October 23, it was learned that there were two men involved in the shootings. One had military training—John Allen Muhammad, forty-one, a Gulf War veteran. The other was Lee Malvo, a seventeen-year-old believed to be Muhammad's stepson, which later proved not to be true.

Festering Anger Communitywide: Punishment for the Good of the Community

Having found the snipers, there was a great deal of anger and a strong desire for revenge. The entire community was relieved and proud of the support received from the protection community. And, especially, the way the different agencies worked together. The citizens of this community responded in caring and humane ways. To live through actual threats and actual events, it is reassuring to know the community is there with its support and help.

There are major lessons that we can learn from reviewing the details of such a horrific true-life story. Whether anger is expressed in a destructive way or in a constructive way is crucial. Not all anger is bad, but when it is acted out destructively, the damage can be communitywide and now, since we live in a global society, worldwide. Dr. Julius Segal, a prominent psychologist, wrote an article in a conference proceeding entitled "Channeling Children's Anger: An International Conference on Children and the Media," held by the Institute for Mental Health Initiatives, Washington, DC, on May 21–22, 1987.

1. Do Not Be Afraid that Anger Will Drive Others Away: Friendship and other close relationships cannot endure if either person is fearful

about the honest expression of angry feelings. By a wide margin, reports indicate that the outcome of their anger is beneficial rather than harmful. This is also true of the targets of the anger. Learning can take place when we hear from others how we are triggering their anger. And if expressed, the very act of talking about your strong emotions and being heard can prevent the destructive acting out of anger.

2. Do Not Suppress Legitimate Anger: Anger is that wonderful energy that needs room. Suppressed anger gets acted out or boomerangs against oneself in self-hate and physical ailments.

3. Avoid Unnecessary and Corrosive Anger: An ancient Chinese proverb taught that "the fire you kindle for your enemy often burns you more than him." Keeping in a state of anger is not only unhealthy emotionally and physically, but it also prevents joy and growth.

4. Recognize the Difference between Thoughts and Actions: There is a gap between our fantasies and how we behave. All humans have a "dark side" that can cause distress, shame, guilt, and even disgust. But angry thoughts need not be the same as destructive actions. Fantasies never hurt anyone unless they are acted out. But disturbing thoughts, when discussed with a confidante, can lead to insight and understanding of what is troubling us and a more uplifting feeling of possibilities. The main purpose of creatively, constructively, expressing anger is to improve a situation or a feeling, not to get revenge.

5. It Is Possible to Accept the Angry Feelings of Others: Not only is it important to express our feelings productively but we can also learn to listen empathically. Alerting people close to us that we are willing, able, and even heartfelt about listening to their angry feelings will go a long way in preventing angry outbursts and destructive behaviors.

6. Anger Energy Can Be Converted into Social Action: Learning to use anger in the service of larger than personal causes is good for the community. Anger can be worn as a victim's badge that encourages chronic aggression. The results will be deteriorating or even violent behavior toward others. Or, anger can be used as an opportunity for growth. This is what prophets of old did when they transformed their wrath into working for social change. And that is what Civil Rights leaders did (and do) when they redirect their outrage at discrimination into new laws and opening doors for all people.

In our own lives anger can be converted into constructive action, by effecting change in ourselves, our friendships, and in our communities.

Used purposefully, anger can be the springboard for separating the essential from the secondary, the important from the unimportant. The goal is to decrease the potential of anger to do harm and to promote the constructive and growth-enhancing potential of this powerful human emotion we all experience.

CHAPTER 10

The Anger-Violence Connection

Expressions of anger, as we have shown, can have either positive or negative consequences. On the one hand, anger can energize a person to right a wrong, adjust an imbalance of power, resolve a conflict, or change a situation for the better. On the other hand, expressions of anger can be futile, or even counterproductive, occasionally in the extreme. Social problems, including substance abuse, school failure, runaway children, teenage pregnancies etc., can in some circumstances be the consequences of anger. Health problems may also be harmful consequences of mismanaged anger. In this chapter we explore one other profoundly negative, but hardly inevitable, consequence of anger: violence.

Violence Entertains

From the times of the Romans who crowded their arenas to watch a lion devour a human victim, or the Spaniards who shouted "OLE" at their bull fights, to the British who packed the hillside by the Tower of London to watch a royal beheading, to our own times where a boxing match is still a big draw, people seem to enjoy vicarious violence. We like reading books involving violence, we enjoy going to movies about violence, and news outlets provide the excitement of reporting on violent acts every day. There is no escaping the focus on violence. One new example of this popularity of violence might be hip-hop music, which has emerged over the past twenty-five years from a gritty New York neighborhood to become a global phenomenon, with sales of the music reaching billions of dollars and hip-hop influencing styles of clothes, language, and other social trends. The violence of this music has entered the mainstream, as reported by Amy Alexander in the *Washington Post* (April 5, 2007). Although women are the primary target of this pop art, paradoxically, women are also the greatest fans.

Why such violence, experienced vicariously, is enjoyed is not really understood, with the empathy of the audiences split between the victim and the perpetrator. There is the element of unreality and of control because we can choose to shut our eyes or turn off the music.

Real Violence

Yet, when violence is acted out by youth who cannot draw a clear line between fantasy and reality, and when violence is acted out by adults who have so many role models for the "how to," we become alarmed, we become angry. We probably need to do some RETHINKing as a society!

Scenes such as the one we witnessed in real time at Columbine High School so dominate our thinking about anger-generated violence that parents all over the country were terrified. Not only were they deeply concerned about their children's safely, but a secret terror also still grips some hearts as they experience angry outbursts from their own teenagers. Parents may wonder, "Could my son turn into one of those rampage murderers?"

Schools have increasingly become stages for violent outbursts, with the tragic events at Columbine one extreme example, and school-age children are increasingly frightened by the possibility of violence intruding upon their own schools and lives. Fights that a generation ago would have ended with nothing more serious than a black eye or a bloody nose now frequently result in serious injury or even death. The ready availability of weapons in many cities and towns surely contributes to the elevated level of violence. The Outlook Section of the *Washington Post* (Sunday, April 22, 2007) had an article by Jonathan Safran Foer, titled, "Some People Love Guns. Why Should the Rest of Us Be Targets?" that presents these facts about guns: Guns kept in the home for self-protection are forty-three times more likely to kill a family member, friend, or an acquaintance than to kill an intruder. For every justifiable handgun homicide, there are more than fifty handgun murders, according to the FBI. The expanded right to carry concealed guns makes us even less safe. And some 3,000 children are killed by guns each year.

The ready availability of weapons surely contributes to the elevated level of violence, but it is not the entire story. Some acts of violence do not begin as simple arguments, but originate instead in a deeper, darker, place in the human psyche. Such violence, when it results in death, is more random and cold-blooded, and has been aptly called "rampage murder." But let us be careful with the concept, "cold-blooded." Actually rampage killers are burning with anger, rage, and hate. And that fire is further fueled by the belief that their rage is the result of what other people have done to them. They are not responsible for their behavior; others made them do it. But, people who carry out these kinds of acts often have a history of emotional illness, which has not been adequately treated.

Rampage Killing

We are concerned with the anger that turns into violence. There are some clear descriptions of people who have turned anger into violence and even into rampage killings. Most rampage killers are men and most showed mental health problems, being on psychiatric drugs, but, more often, were sent for mental health counseling. They show depression—often seen as suppressed anger—and think others are intent on harming them. And they often make attempts to commit suicide—an extreme reaction to depression.

They are, of course, troubled people, whom the Mental Health System has failed. We don't see them as dangerous, just peculiar. However, they frequently give warnings about their intent to harm a specific person or a specific group. They make general, even targeted threats. Their behavior changes before killing. They display violent behavior and they often show their weapons in public. These rampage killers are loners even though they almost always let someone know their intentions.

Jim Davis, whose coworkers had nicknamed him Psycho, warned his colleagues at a tool warehouse in Asheville, North Carolina, "If they ever decide to fire me, I'll take two or three of them with me." His employers fired him and feared he would respond with violence, but did nothing. Nor did the employees ask for protection or work out their own protection. So they were not prepared when Jim Davis came back and took his revenge.

The Special Case of Teenagers

Teen rampage killers are different from adult rampage killers. The teens have accomplices and give verbal warnings of their intentions. They are often goaded into the act, but, more commonly, helped. In a teen shooting of a popular basketball player that took place at the high school in Bethel, Alaska, Evan Ramsey, the killer, gave plenty of warning and was helped. He told classmates to be on the mezzanine of the school lobby to witness his "evil day." And one fellow student showed him how to load the gun just the day before, while another carried a camera to take pictures of the event, and then forgot to use it.

These young killers often asked for help from one or two others, received it, and boasted about their plans. They also shared their feelings of anger and hatred for a particular person or for a specific group of people, like the jocks. Having someone to share planning the rampage with gives them the courage and the anger energy to carry out the killings.

Like adult rampage killers, the teen killers had histories of emotional disorders, as well as problems with managing their behavior. Many times, teen rampage killers are "getting even" with some person or some group. Most of the time this revenge is fantasized into: "He'll get what's coming to him."

But the line between fantasy and reality can disappear. In the Columbine killings, where teens talked and planned together, they were "getting even" with their classmates who kept them out of their cliques. The classmates included those who were popular, and those who had ignored them or made fun of them. All their needs for peer approval, acceptance, respect, or feeling competent, were violated. Anger into violence into killings was the "getting even."

Jamie Rouse always dressed in black. He walked up to two female teachers who were chatting in the hall, and without a word shot each of them in the head. One teacher was gravely wounded, and the other died. Then Jamie smiled and aimed at the school's football coach. But a student, Diane Collins, happened to cross his path. A bullet tore through her throat. She was sixteen when she died that day.

Jamie had a long history of threatening others, even holding his own brother at gunpoint. His parents punished him for this act by taking away his gun. But, he was giving warning signs regularly and no one was looking. In his senior year, Jamie submitted his entry for the yearbook: "I, Satan, James Rouse, leave my bad memories here to my two brothers." By that time, Jamie was working nights, taking something to stay awake, and something to get to sleep. He was listening to heavy metal music, cranked very loud because it drowned out the voices in his head. He later told psychiatrists he heard voices all the time.

The spring before the shootings, he got into a violent fight with two other boys at school. But when the teachers broke it up, Jamie would not calm down. He was totally out of control, saying, "I will kill you!" The police became involved after this incident. Jamie faced juvenile charges and was suspended for three days. When hunting season started, his parents gave him back his rifle. Later, after the killings, his mother said it never occurred to her to get counseling for her son. No teacher had been close to him since elementary school; and adults who noticed his antisocial behavior did nothing. Teenagers who were familiar with his peculiar, even dangerous behavior, did not tell.

The fear and anger these rampage killers generate in the general public are justified; however, when a child is having trouble with schoolwork, with social relationships, and with managing anger, this is all the evidence needed to intervene with appropriate help.

Recently in the news (CBS, April 16, 2007) was another act of rampage killing on the campus of Virginia Tech University, in Blacksburg, VA. Thirty-two were killed and more were wounded by a student named Cho Seung Hui. He killed himself as well. After the shooting, as police and community attempted to understand what happened, a portrait emerged of a loner who would sit in the back of the classroom and never participate. He was described as "one of the most disturbed students" ever seen. He had sought bizarre expressions in literature; he was angry, menacing, disturbed, and "so depressed he seemed near tears" (*Washington Post*, April 18, 2007). A teacher said she recommended counseling, "But you can't force someone to do something they don't want to do." His parents are described as good and religious people. His mother wanted him to accept religion and it was a huge contention between them.

The day after the shootings, it was learned that Cho had mailed a package to the University between his early morning killings and his later ones. The package contained pictures of him in which he showed his rage as he brandished his guns. Again, he was not at fault for what he did. It was others who made him do it; it was their behavior.

These chilling tales are in everyone's awareness, but fortunately they occur rarely. Only one-tenth of 1 percent of the population are such rampage murderers, but they highlight the terrible gaps in the mental health delivery system. And the feeling of utter helplessness of those who know something is wrong but do not know what to do abut it.

However, at the same time it is important to remember that most mental health patients, in treatment or recovered, are neither violent nor threatening, so as not to confuse them with those who commit such grisly crimes. With proper medication and psychotherapy treatment, people diagnosed with such serious mental illness are no more likely to commit crimes than the rest of us, and can lead productive lives in society. With treatment, such patients can learn skills for managing their anger and not resort to killings.

Gang Violence

Gangs are a major source of violence, even though violence by individuals is more common. Gangs form when the experiences in their homes and in their communities create feelings of insecurity in what is experienced as a hostile, aggressive environment. The members develop a negative orientation toward people, believing that aggression is normal, unavoidable, and even good. They also feel aggression is unavoidable, even good. Members of gangs usually have limited social skills and a great deal of difficulty in school learning. They find comfort and strength in the gang. It meets their need for a sense of identity, their need for feeling effective and in control. It meets their need for protection and feeling safe. Gangs develop a sense of strength and power, protection of turf, and demand respect from others. They identify other gangs as outgroups and intensify the difference between "us" and "them." Gang violence results from real or perceived conflicts between gangs. The role of anger is to provide the energy to engage in conflict, in destruction, and even in killing (Ervin Staub, Cultural-Societal Roots of Violence, *The American Psychologist* (February, 1996): 117–132).

Anger management for gangs is different than anger management for individuals, even though they are all dealing with unmet needs that move them to loss of control and to violence. Unfortunately, there is no clear danger signal to alert you that a situation involving anger could turn into a situation of violence. There is no natural flashpoint that is the same for all people in all situations. Some encounters, like tripping someone, can end in apologies or lead to physical combat. Yet some clever approaches in working with juvenile offenders can be adapted to gangs before the members get in trouble with the law.

RETHINK for Teens

The RETHINK acronym has been used in programs for aggressive teens as well as for teens with behavior problems. The focus of the training is on Thinking in a different way. It includes, Recognizing feelings and anger triggers, Noticing what experiences rouse anger, and what acts to help as calming agents. The Thinking also involves problem solving skills and how to use them to deal with situations that trigger anger. The emphasis is on Thinking because that is where the power to change perceptions of what is happening resides, and that is where making decisions about responding are made, and that is where management of the expression of feelings is acquired and maintained. Even when your perception of what has happened is accurate, Thinking allows you to make decisions on how to bring about needed clarification or changes and therefore, changes in behavior and feelings. You can use the anger energy creatively to resolve the problem. But sometimes your feelings continue to remain, say, in a state of fear, even though you have worked through your thinking that makes it clear your don't have to be afraid. The person is not going to harm you—that seems clear enough—but you still have feelings of fear when around him. Feelings can be strong and even defy thoughts or evidence to the contrary. Time may be needed to calm the fears.

The program includes learning how to self-regulate, acquire coping skills, and Notice how to calm down through relaxation exercises. Teens learn to Integrate respect with their expression of anger and to Hear what the person making them angry has to say. They learn how to communicate with words, not knives or guns. Managing anger does not mean avoiding the feeling of anger. Anger is an important signal that changes need to be made. But what the teens learn is to moderate, manage, and prevent the anger to aggression patterns. They learn to draw on problems solving skills to deal with experiences that become anger triggers.

Similar courses have been taught to junior high school adolescents. RETHINK can be applied to any age group with similar outcomes of improved communication skills, problem solving skills, and greater management of feelings and behavior.

Negative Influences on Anger Reactions

If you are having a "bad day" you are more likely to react with anger than if you are having a "good day." But much more depends on how the rest of your life has evolved. How you react depends somewhat on previous exposure to violence. Did you see little of it? Did you see a lot of it? Was it part of your daily way of living? You are more likely to use violence if you see it as a routine, not extraordinary response.

Early life experiences will also influence the extent or reactions moving from anger to violence. The more abuse and violence children experience in their homes, the more likely they will imitate these behaviors. Role models play an important part in socializing our behavior. Children raised in violent homes and in violent communities have difficulty finding role models who can help them learn to manage their impulses. When we have not learned how to manage impulses it is more likely we will lose control and act out our anger. And those children who lose control easily wind up with low self-esteem, self-hatred, and lack of hope—all of which can create conditions leading to violent reactions.

Adding insult to injury, not learning how to moderate aggression, leads to free-floating anger, just looking for a target. Such feelings can easily trigger striking out at people who are close. Alcohol and drugs play their roles in moving anger into violence. And of course, easy access to guns contributes to violent behavior.

High levels of "arousal," signifying being emotionally and physically stirred up by all the stimulation around you, will influence your reactions. For example, if you are at a basketball game, at an active bar with dancing and loud music, or at a big party where everyone hangs loose, you tend to experience arousal. When you are in this state of arousal, even if you are happy and enjoying the stimulation, you can be moved quite easily into acts of violence. Fights break out between different team spectators of games. Fights break out between members of different teams. This is particularly true in hockey, probably the roughest sport. Fights break out at the bar, at the party. It takes little to trigger violence. The participants are, for the most part, not habitually engaged in acts of violence, and they often are shocked to see what they have done.

Violence in the Home

Two forms of violence, more commonly referred to as domestic issues rather than as part of anger to violence acts, are domestic violence and child abuse. The reasons for these separations probably are historical. For many years domestic violence, mainly toward women, was seen as a domestic problem that should be resolved within the home or with some counseling or, perhaps, some court intervention. It is only recently that it has been classified as violence. And the leading cause of injury among women is being beaten by men they live with. The man almost always explains, as if it is self-evident, "She made me do it." That "she had it coming to her" is the deeply embedded belief in the mind of the batterer. In the context of intimate relationships, a person with a shaky sense of his own worth can read criticism and disparagement into acts that may have not been intended. A total mobilization in a fight between a married couple can develop rapidly, with primal thinking leading to a breakdown of normal inhibitions, and physical abuse following.

Frequently, even when there is no intentional put-down spoken, a re-mark can be interpreted as disparaging. Power struggles are inevitable in couples' relationships. When either partner tries to adjust the power imbal-ance by becoming angry or resorting to insults, with full knowledge of their partner's vulnerabilities, the pain they inflict with their words can be an-swered by physical assaults. Common beliefs among abusive husbands are:

Physical force is the only language my wife understands.
Hitting is the only way to get her to shut up.
Only by inflicting pain can I get her to change her abusive behavior.

The conviction that the abuser is really the victim is firmly established in the minds of most of these offenders. Any inhibition against violence is overcome by the thought that "she really deserves it." Although assaults on the self-esteem can lead to common domestic violence, imagined or real infidelity is what arouses anger and jealous rage to the highest level. The most common cause of homicide within families is suspicion of other's sexual relationships. In such cases even some juries will concur that "she really got what she deserved." When a person's fear about adequacy is aroused, fears of being lied to or jerked around and being made a fool of frequently stimulate violence. And, of course to no productive end.

Violence against Children

Child abuse has historically been seen as a domestic problem, with re-moval of a child from the home as the last resort. The label, child abuse, tends to cover the violence involved. Child abuse is a leading cause of death among children under the age of five. There were more than two million cases reported in one year alone, and experts estimate that three or four times that number went unreported, in spite of the laws requiring such reporting. Contrary to greater violence by men in domestic violence cases, violence against children is committed more by women, the moth-ers. Unresolved anger plays a major role in the abuse of children. And, as you know, the extreme expression of anger is violence. Abusive parents are angrier, more aggressive, and more rejecting of their children. When the link between anger and violence is seen, then the link between anger and child abuse becomes clearer. Some parents are roused to anger more quickly than others, but they also are less knowledgeable about child de-velopment and child rearing. They use inappropriate discipline techniques for the child's level of development or have unrealistic expectations of their children. Abuse of children by parents involves similar misperceptions as we have seen in couples' relationships, where threats to self-confidence or to one's competence cause destructive reactions. If a child does not obey, it is interpreted as a sign of disrespect and a fear that "I am not a good mother" can be aroused. Especially if the parent was herself subjected to abuse, her learned response is to react with harshness and even violence.

For both kinds of violence, anger management is critical. Increasingly courts are requiring those who engage in domestic violence to enter anger management programs. And, increasingly, parents or caregivers who engage in acts of violence against children are required to attend anger management sessions.

In using RETHINK to address violence in the home, it becomes clear that parents who tend to abuse their children need to deal with their own anger before they can do much to change their behavior with their children. A program the authors developed has been used to help parents who tend to abuse their children. And here are some of the questions that help parents or, indeed, anyone, get ready to RETHINK anger and angry, even violent, behavior. Can you remember the most recent time you were angry?

Why do you think you were angry? For example, did you feel your pride was hurt, you were put down, you were humiliated, or you were the target of someone else's anger?

Was anything else going on in your life that added to your angry feelings—problems at work, lack of time, feeling overly tired, or family conflicts?

How did you express your anger?

How did it end up?

Was that a satisfactory ending?

What does your child do that triggers your anger?

Can you describe a recent time you were angry with your child?

Who was angry?

You only?

You and your child?

Others?

How was the anger expressed?

How did it end up?

Was that a satisfactory ending?

When parents begin to understand and manage their own anger with RETHINK skills, then they can Recognize their anger when a child does something to rouse it. They can Recognize when their child is angry and help the child learn to manage the anger. Clearly, child development information is needed. If a child of three is expected to sit quietly and is not allowed to move around exploring the environment—he might knock a lamp down—the child will become angry with the constraints. The parent, who is making unrealistic demands on the three-year-old, does not recognize the need of the child to explore and only experiences the anger she herself feels.

The Genetic Explanation

It is not uncommon for people to believe that some children are born with the inclination to become angry quickly and to act out in violence. They believe that such anger is in the genes and that it is almost impossible to do anything about what has been determined by nature. It is tempting to believe that, as it provides an explanation for violent behavior. But, what is really involved here is the heredity/environment issue, the nature/nurture issue. Certainly genes are basic to being a human and determine a great deal about us. But do they determine how we behave or does the environment have something to say about that?

Scientists traced the roots of depression to a specific interaction of genes and the environment—the nature/nurture issue. (Thomas R. Insel, Director, National Institute of Mental Health. Influence of Life Stress on Depression, *Science* (July 18, 2003) 301: 386–389.) The prevailing belief was a genetic cause for depression. But when some subjects of the study who had the gene for depression were found not to become depressed as a result of traumatic experiences in life, it was concluded that the interaction of the gene with the environment determined the outcome. In other words, nature and nurture interact to determine what happens to individuals. Genetic variations affect how people respond to stress, with some being vulnerable to depression and others being more optimistic. But the environment is able to counter the genetic tendency by experiences and guidance in daily living. For example, self-confidence and optimism are more likely to benefit a youth who has a tendency to become depressed when trouble emerges. Management of impulses, responsibility, respect, and empathy and caring for others, are more likely to benefit a youth who has a tendency to become violent.

Gender and Violence

Although girls are now becoming more aggressive and even sometimes violent, there is no question that boys are seen as more violent than girls.

Boys form the gangs that engage in acts of violence; boys play more video games involving violence; and boys engage in more physical solutions to problems and aggravations. Society has different expectations from boys than it does from girls, especially in terms of feelings and behavior. In many ways, boys are encouraged to be aggressive, even engage in violence, as an appropriate response to feelings of fear, anger, or vulnerability.

But, society is not in tune with the reality of what boys actually feel and want to do. Interviews with boys identified some of the expectations society had for them that do not apply to girls and, indeed are contrary to what boys want (*Canadian Boys: Untold Stories*, 2002):

1. They were not given much support from parents and teachers and yet were expected to deal with their problems on their own because that's what is expected of males.
2. They have a harder time growing up than girls because they were expected to be tough, participate in sports, and constantly prove themselves. If they are highly intelligent and don't engage in masculine activities, they are called "nerds." (The overwhelming success of the Harry Potter books, where Harry is clearly a "nerd," gives some idea of how much children and youth want and need more than tough, male behavior as a role model.) They feel parents protect girls more than boys and that boys were left alone to engage in more risk-taking behavior. And they feel that parents punish boys for not living up to the conventional standards of masculinity.
3. They feel boys are expected to fight when challenged and are discouraged from showing their feelings, except feelings that express anger in the form of aggression. The astounding fact is that when feelings are not identified and labeled, all the emotions converge into anger!
4. Boys want more understanding so they can be themselves and not try to be what parents, girls, or other guys expect them to be.

Recognizing Feelings

It is difficult to Recognize feelings, especially for youth. And, as has been stated, this difficulty is very often due to the expectations of society as well as early learning patterns. So, it is critical to begin early in children's lives to learn how to label their feelings in order to enhance development as well as helping them when youths to deal with anger-producing situations. Youth who label feelings say the following: I feel sad, concerned, angry, frightened, belittled, ignored, controlled, encouraged, protected, manipulated, rejected, approved, accepted, loved, good, bad, optimistic, self-confident, safe, insecure, etc. When youth know their emotions, have words for them, and recognize when the emotions are felt, they can think about them, talk about them, and learn how to manage strong emotions in productive ways. One sure-fire way to manage feelings is to stop and think, before acting. Good questions to ask before acting are these:

1. What am I feeling? (I'm feeling angry and humiliated.)
2. What about the event that triggers these feelings? (George seems to have deliberately ignored me when I tried to ask him a question about a class assignment. He actually said, "I don't have time for you.")
3. What can I do so that the feelings will not make me do something I will regret? (I can calm down so that my feelings don't take over, and think about what I can do so these feelings are used constructively.)
4. How can I approach the person who has roused these feelings? (Do I share my reaction? I can even keep it light and say: "Hey, that remark has me spinning. It would be cool if you could tell me when you have time to answer my question.")

Recognizing feelings is an important part of social interaction. No one wants to be isolated from others unless there is a critical reason. Most youth want to interact with others, especially other youth, and many are not aware of the skills necessary to succeed.

Social-Emotional Intelligence

Many of the institutions that are involved with youth do not emphasize social-emotional intelligence. This is particularly true of the schools, which are more focused on cognitive and academic parts of education. The schools want mastery of reading and math, and, in high school, more specific academic subjects. States and the federal government are in accord with this focus. Further, states are required to test students to decide if they are ready to graduate, having met certain standards, especially in the designated areas. And the federal government makes decisions about funding states to help in the educational endeavor.

Teachers, who are trained in particular subjects for middle and senior high schools, have little time or interest in the social-emotional intelligence of students. This situation is understandable, but does not help children learn how to manage their emotions. If we understand that violence can happen as a result of mismanaged emotions such as anger, rage, and other feelings, and that many families are unable to provide the necessary skills that are important in managing anger, then it becomes imperative that our schools and our communities teach such skills. These skills are also necessary for teachers who have students who cannot pay attention, who are angry, and who cause problems; indeed, drop out of school. It is recommended that teacher-training programs need to include information about the social-emotional development of youth, and about the role of anger. In the long run, it would be cost-effective and valuable in terms of human capital.

What is Social-Emotional Intelligence?

Social-emotional intelligence involves the ability to motivate oneself and persist in the face of frustrations; to control the impulses and delay gratification; and to keep distress from swamping the ability to think, empathize, and hope. Such intelligence is manifested by people who know and manage their feelings well, who read and deal effectively with other people's feelings, and who are altruistic and willing to help others. (Daniel Goleman, *Emotional Intelligence: Why It Can Matter More than IQ*. New York: Bantam Books, 1995) provided a test for the reader to determine social-emotional intelligence:

I am aware of what I am feeling.
I know my strengths and weaknesses.
I deal calmly with stress.
I believe the future will be better than the past.
I deal with changes easily.
I set measurable goals when I have a project.
Others say I understand and am sensitive to them.
Others say I resolve conflicts.
Others say I build and maintain relationships.
Others say I inspire them.
Others say I am a team player.
Others say I helped to develop their abilities.

Outsiders and Social-Emotional Intelligence

Goleman's list, while descriptive of an individual, does not include the critical role of outside community help and supports. Clearly, it is desirable that parents need to be involved in promoting social-emotional intelligence, but when parents have not learned the skills themselves, then, surely the teachers need to play a role as well.

Workshops for Teachers

Many teachers are concerned about problems they have with youth and are more than willing to attend workshops that focus on ways to help them interact with and help youth. Numerous anger management classes designed by the authors have been conducted with teachers, youth service providers, and community representatives. These seminars have been conducted throughout the United States as well as internationally. One of the authors has conducted workshops with teachers to address these problems, providing American Psychological Association Continuing Education credits. A pretest was provided at the beginning of the workshop, which asked the participants how they would deal with a problem in the school with a teenager. They were asked to indicate:

What happened?
What did you do?
How did you feel?
What did the youth do in response?
How did the youth feel?
What was the outcome?
How are things today?

At the end of the workshop, the participants were given the same example they reported at the beginning and indicated what changes they would make. The responses were as follows. Help the youth to:

1. Find role models to demonstrate how to deal with the problem.
2. Feel more empathy for oneself and others in a common problem.
3. Talk to others, share thoughts, and feelings.
4. Manage one's behavior when considering doing something unacceptable or out of anger.
5. Seek help from those whom one trusts.

These changes suggest that after the workshop, teachers focused more on interpersonal relationships when appropriate. A follow-up of the teachers six months later indicated they were continuing to use what they had learned.

If you work with teens in any capacity, think of an experience you had with a teenager that involved anger and other emotions:

What happened?
What did you do?
How did your feel?
What did the teenager do?
How did the teenager feel?
What was the outcome?
What changes would you make if you had the same experience now?

Sixth-Grade Line

Other workshops conducted in a school including both elementary and middle-school aged students, made quite clear that the line is drawn at Sixth Grade. Up to that level, teachers are very involved with the interpersonal relationships of the children, while from Sixth Grade and higher, the teachers want to focus on academic subjects. The concern about students is more on expecting good behavior than on interpersonal relationships. With the emphasis on subject matter, youth are left to deal with their own interpersonal behaviors on their own.

> A teenager is dropping out of school. Here is his reasoning: I don't like school. I don't like my teacher because he is always yelling at me for not getting my homework in. I don't like to do the homework because I don't understand how to do the problems and I don't want to admit I can't do them. That makes me look stupid and I don't like to look stupid. I am failing and so I might as well drop out.

The teachers often play a critical role in the lives of students, especially when students have serious problems at home. They are not only role models, but they are also often the only supports some students have who help them deal with their problems, and their anger. Ruth Simmons, the President of Brown University, was brought up in poverty and her family could provide her with little help as she showed a great interest in reading. Some teachers recognized her intelligence and ability and were especially supportive of her when her mother died. She was encouraged to continue her studies and helped in finding financial support to pursue advanced studies. She says:

> If it hadn't been for teachers, I don't know what would have happened to me.

That is a great tribute to teachers who clearly went beyond academic achievement in showing a caring concern for the student. Not all students need this kind of support. Many need help in recognizing feelings, especially their own; learning to express anger without causing dangerous outcomes; and learning how to resolve problems that enhance life rather than diminish it. Teachers can be role models of acceptable behavior, and of ways to deal with anger; they are teachers of these things. Subject matter and behavior cannot be so easily separated.

Conclusion

Violence is a serious problem in society. When anger is expressed in the extreme and violence, abuse, and other destructive behaviors result, we often feel powerless. However, given that anger is a universal emotion that occurs daily in all kinds of human interactions, we are presented with an opportunity to do something before the anger-violence cycle takes hold. By teaching children, youth, parents, teachers, and others who work with youth, skills such as anger management and emotional intelligence, we do much toward creating a more peaceful and productive society.

CHAPTER 11

Cultural Differences

Generate Fear Misinterpretation and Anger

For most people, cultures tend to fall into the category of "the other." And, as is generally accepted, the concept of "the other" is fraught with the potential of ascribing to "the other" characteristics and behaviors we reject or deny in ourselves, including violence, cruelty, terrorism, and inhumane behavior. When we assume these undesired qualities and behaviors in others, we react with fear and anger. We almost always feel anger toward people who make us afraid.

There are no cultural differences in physical responses to fear. Everyone who becomes fearful reacts by sweating, hyperventilating, heart beating too fast, a sense of anxiety, anger, or a combination of these. Nor are there cultural differences in what makes you and "others" fearful and angry. You have been offended, belittled, threatened, betrayed, cheated, ridiculed, or disrespected. The culture determines what constitutes evidence of these unwanted experiences. Members of one culture will see showing the sole of a shoe when sitting in front of another person as an act of disrespect. In another culture people will see a foreign woman talking to a local man as being offensive. Learning the taboos of a culture is required for all diplomats.

Acquiring Culture

Culture is acquired. It is learned from infancy. As one wise person observed, "Culture is the pearls on the road to ease the arduous journey of life." Culture contains all the habits, beliefs, values, manners, and even thoughts about the world. You just assume as a child that this is the way things are, the way things are supposed to be. Grandpa makes final decisions; children are free to play until age five; mothers do not appear in public without complete coverings; and boys go to school.

Or there can be a completely different experience that children assume is the only way. Mothers work; the children go to school; fathers are involved with their children; and decisions are made by the whole family. These different cultural practices may rouse fear, as misunderstandings raise the stress level. And fear reactions, now accompanied by anger, will certainly appear when cultural conflicts cause a person or group to feel offended, belittled, threatened, betrayed, cheated, ridiculed, or disrespected.

For example, if in one culture people assume that the father will make all decisions regarding the health care of his children, he will be angry when a doctor or nurse takes actions he has not authorized. He may not be at the doctor's office and his wife may have accepted what the doctor or nurse did, but the anger will be there. The threat to culturally determined power relationships rouses his fear of losing power and feelings of anger are responses to his fear.

The Challenge

One school system on the east coast of the United States has seventy-eight languages being used by children. These languages, for the most part, reflect different countries and different cultures. The idea that anyone, let alone the teacher, could understand the languages or the cultures of these children is unrealistic. But, if the teacher knows something about what tends to make children fearful and angry, and she assumes there will be cultural differences in that, she has a chance to keep feelings of fear and accompanying outbursts of anger at a minimum. The same is true for adults at a meeting, service providers helping individuals in need, and attendees at a social or political gathering. If many cultures are represented, the challenge is the same. What do you need to know about cultural differences that will limit misunderstandings leading to fear and anger, and that will enhance good relationships? The importance of using the RETHINK skills Hear and Empathy are basic to helping in assimilation, in acculturation, and in reducing, or even eliminating the fear and anger. These skills must be used by family members as well as by service providers.

Cultural differences to note

The major and basic dimensions on which cultures may differ are on the extent to which a cultural group stresses individualism more than collectivism; independence more than interdependence; separation more than family affiliation; acquisitions for self more than generosity; self-fulfillment more than interpersonal harmony; and sexual equality more than male dominance. These characteristics are not exhaustive nor are they fixed. They sometimes change, especially when there is an advantage to change. Some cultures, for example, that prefer cooperation to competition have learned to become competitive in the world market. And families that are within a society stressing cooperation often hire tutors for their young children so they can compete for entry into the best schools.

But, even when these differences are accepted, disagreements exist. Members often say that "only some people believe that" or "live like that," or "only a certain class lives like that." There are differences that show up in interactions with people who do not want to dismiss the differences; they are the mark of the culture, and are offended by any violation.

Cultural differences in behavior triggering fear and anger

While there are too many cultural differences to note here, the most clear-cut cultural differences that can trigger anger reactions include these:

Standing close to people shows acceptance—vs.—Standing close to people shows an invasion of space

One cultural difference that has meaning is in how close you stand to someone you are talking to or working with. In many cultures they believe it is appropriate to stand quite close to a person when interacting. It may be seen as an expression of acceptance, trust, and comfort. In other cultures they feel it is appropriate to stand farther away when interacting. It is seen as respect for personal space and recognizing limits to informality. It also prevents that most annoying "In your face" feeling. These two views clash constantly and you learn to sense how the person you are talking to is reacting to how close you are standing. If you do not adjust your distance, you may find you are abandoned, ignored, or even treated with an angry dismissal.

Touching others shows caring—vs.—Touching others invades privacy

The physical contact between people is another area of cultural differences. Members of some cultures like to touch others, hug them, and express all kinds of emotions of pleasure. In other cultures they may find this an invasion of privacy or an unseemly expression of feelings. Often, there is resentment and anger from both because their cultural ways are being disrespected.

Groups of young men gather for social purposes—vs.—Groups of young men gather for destructive purposes

Immigrant young men are particularly vulnerable to culture conflict, often leading to fear and anger, and escalating into violence. A group of youth from Central America tended to hang out at the corner near a grocery store. Now, this is very common behavior witnessed by anyone who has ever been to Latin America—the plaza being the gathering place for social purposes. Besides, they like to be out where they can see people. They may even like to flirt a little. *Que hay, rubia?* (How you doing, blondie?) was a phrase often heard by a young American woman working in a Latin American country. Nothing to fear; no harm is meant. Nothing to be angry about. It is casual and informal.

In the United States, some people were intimidated by the presence of young men near a grocery store and called the police. In the United States, any group of young men may be seen as trouble; especially if they are darker and don't speak English well. As soon as the police intervened, the entire environment changed. The young men were not just having a social interaction; they were accused of loitering and ordered never to gather at that place again. They were given no alternative place to hang out; besides there was no community center or park available. The young men were angry and insulted. They, unfortunately, took out their anger by keying cars that came around the store and stealing whatever they could from parking lots. They had been assumed a danger without cause, had no one to speak for them, and in their sense of unfairness and hopelessness, they turned their anger into destructive behavior. The language barrier added to the entire tragic scene. No one had any sense of cultural differences that made their original behavior absolutely acceptable. No one explained why that behavior was seen differently here.

Stereotyping versus Flexibility

It is easy to think of some people in terms of stereotypes and to do so is common when interacting with people from other cultures. Stereotyping is used to categorize people, assuming certain behaviors and attitudes. Now, everyone engages in some stereotyping. Children are such and such. Women are such and such. Men are such and such. Youth are such and such. Older people are such and such. You can get trapped into stereotyping, or you can use it as a starting point and then change it as you interact with the "other" and get to know the "other" better. When you are familiar with the concept of cultural differences and have built some expectations of behavior by stereotyping, you can verify or change your perception of the person. Flexibility is needed.

Communication style should be frank and direct—vs.—Communication should be guarded and indirect

Differences in communication styles cause many conflicts and generate much fear and anger. If you disagree with someone, do you just say, "I don't agree with you, and here is why," or do you say, "You must be out of your mind to think I'll go along with that!"

It is important to Integrate respect and empathy when dealing with cultural differences. Saying what you want in the way you want often prevents you from being aware of how others feel about what you are saying. In some cultures, it is an insult to be frank and direct. Watch diplomats. They are experts in knowing how to be indirect, using all kinds of speech devices to communicate acceptance and nonimplied criticism.

Gender roles are clearly defined—vs.—Gender roles are flexible and interchange-able

A common area of differences among cultures involves gender roles. Are gender roles the same or different, for example, in terms of authority and competence? A woman who was Director of an organization devoted to conducting research to address problems of minority groups, had organized her unit into two divisions, one to address issues concerning African-Americans and the other to address issues concerning Latinos. She selected as head of each division a member of the designated minority group and held her first staff meeting, involving all those working in the two divisions.

What she hadn't expected was the open hostility and expressed anger of the Latino division head, Ramon, an immigrant who had been successful in making the transition to a professional life in the United States. But, it became clear he could not tolerate a woman being his boss. His cultural background found it not only unacceptable, but also insulting. So he spent the entire meeting being critical, snorting his disapproval, and disagreeing with everything the Director suggested or discussed.

The Director had lived in Latin America for a few years and was fully aware of the difficulty men there had when a woman had authority over them. She felt Empathy for him so she said nothing as he tried to disrupt the meeting; instead she continued with her agenda.

When the meeting was over, she asked him to stay a minute. He clearly did not want to, so he propped himself on a table, crossing his legs in a defiant position. She said, "Ramon, I know this is difficult for you. But I need you. I cannot deal with the issues of Latinos without your help. I am no threat to you or your authority in your division. If we are going to help minority groups, we have to work together."

His response was totally unexpected. He said, "You could have reprimanded me. You could have reported me to the head of the organization. I am grateful to you for talking to me directly. I will give you no trouble." He smiled and left. Indeed, there was no trouble.

She was not only surprised, but also really glad she had not expressed the anger she felt as he acted out his anger in the meeting. This was one time when holding back the expression of the anger and using the energy in a creative way to deal with the situation, paid off.

Competition—vs.—Cooperation

Competition is characteristic of Anglos and cooperation is characteristic of Latinos. Or so it is said. Two men, one an immigrant from Mexico, the other a labeled Anglo, received money from a foundation to study the cultural differences in high school students in terms of cooperation and competition in undertaking an assignment. The high school students were about an equal mix of Latinos and Anglos. The Latino cultural value is generally on cooperation with competition being seen as causing fear, conflict, and anger in interpersonal relationships. Anglos, on the other hand, are said to see competition as stimulating and challenging, with cooperation favored by those reluctant or unable to compete.

They studied with the same assumption: Latinos would use cooperation with other students as the primary means to do their assignment; Anglos would engage in competition with other students to do their assignment. And the assumption held up.

However, a member of the foundation thought something was missing. He knew, for example, that people often switched from being cooperative to being competitive, depending on the situation. In basketball, for example, players are cooperative with each other but competitive with members of the other team. He thought one way to find out what might be missing was to see if there was a relationship between intelligence and cooperation or competition. The class assignment relied more on intelligence than physical ability and seemed a good way to go. The researchers were reluctant to do further analysis. They had supported their assumption and felt they met the requirements of the foundation. With a little persuasion, however, they did the analysis. But they did not like the results. The more intelligent (in terms of IQ tests) the student was, the more the student used both cooperation and competition (as seemed useful) in doing their assignment.

The risk of assuming specific cultural differences is to overlook or ignore evidence of flexibility of cultures. *No culture is rigid in its values.* There may be some exceptions to that fact, but not many.

Communicating Across Culture Barriers

Avoiding encounters with people who have different ideas of expressing their feelings may prevent conflicts, but it does not help in learning to interact so that you can communicate what limits you are able to accept, without disrespecting the culture. As the following anecdote demonstrates:

> A teacher in an early childhood program does not show up for class and the children are upset. She does not call in either. When she shows up the next day she says some relatives came to see her and she had to spend time with them. She was admonished for not assuming more responsibility for her job and her answer was, "Well, take it out of my paycheck." Her supervisor said, "You miss the point. The children need you." The supervisor took the opportunity to address different cultural expectations.

Unexpected Differences among Subcultures

One does not have to go as far from the dominant culture to find surprising clashes and anger that is distressing.

> Claire and Clarence were both born in the United States, went to the same college, and were brought up in the same Protestant faith. At their wedding a terrible violation of the groom's family's sense of propriety occurred when a champagne toast was proposed by the bride's father. Clarence's family did not approve of alcoholic drinks and their religion reinforced that view. They were taken by surprise at the toast. They believed that offering an alcoholic beverage at a wedding was sinful and shameful. How could their son do this to them! They felt betrayed. Didn't he know and share their beliefs? If this crisis had been anticipated, a family split could have been avoided. At the wedding it seemed too difficult to Rethink this anger-provoking situation at the time it occurred. It took much effort and time to heal this family wound.

Weddings are occasions when feelings are intense and surprising anger can erupt.

The marriage between Dorothy and Duane was interfaith, but all the details about the differences had been worked out. However, when the bride's mother and the groom's mother arrived for the family photographs in exactly the same dress (and very different shapes), the chubby mom was humiliated and angry. Couldn't the groom's mother find something different to wear before the first photo was shot, she demanded? This crisis occurred before the guests arrived and there was no time to use some Rethink skills. Everyone had to be calmed down, and this time some champagne helped. Lots of respect and humor also helped them reframe the incident. They said it was providential, an omen, that the two mothers had picked the same dress. It was a symbol of harmony for the future. They laughed a lot and the chubby mom told the story often. The irony that all the differences had been worked out and the trouble arose from the same taste that both mothers had displayed in choosing the same dress, added to the humor in the retelling of this family saga.

Weddings where the bride and groom come from the "same cultural background" may still be fraught with dangerous outbursts of anger. In one instance of an orthodox Jewish wedding, one of the families was upset or rather, outraged about men and women being seated together, whereas the other family hadn't given that issue a thought. Such differences in belief systems are especially surprising when the two "cultures" are nominally the same. Sectarianism is great even between very similar subcultures.

Seating arrangements are among the devils in the details at many weddings and other events where some guests can feel offended by what they consider an act of disrespect when they see with whom they are being classified, or how far from the head of the table they have been placed. It would be nice to be able to avoid all such anger in advance by understanding the cultural nuances that each guest brings. The offense is usually not intentional and seems like a mere detail to the hosts, but the anger generated can be painful and may be hard to recognize.

Americans Abroad

We will consider at some length the issues of immigrants in America, particularly the Latinos. However, when Americans are the foreigners, they may be surprised that they give offense. This anecdote demonstrates how not knowing a detail of the culture can cause anger and resentment.

When the Langs went to live in a Mediterranean country, they were delighted with their new apartment. It had a charming playground outside and they sent the children out to play while they started unpacking and settling in. The children, so long restrained in transit, were happy to be free to run and exercise. They shrieked with glee in their new playground. All too soon, a stern voice was shouting at them in a foreign tongue and a man shepherded them back to their new apartment. No one, said the native, lets the kids out to make noise during the siesta hour. How inconsiderate were these newcomers? The Langs were embarrassed and apologetic. They tried to express their respect for their neighbors but it took a matter of weeks before the natives could rethink their anger at the "ugly" Americans.

Cultural differences can engender fear, misunderstandings, anger, and even violence. Being prepared for the differences can go a long way in prevention and skills in managing anger, one's own and that targeted at us can make a difference.

Immigrant Fears and Anger in a New Culture

The number of immigrants, especially from south of the border, is already beyond thirty million and growing, with few accurate numbers to determine just how many. You can go into a hairdressing shop, a grocery store, see a cleaning crew, and even construction workers, and you will find Latinos providing the services and doing the work. One young woman, twenty-three years old, came into this country with her family illegally when she was twenty, and now wants to go back to her country of origin to get married and bring her husband back with her. Not a chance. She will not be able to return because she has no green card and, try as they did, her fiancé could not get a tourist visa to enter this country. She left, knowing she will never see her family again and going back to the life the family took such efforts and risks to leave behind. Her sadness and anger were combined and she found herself crying a great deal. Many immigrants, especially those who entered illegally, face a life of fear and anger.

A Study of Three Latino Groups

A study was conducted under the supervision of the authors and supported by the Center for Mental Health Services, National Institute of Mental Health, and the U.S. Department of Health and Human Services. The study consisted of conducting focus group meetings of three Latino populations: one in Los Angeles, CA; one in Miami, FL; and one in New York, to learn of the problems they faced that roused fear and anger. Those in the focus groups included, in separate meetings, the parents, the youth, and the service providers.

Parents and youth from each site identified the problems that roused fear, anger, and, often, violent reactions: The range of problems extended from grasping the language, dealing with crime and drugs, to youth needing parents, teachers, and service providers, as they adapted to the new culture.

Grasping the language

The Latino immigrants had difficulty finding jobs, reading papers, or filling out forms, as their English was not adequate. One woman, who finally was able to get away from her job in a hotel long enough to attend the focus group sessions, shared this story: she was living with her sister and her sister's two children. She had left her two children behind with her family in Bolivia. She said she was earning good money and sent money back to Bolivia to help her family there. We talked about the importance of learning English to help her find a job more in keeping with her education and experience; but she claimed she was not able to attend classes at night because her sister worked then and she needed to take care of the children, and she needed to work at a hotel seven days a week to earn enough money. She was angry about this series of roadblocks, but it had converted into a general state of mild depression. The only RETHINK skill that seemed possible was to Hear with Empathy what she had to say. When she was seen at another focus group meeting a couple of days later, she indicated that she had asked her sister to give her some time from caring for the children to go to a nearby library, where they were teaching English. The sister was delighted!

Poverty

Although there is a high rate of employment among Latinos, poverty is widespread. In one neighborhood, there were five men living in a one-bedroom apartment, getting jobs where they could, and hiding their illegal status, but finding enough money to pay the rent each month. Their families were not there. These were men who wanted to improve their lot in life as well as of their families back in the countries of origin. They sent money orders to their families every week; you could see them lined up at the Post Office every Friday. Anger is readily aroused in such stressing conditions.

Crime and drugs

Many Latinos live in neighborhoods with high crime rates, with many of the crimes associated with drug trafficking. Those are the neighborhoods that offer cheaper rent and where there are other Latinos for social life. But the crime rates are high, and Latinos become victims of or participate in the crimes.

Discrimination within Latino groups
Many people assume all Latinos are alike and work together easily. Actually, there is a great deal of discrimination among Latinos from different countries or even from the same country. These differences are often based on color of skin, socioeconomic status, or culture. There are common fights among youth from different Latino groups as they organize to protect themselves from expected violence. In Miami, there are many issues related to ethnic, racial, and cultural differences. The recent influx of Salvadorans and Guatemalans has created a difficult situation for the long established Cubans. The community is struggling with this problem.

Absent/noninvolved parents
Parents may be holding two or three jobs to make enough money to support their family here and the families left behind. And with the language barrier, it is difficult for parents to attend school or community meetings that involve their children. The children are left to the care of the older children or, indeed, left to watch television, do homework, or go outside and join a gang that may or may not be well-meaning.

Poor communication between parents and children
Communication problems are especially difficult when the children and youth are being integrated or are at least comfortable with the new culture. The children and youth want to accept and behave with the different standards, such as expressing their opinion and disagreeing with the parents. They want to become American and resent being drawn into the problems their parents had with their country of origin.

Attending a focus group that included both the parents and their teenagers, it became clear that there was a conflict between the parents and their children regarding support of a political problem in their country of origin. The parents wanted their youth to be willing to fight for or at least be supportive of a change in government in their country of origin. The youth claimed they didn't want to be caught up in those problems; they wanted to become American. The clash between the parents and the youth was palpable, much anger was expressed, and the parents finally accepted the fact that their youth, indeed, had to become American.

Peer pressure on the children and youth

Many parents become increasingly aware that their children and youth are being more influenced by peers than by them. They see the children and youth taking on new values and new attitudes toward discipline and their obligations to the parents. They feel they have lost the authority over their children and youth that their culture determines is necessary. They feel fear and anger as they see their authority being challenged.

Drugs

When drugs are so easily available on the street, it is difficult not to get involved, either at the selling or use ends. And the temptation to youth to earn money for themselves or for their families is hard to resist. Youth, especially, have not developed a full sense of consequences of behavior and so are easily seduced into the business. It is exciting because there is enough risk and fear to bring the adrenaline rush, so much a part of the attraction of fear. Parents who fear for their children's well-being are angered by this situation or drugs in their neighborhood.

Fears and anger

Many Latinos live in fear of being found out as illegal immigrants. And, while they have that fear, they are also angry because they are so vulnerable. And this anger easily turns into acts of violence. Unfortunately, the acts of violence are often carried out against other Latinos. It is not easy to find a way out of their situation; yet they want to stay here.

Clash of Behavioral Expectations between Traditional and American Cultures

The American culture is generally democratic, while Latino cultures are more authoritarian. In an authoritarian family, children will be given very little input even when the decision directly affects them, and the same is usually true for their mother. This lack of democracy may well be countered by a great concern on the part of the parents that their children be well protected. The family may have a highly developed system, handed down generation after generation, of decision-making for the benefit of the child.

One youth in a focus group told about plans he made when living in Puerto Rico, to go to medical school on the mainland. He was asked which one he would be attending. He replied that he didn't know yet because he was waiting for his relatives to hold a meeting to make that decision. The focus group leader was very surprised and asked how they would know enough about the medical schools to make that decision for him. He shrugged his shoulder, and said that would remain to be seen.

Youth having too much unsupervised time

With parents working, with the youth not being involved in after-school activities, they are left alone for extensive periods of time that need to be filled. There are few or no sports or recreation facilities available. And libraries, where many Latinos do their homework, are few and far between. Further, there is lack of services and/or knowledge of how to use them. At one service center, the youth hang out just outside the center, rather than go in to get the help they could so well use. What do you do with all that time? The youth themselves complain that their parents are not available and are not involved in anything the youth are interested in. Parents don't attend school activities or join the PTAs; they are insecure about their limitations. The youth feel their parents are poor role models for how to behave in this new culture.

Need to be Protector of Family/Parent

Many youth feel they need to protect the family, especially from the risks and fears of dealing with the various systems—transportation, stores, authorities, or social services. And the youth are often in the position of having to make decisions for their parents when they are not always sure they are qualified. It is a heavy burden. Service providers added some of their own indicators of the things that caused fear and anger, and even violence, among Latinos. They expressed Latinos' lack of knowledge of rights/expectations as an American resident/citizen. Between not under-standing the bureaucratic systems, fear they won't be listened to or taken seriously, the lack of local language ability, and you have a formula for po-tential disaster. Certainly, Latino groups are formed in most major cities, and some play a powerful role in providing services for the families.

Further, there is also fragmentation of the Latino community. Latinos from different countries have different cultures, a fact well documented by gangs of teens representing different countries, and carrying out conflicts brought with them. The churches often play a decisive role in becoming a community center for Latino families, with certain services conducted in Spanish. For the cultures that stress family and community, this frag-mentation of the historic community rouses the fear of lacking support in times of crisis, and anger at being put in such situations.

The legal status of the immigrant is a continuing problem and the level of education, with segregating Latino children from their classmates and treating them as second-class citizens, increases difficulties. Teachers do not call on them in regular classes, apparently so as not to embarrass them, but some Latino students complain that the teachers do nothing to help them. And the bullying that goes on against Latinos expresses the general attitude of fear of "the other" and anger toward "the other" in irrational ways.

Feelings of anger and anxiety

Teenagers harbor a great deal of anger and anxiety, as they perceive that they are treated unfairly. They know they are vulnerable to arrest, to police harassment, and to being perceived as dangerous and they resent such treatment and expectations. Their dread of unfair treatment easily moves into anger and subsequent acts of violence. The human being needs to be respected, the human being needs to feel safe, the human being needs to be accepted, and the human being's needs to connect are threatened.

Differences

Some interesting differences were found among the four Latino youth groups and are worth noting. The New York youth were very invested in personal responsibility. There were specific gender biases: males felt responsible for protecting their mothers, while girls were found to feel responsible for care taking. These New York youth trusted authority figures as dependable and available and were more comfortable in using community resources than were the youth in the other cities.

The Miami youth lived with a significant degree of distrust of authority, dysfunctional family relationships, and limited resources. They were familiar with violence and indicated they would counter aggression with aggression. They described a general sense of futility. They felt their parents abandoned them after they reached a certain age because they were too much trouble. They were angry.

The Los Angeles parents acknowledged the dangers children face in the school system and on the streets. The study reinforced what is already known about Latino families and communities. In particular, the importance of family relationships and youths' reliance and need for parents to guide and direct their behaviors. These young people identified the importance of adult mentoring, the significant role their schools and teachers play in their development and adaptation, and their desire to receive such support. Furthermore, these young people emphasized the importance of being able to exercise some independence and planning for their future, but within these guiding adult relationships. They consistently emphasized that they wanted to integrate into the mainstream culture, while still maintaining a strong connection to their original cultural identity. It should be pointed out, however, that the children of most immigrants increasingly become part of the mainstream culture, with their own children having little involvement or desire for involvement in their original culture.

Special problems with parents

Most of the attention of the study was on youth. However, it became clear that parents had some problems of their own, independent of the youth. And these problems almost always involved anger. For example, Latino women are often subject to somatic ailments, often as a result of their suppressed anger, while the men are enraged at their feelings of helplessness and often act out by drinking or becoming violent. The women become ill, or more commonly, have continuing headaches. The headaches are relentless and paralyzing. The men feel emasculated because all of a sudden they are no longer the provider; they are depending on the women. This triggers a cycle of anger and violence. The legal repercussions of domestic violence charges are often considered to be deterrents to reporting, since such charges can lead to deportation.

Overall, however, the immigrants in this study could deal with their fears and anger if they had support, developed safe and connected relationships, had adequate services provided, and had an overall belief that they would be accepted in the dominant culture.

What Rouses the Fears of Different Cultures?

Throughout history, in cultures and countries, people have always feared "the other." Although complaints are often expressed in terms of job competition, expectations of criminal behavior, requiring the country to spend money meeting the newcomers' needs, and refusing to become integrated into the larger society, these excuses are used to build barriers between natives and new comers. And it is the barriers that, in fact, become the basis for conflict and anger. If you fear criminal behavior and expect it, you are in a position to react whether there is real cause or not. Being afraid makes you alert, often overly alert, where danger is seen when none exists. Police are aware of how easy it is to overreact to any action on the part of a potential criminal. A Latino friend claims that when he is stopped by a policeman, he sits and waits for instructions. He knows that if he makes a move, he is in real danger.

Difficulty of Assimilation

Any person from a culture that reflects thousands of years of use, and testing, and changing, and that is integrated into the lives of every family from the day of birth of a child, will have difficulty in assimilating. Too much of who each person is, too much of who a group is, too much of what is important and respected, is at stake. The American culture is no exception. Even though there is the reality of many cultures within the nation, there is a recognizable American culture. Ask anyone who travels around the world if Americans are not recognized as Americans. Cultures that are flexible enough to take what is good about the new culture and integrate it with the more traditional, benefit from the new, while cherishing the old.

The concept of biculturalism has received much needed attention and is another response to being an immigrant (see F. Infante with Alexandra Lamond, Resilience and Biculturalism: The Latino Experience in the United States. In *Resilience for Today: Gaining Strength from Adversity*, Edith H. Grotberg (Ed.). Westport, CT: Praeger, 161–188, 2003). By maintaining what is desired from the traditional culture and taking what is helpful and desirable from the new culture, the newcomers can have the security of the valued and familiar culture and select what is useful and beneficial of the new culture. The RETHINK skills are integral to this process. These skills must be mastered not only by the Latinos, but also by those in the dominant culture.

The community needs to RETHINK what it is doing to help the immigrants become integrated into the American culture without giving up their primary culture. Each skill has a role in addressing the problems. Recognize what is making the Latinos or the "others" angry. Empathize and Hear what they are saying and doing. Integrate respect and caring when communicating. Think about each problem in a different way—it is not always a cultural thing: it is a universal human thing. Notice what calms all involved. And, Keep to the issue at hand, not bringing up other experiences or biases.

CHAPTER 12

Change Comes from Practice

Change is never easy, especially when it involves altering the way we think about things. The way we think is so much part of us, our whole sense of identity seems at stake when we modify our thinking or our behavior. However, we often recognize that what we are doing is not only nonfunctional, but, indeed, is also causing us great harm. "How did I end up losing friend after friend, every time there was an argument? How did I wind up losing a job any time I dealt with a nasty customer? How did I wind up losing my best love just because I yelled at her?" In order to move out of a rut, and have experiences that enhance our lives, we have to be able to examine our thinking and recognize when our thinking and behavior are detrimental to our aspirations.

But there are indeed specific obstacles to change, which different people experience in different ways. In some sense, what we are calling obstacles to change are actually defenses against some perceived threats if we change, so we persist in thoughts that were originally protective. Identifying the things that get in our way as we want to change becomes complex and often difficult.

Thoughts as Obstacles to Changing Anger

Here are some thoughts that may well prevent you from making changes in how you deal with anger:

—Someone else is causing my anger. She is mean, stubborn, inconsiderate, selfish, and doesn't understand, and so I get angry!

—It is clearly someone else's fault, how can anything I do, like "RE-THINKing," make a difference?

—Anger works for me. I get what I want. What harm does it do?

—What else can you do when you feel attacked? You have to fight back or people will walk all over you.

—I AM NOT ANGRY! People get so ugly when they are angry. I am not an angry person.

—I am not interested in "feelings." I don't recognize feelings in myself or in anybody else.

—Anger just goes right by me.

Overcoming any of these obstacles is really difficult. We are all experts at resisting, but here are some ideas that can help when you are ready to try change.

Obstacle 1: It's someone else's fault!

You firmly believe that other people are responsible for causing your anger. How many times have you said, "It's your fault that I'm angry. You made me angry. I would not have hit you if you didn't make me so mad. You need to watch your behavior. You are out of control and my anger is the only response you deserve!" Projecting the responsibility onto someone else for making you do something dangerous or unacceptable is common. Do you hear yourself saying, "He started it. He deliberately tried to get my goat. It worked and he deserved whatever happened to him."

When the other person is held responsible for rousing your anger, it permits you to retaliate, get revenge, and in any way you choose.

A Case in Point

A court case involved two adults who were suing each other for damages to their respective cars. They were neighbors and had a common driveway to their separate garages. One of the neighbors, Mrs. Jones, had the habit of parking in the driveway, preventing Mrs. Smith from getting her car into the garage. Mrs. Smith had talked to her neighbor about this many times, with little success. So, the next time she saw the Jones' car parked in the driveway and blocking it, she took her car key and made scratch marks on the side of the neighbor's car. When Mrs. Jones saw the damage to her car, she went ballistic and was sure her neighbor had done this. So she waited until she saw her neighbor's car in a place available to her, and did the same thing:

used her car key to scratch the car. Now, both were furious and confronted each other. Mrs. Smith, who had been angry about being blocked and had done the first scratching, yelled that the other woman started the fight by blocking her car. It was her fault and she got what she deserved. Mrs. Jones responded that she was clearly not responsible for her behavior because she was only reacting to what had been started by her neighbor.

They wound up in court, where the judge agreed both were responsible for the anger outburst and the resulting damages and they could pay for their own car repairs. "Grow up! Be responsible for your behavior!"

That was the message from the judge. Might the judge be talking to you?

The basic problem in accusing others of causing you to be angry is the lack of respect you feel or show others. They are the problem. They are the bad guys. You are the good guy. This is an attitude problem. And to change the way you deal with anger, you will want to start with the skill represented by the "T" in RETHINK.

Think about others in a less stereotypical way. Human beings are not all alike. They are individuals, and as such, deserve respect. Then the Integrate skill comes into play. If you respect others, you will be able to integrate that message with your expression of anger. You will also want to Think about the situation causing your anger and identify the steps that lead to your blaming the other person for your behavior. Do you really want to be so prone to anger? Is it really so hard to manage your own behavior? And do you want to give someone else all that power over you? Did Mrs. Jones have to respond as she did? Was Mrs. Smith powerless to do anything other than what she was "made" to do? The person who seems inflexible and places all the blame outside himself can learn important lessons about managing his own anger. You can say to yourself, "This is a human being I respect. I will show it as we are in a situation involving anger. And I will manage the way I express my anger. I am in charge of myself. I am responsible for myself. Blaming anyone else for my behavior is demeaning to me." When you can talk to yourself that way, you will be on your way to mastering Rethink and overcoming the first obstacle to change in your anger style. You will feel stronger and more in charge of yourself.

Obstacle 2: How can anything I do make a difference?

Feelings of fear of one's own anger as well as fear of loss of love, all keep you locked in an emotional prison. Also, if it seems clear to you that someone else is at fault, you may feel you lack the power to change anything. Perhaps you lack the confidence and sense of inner strength to change anything. You may think, "I don't have the intelligence or words or energy or nerve," or whatever you think you are lacking to manage the moment effectively.

Many of us learn to fear our own anger, not only because it brings about disapproval from others, but also because it signals the need for change. With the fear we tell ourselves, "He will just blow up," or "It's not worth the trouble," or "If I say something it won't matter anyway," or "I better pick my battles and this is not the one; I don't know if I am right about the issue."

We tell ourselves these things because it is a way of rationalizing our own fear and foregoing a push into an unknown territory, even when every part of our body tells us change is necessary. In some instances, holding on to anger helps avoid some frightening new experience or relationship:

> If Joe holds on to his anger then he doesn't have to get serious with the women he dates. Joe explains the reason he can't get serious is not because he doesn't want to but because women are so bossy or he just can't find the right woman. He is angered by each woman he goes out with and gets to know.

We often feel inept at expressing anger or make all kinds of excuses to shy away from saying what is on our minds. Frequently we feel injured and withdraw rather than address the person who has hurt us. We justify this behavior by telling ourselves that we need to protect the *other* person. We want to preserve harmony in our relationships and fear that if we *really* state what is on our mind the relationship would fall apart. With this withdrawal and fear comes a loss of self, our dreams, our own sense of competency, and our own sense of worth. Not wanting to risk our security (even if it is minimal, it's all that we know) we live with a kind of emotional paralysis.

Do you tend to process information rather slowly? We certainly know that we often have a better understanding of what happened, what was good, and where something went wrong, after we have had time to re-examine the event. Some people do this more slowly than others and often realize they would have acted quite differently if they had more time to think about it. Do you have trouble changing your behavior when a situation requires it?

> A woman was to attend a meeting in a building she was not familiar with. "I went to the building announced in the e-mail they sent me, only to learn from the note on the door that the meeting had been moved to another building. I did not know how to get to that building and had to stop at a gas station to get directions. Now I was late for the meeting and knew doors

would likely be closed because the meeting was being televised. I don't like being late. It makes me look unreliable. I was angry. When I got to the correct building, I saw that there was no parking available on the street and had to go down a block to find a space. I was beginning to feel very tense and ready to snap at someone. But I walked back to the building and saw two doors, separated by several hundred feet. I went up to one and pulled it, only to see it was locked. My anger was escalating and I could feel my back begin to ache. Before walking to the second door, however, I saw two men on the sidewalk talking, and decided to make sure I would get the right entrance door. "Excuse me, how do I get into the offices of this studio?" One of the men, clearly angry with my intrusion, sad sarcastically, "The door's right there, can't you see it?" Now I was more angry and frustrated than ever, and shot back, "That's a door right there, too. You don't need to get sarcastic!" He immediately apologized, but I was not flexible enough to acknowledge it. As I walked to the correct door, I felt bad that I had not been able to acknowledge his apology, but I wasn't going back to him. Enough, already! But I will remember what happened and be more flexible next time in RETHINKing what is happening and respond more appropriately. These anger experiences can really be learning experiences.

This woman felt especially helpless with the company that had given her wrong instructions and felt frustrated and angry. She snapped at the men on the sidewalk but felt she couldn't do anything about the real cause of her anger. Her anger had been misplaced.

You can lose your flexibility when you are caught in a strong emotion, like anger. So you need to Recognize not only your anger, but also the level of anger you are experiencing. Perhaps more important, however, you will need to Notice what calms you down. It is calming enough to respond to a changing situation with a change in your behavior. If your anger tends to control your behavior, then you will need to practice calming techniques, such as deep breathing or humor, so that they are available to interrupt your anger, or at least reduce it enough for you to respond with flexibility to a difficult situation. The way you Think about a situation needs to change as the situation changes. Anticipating what will trigger your thoughts of powerlessness can help you rehearse so that you won't feel stuck the next time a similar situation occurs. When you can be flexible even when you are angry, you may be able to see some humor in what seems a troubling situation. Here is a story of a young mother, Pam:

Pam was working out to keep her body supple and in shape. "Step, cross, step, kick; step, cross, step, kick." With each kick Pam lunged forward with her mop, cleaning another section of the kitchen floor. She felt jubilant. This was the way to go. Put the kids down for their nap, start up your favorite music, practice your aerobics routine, and clean your kitchen floor all at the same time. She was taking the latest advice to heart. "Take charge of your life!"

Then Pam did one swift turn and shrieked, "Dennis, what do you think you're doing?" Her two-year-old stood right behind her, ketchup bottle in one hand and mustard squeezer in the other. He was creating chaos more quickly than she had been cleaning. She was flooded with terrifying thoughts. What a monster she had given birth to! A life of crime often started with acts of vandalism like this one. Was this the kind of thing that that eleven-year-old who was just convicted of murder...?

She stopped herself as she saw that her screech and her anger-contorted face had terrified her son. He had never seen his Mom like this. He was howling and crying real tears. As Pam picked up her darling toddler and snuggled him close to her, she glanced at the kitchen floor. She found that she was not just developing flexibility in her body, but in her mind as well.

Then she wondered if the artist Jackson Pollack's mother had ever had a moment like this one, when she saw her little boy spreading colored liquids around the house. She amused herself with this thought and calmed herself with these musings and even created a family myth about her son's great talent. With Dennis still in her arms, she ran for her Nikon. She would take a picture of this floor, blow it up real big, and display it as his first art exhibit. The label would read, "Untitled: Early Work of Dennis Menacci—Age Two—Mixed Media: Ketchup and Mustard on Linoleum."

She was laughing with Dennis as she started taking pictures, assuring him that he was a fine artist, but next time, "Let's use paint and great big sheets of paper, O.K.?"

By the time Dad came home, order had been restored and the family myth of the great art exploits of Dennis had been started.

When you can get a different perspective, loosen up and laugh, then you have your flexibility problem well under control. You may find you are not as powerless as you had felt in the first moment of panic. Anger can be paralyzing but with mastery of RETHINK skills you can overcome this common obstacle.

Obstacle 3: Anger works for me

With the notion that anger works for you, a kind of tyranny can evolve:

George was a very strong and dominant person. He ran a large company and his employees were grateful for the opportunity he provided them to gain such prominence and success. But he wanted things his way. And when he went home, he also wanted things his way, including the neatness of the house, the children's behavior, his wife's cooking, and the type of friends with whom the couple would associate. All people who came in contact with him needed to do it his way. People generally chose to avoid his angry outbursts and so anger worked for him. But after a couple of years, the people closest to him started to drop out of his life. Even his wife threatened divorce.

If you live with a tyrant can you use the RETHINK skills to attempt to improve the relationship? Can you find the Empathy for the tyrant as you recognize there is a sad loneliness that he experiences? Often tyrants will feel bewildered. They have very little insight into their behavior's impact on others. People who may act like this seldom know how else to live. Their only role models acted this way; so they lack skills to do anything else. Now look at yourself. This tyrant part is in all of us—children, men, and women. There are different settings in which we can act tyrannically.

Think of a time when you purposely exploited your anger. You might have been a tyrant. And each time that anger works for you in giving you more power, you are less likely to change and thus hang on to your anger. To change the way you deal with your anger takes great patience, small achievable goals, and repeated efforts, much like working out at a gym. When you can combine Empathy with Integrating respect and Hearing skills, you will find you have broken a pattern that didn't always work for you.

Obstacle 4: You have to fight to protect yourself

Do you wonder what alternatives you can use without feeling vulnerable? Let's tune in to Ed's monologue:

> I don't know what alternative I can use without feeling vulnerable. Anger is a great shield for me. It scares people. It threatens some harm to them. It shows how tough I am. It clearly states: "Don't mess with me!" Now, that is very satisfying, especially when I feel exposed and at risk for harm from anyone who makes me feel vulnerable. I am a twenty-year-old student who has been using this shield all my life and it has worked. I even have friends who protect themselves by staying near me. That gives me a sense of power. But these are not the kind of "friends" I really want. They are too kowtowing, trying to please me. They provide no challenges, no real excitement, and I find myself increasingly lonely and avoided. This sucks. I must find other ways to protect myself from feeling vulnerable. I need to RETHINK my thoughts and feelings and get some skills that are more effective and rewarding than using anger as a shield."

If feeling that you must fight is critical to your sense of well-being, you can change that perception and need to protect yourself, by practicing R for Recognizing what makes you feel vulnerable physically and emotionally, and undercuts your self-esteem, your sense of trust. Make a list of some early experiences you had and identify the perceived threat to you. Might your anger be a cover-up for fear, for insecurity? What do you see as threatening? As you examine the list, you will gradually notice patterns of what threats lead you to respond with anger.

After you have a good reading on the patterns of your reactions, you will find T a useful letter. You can practice Thinking of ways you can feel less vulnerable. If, for example, you feel vulnerable when someone criticizes you, then you will want to learn to benefit from the criticisms that are not threatening, but, in fact, might be helpful. As someone is criticizing you, you can focus on identifying the specific points of the criticism. Then you can assess their value to you—some are helpful; others are irrelevant. After you have done this, you are ready to thank the person for the helpful criticisms and ignore the rest. Now, you have benefited from the criticisms and dismissed the others. You can even thank the person for taking the time and showing enough interest to offer the criticisms. You are not threatened. You don't need to feel anger to protect yourself. This kind of change in behavior is rare and most difficult. When you achieve this level of change, you deserve a reward!

Do you prepare yourself for an angry exchange so that you go into the situation with confidence? Have you considered possible responses of others so that you are not taken by surprise? You will want to develop a procedure for anticipating what might make you feel vulnerable and prepare for it.

Another useful skill you can learn is to Notice what calms you down when you feel vulnerable or in danger, and these feelings make you turn to anger as a protection. Your own special way to calm down will help you feel less vulnerable and therefore less angry. For example, you might want to take a break from the provocation by walking away for a short time so you can collect your thoughts. To avoid responding in your usual reactive way, think to yourself, "What else can I do in this situation besides coming back with a fighting response?" Perhaps you could try to articulate in a calm way what is distressing you. Singing or whistling or some calming distraction will help you focus better as you return to the disturbing thoughts.

Obstacle 5: I am not an angry person

Many people fear that if they admit they are angry, they will be perceived as unpleasant people. This is a myth that showing anger will cost you a friend.

Mary, a teen-age girl, feels terrible because she thinks she has lost a friendship. May had invited Barbara home with her after school. When Mary had some chores to do, Barbara went into the living room and turned on a television show, which she watched attentively. Mary said to herself: "I thought Barbara would at least offer to help me. But no! Instead, she is just sitting there enjoying herself. I can't take this any more. I am going to tell her what I think! I went to her and said, "You could at least offer to help me!" and went back to my work. It was quiet and still Barbara did not come to help. Then a few minutes later, Barbara just walked out of my house. Our friendship was over. I was stunned but realized my anger had cost me a friend. I want to be liked and instead I am an unpleasant person. No more of that! I will not get angry any more."

With Mary's new resolve, she became quite passive, avoiding conflict with her friends. Soon she had a reputation for being dull and lacking any spark. Mary had to learn to accept her angry feelings and to find ways to express anger without turning people off.

Obstacle 6: I am not interested in "feelings"

You may be one of those people who say, "I don't have a clue how to recognize my anger." You may be carrying a load of anger and be unaware of your burden. Are you saying you are content but really feeling lonely? Are you alert or is it more like tense? Are your relationships close or more distant? Are you kidding yourself? It is not uncommon for people to feel burdened without knowing consciously what the feeling is all about. Really smart people too! For example:

Ted was head of a division of a large corporation. "Every time there was a staff meeting, I prepared for confrontation with certain members of the division. I prepared myself for this by practicing what I would say when a staff member challenged a decision I made or an action I took. I practiced it in my head and had all my comments lined up. When the meetings began, I was ready. However, I did feel tense and noticed I was sweating as if I were entering some contest, but I accepted this as part of the job.

When I arrived home after these sessions, my wife would often say, "Oh, something must have happened to make you angry." For example, she might ask me to take out the trash while she got dinner ready and I would ask why she couldn't do that some time during the day. She would then ask me: "What was it today that got to you?" My tart reply was, "Don't be silly! Everything was fine. I had a staff meeting and I was able to get the results I wanted."

Her response was: "You seem to be paying a big price for that. Aren't you aware of how tense and angry you are? Can you see what it is doing to you? And I hate that you are so short with me."

Ted walked out of the kitchen feeling really annoyed and sat down to think about this. His wife had never spoken to him like this before. She was a pretty sharp woman and he could usually trust her feedback. Maybe there was something to Recognizing his anger. He started to pay attention to his physical symptoms as a way to find out what triggered his anger, and what calmed him down.

It is not always easy to identify and label your own feelings and probably harder to do that for others. It is not clear to what extent thoughts control feelings and feelings control thoughts. Once you engage your mind by trying to identify feelings, however, you are beginning the process of understanding them rather than being ruled by them. Anger often results from a tangle of unsorted emotions, so learning about your whole emotional repertoire can be helpful.

There are many problems with inhibition or denial of feelings. *The more we do not say what we need to say, the more we store up our anger, either consciously or unconsciously, the more these feelings can turn to rage.* Rage always finds expression, either as an external explosion, or as internal depression. Rage is out-of-control anger. We talk about "blind-rage." Rage can bring about destructive consequences, pushing people away rather than changing the things that need to be corrected. Or people can easily discount your concern and not consider your complaint on the merits. Often, the more you rant and rave the easier it is for the other person simply to disregard you. Nothing changes, except you feel worse about your relationships.

If you decide to work on getting unstuck, change is never easy and certainly won't happen overnight. But here are some suggestions that will be helpful in your attempts to get free from your destructive anger.

Anticipate Anger

How you anticipate a situation will make a difference. What you think will happen can either heighten emotional intensity unnecessarily if not unrealistically, or lessen the impact of even the worse situation. People with fear of the dentist often raise their anxiety to unimaginable, indeed, unreasonable, heights even before they get out of their cars in the parking lot. The same is true for encounters where anger is anticipated. As a matter of fact our anger worry can be all for naught. Take for example:

Bob is bringing his car in for inspection. As he waits his turn at the inspection station, he notices a crack in his taillight. From his experience he knows that his car can still pass, but it's something of a judgment call. What if one of the inspectors decides to make it an issue? Bob starts to stew, imagining the quarrel to come, failing inspection, and having to miss work and come back. By the time his car reaches the inspector, Bob is anticipating a major argument with the "incompetent" inspector over the cracked taillight and is imagining calling supervisors and writing a complaining letter to city officials. The inspector politely asks Bob to get out of his car, but by this time Bob is ready to jump out of his skin and looks surly if not downright hostile—his heart is racing and he is sweating. Bob is surprised, relieved (and not a little bit embarrassed) when the inspector says: "You have a cracked taillight. I am going to pass you this time, but please get it fixed."

If only Bob had known that when anticipatory anger and stress are addressed through self-talk or some other method, the actual event and the aftereffects seem to decrease. It is surprising but true that the body reacts differently to anticipatory stress than actual stress, and there is some thought that anticipatory stress actually might be *more* hazardous than the anger and stress of the actual event. The imagination can be more powerful than the reality. But anticipatory anger may be useful if it leads to preparation or some constructive action.

Planning for An Anger Exchange

Whenever possible, it is extremely helpful to prepare for an anger exchange, and learn how to "live through" the conflict and ultimately learn from the experience. The most common knee-jerk reaction to anger is either to shy away from it or go after the person with a vengeance—the fight-flight reaction. Although there is thinking involved, it is usually automatic and frequently the reaction can be destructive. So many times when people look back on the anger exchange, they say, "I wish I had said . . ." or "I should have done . . ." or "I am sorry I called her. . . ." They can even spend hours talking to themselves, going over (and over and over) the exchange, desperately trying to get a handle on the conversation in an effort to save face. Regretfully, many people feel devastated by anger exchanges. They are so humiliated or hurt that they wonder if they will ever recover. Or many people fear the anger exchange so much they will avoid it at all costs. We have a friend who told us she will never speak up when she feels incensed because the minute she even considers expressing her anger, she sees blood, knives, and people screaming. This was her childhood experience and she is petrified that she will only reexperience it today.

In planning for an anger exchange, here are some guidelines:

1. Identify the problem or the issue and describe it in your own words. Do this with someone else or to yourself.
2. Design in your head solutions to the problem. What are some of the ways to deal with this problem? What obstacles need to be overcome? Call on your own inner resources as well as others to help you come

up with a couple of different ideas. Other people can often help you gain a clearer perspective.

3. Practice or rehearse the discussion. Use positive self-talk and "I messages" as you rehearse. Practice in front of a mirror. Record yourself and play it back so you can hear what you sound like. Rehearse in front of a confidante. Or you can write down your thoughts and feelings as if you are composing a letter to a person. Modify the solutions you come up with, thinking through the consequences. You can rewrite the "script" as many times as you want until you feel comfortable. Remember to have Empathy for the other person as well as for yourself. Also, think through strategically such things as timing (when would it be best to have the exchange), who else should be around, and should the interaction take place in person, over the telephone, or by e-mail? Can you find some humor in the situation? Can you find some humor when talking about the problem? But, be prepared for surprises in the final interaction! They happen!

4. Take action. Put the solution to the test. Have the exchange. Here are some guidelines for living through such an anger exchange: Use the RETHINK skills that you have learned about throughout the book. Recognize that you are angry. Say it to yourself. Label your feeling "I am very angry right now." Then move a step back both physically as well as emotionally. Practice calming down and give yourself an assignment like "breathe deeply" or excuse yourself for a moment, walk a little and then come back (very hard to do but it is doable). Talk to yourself to help calm down. "I have the ability to handle this" or "I am strong and I respect myself and I will treat the other person with respect and clear words."

Living through An Anger Exchange

Start to think and make a plan. What do you want to accomplish? Answers might include: I want to be forgiven for changing my plans. I want her to understand that just because I changed my plans doesn't mean I am a bad person or that I am undependable. I would like for her to see it from my perspective; that is, if she were in the same situation she also would have changed plans. I would like for her to be generous to me and cut me some slack, since 90 percent of the time I am a loyal, dependable, and loving friend. I am available to her and her family in ways that enhances their lives. She can give me leeway to be imperfect.

As you are living through the anger exchange, watch for your own critical voice and find Empathy for yourself.

Finally, assess the outcome. Frequently anger does not get resolved in one discussion. It takes time and often many discussions until you can work it out. Keep trying. The rewards are worth the effort.

Practice

Like any skill you want to master, you need to practice. You will want to master ineffective anger reactions, the kinds of responses that add to problems rather than resolving them. And you will want to practice mastering effective anger reaction, the kinds of responses that enrich life. But it helps if you know enough about yourself to make decisions of how to practice.

Getting to Know Your Own Anger Style

Can you identify your anger style? Are you quick on the trigger, do you shout, are you physically aggressive, or do you say threatening things such as, "If you weren't my sister, I would stick a knife in your heart?" Alternately, do you cry, sulk, not want to talk to anyone, withdraw into yourself, or into your room or your bed? Do you find solace in a refrigerator, a bar, or drugs? Or are you an exercise junkie who retreats to hours and hours of exercise? Do you keep thinking and reworking your every insult, betrayal, or provocation, thus hanging onto your anger? People who fly off the handle or are hypersensitive often suffer from shaky self-esteem. Can you relate what triggered your anger to a put down?

Activity: How effective is your style? If you have a short fuse then you should practice noticing what works to calm you down before you respond in an anger situation. If you find it hard to express anger, then you might want to practice developing a way to talk about your anger. If you ruminate about your anger, then practice interrupting your thoughts by giving yourself a command to "STOP" and then tell yourself to KEEP *only* with the present problem and move toward solving this problem, substituting a list of positive options for the list of offensive actions that were so hurtful.

Calming Yourself

Activity: When you feel angry during the upcoming week, tell yourself, "I am going to calm down. I want to manage this situation in a helpful way. I will start by taking a few deep breaths."

Activity: Create your own list of ways to RETHINK a situation. Put your list on a three by five card and carry it with you for quick reference when you need it.

Activity: Create you own personal anger management hotline "life guards"—make a telephone list of trustworthy anger confidantes—people who will come to your emotional "rescue" should you need it.

Activity: Declare a "free-feeling zone": a special place (room or park) where you can allow yourself to go in a time of anger.

Hearing and Empathizing

Activity: Think of a recent situation when you were feeling angry. Was there someone who heard what you were saying and understood your feeling? How did you feel about the support? Now, describe a situation when you would have appreciated someone hearing what you were saying and showing empathy. What would you have liked somebody to say to you that showed understanding? How do you imagine that you would have felt? How would empathy be helpful to you and to the one showing you empathy?

Last, describe a situation where you practiced reflective listening. Reflective listening involves listening to what the angry person is saying, while thinking about the situation from a more beneficial perspective, as well as thinking about the anger style of the angry person. To be helpful, it is important to know something about the angry person.

Activity: Practice using empathy and reflective listening within your daily life. Notice when you have a number of feelings in response to a situation. What are they? How do you understand the range of feelings you experience? How do you use these feelings to resolve a conflict? Look for expressions of empathy you experienced during the week.

Integrating

Making "I" statements. When using "I" messages, we are communicating our indignation to another person. We express our anger by describing the behavior that is triggering our anger, not by attacking the person. Here is an example of phrasing "I" messages:

1. State your feelings about the possible consequences of the behavior ("I feel . . . ").

2. Describe the behavior you find annoying ("When . . . ").
3. State the consequences ("Because . . . ").

The format could look like this:
I feel _____, when _____, because _____.

Example: *I feel* irritated *when* the radio is playing loudly, *because* I can't concentrate and complete my work.

Making "I" statements will give you a chance to express what you are feeling and lower the chances of adding fuel to the fire by hurting or diminishing the other person. It requires a special kind of courage to make an "I" statement in the heat of an argument, because it involves taking responsibility for your own feelings and thoughts, not resorting to blaming the other.

Words matter in any relationship. Remember to Integrate an assurance of love and respect even when you feel angry and disappointed. Reprimands, discipline, and corrections all can be expressed with respect, so that vulnerable children, students, and employees, will be able to accept the criticism without shame and humiliation. With partners or people you love, integrating messages of love along with anger can be challenging but certainly worth the effort.

Example: "I am angry because of your thoughtless behavior this afternoon. I know you are usually extremely considerate and caring. But, today I was really inconvenienced and was late for my meeting when you left with the keys to my car. I assume it was a mistake, so let's make a plan where to leave the keys so it doesn't happen again to either of us."

Activity: Try to develop a vocabulary for expressing anger. It will make it easier to maintain the respect you have for yourself and for the target of your anger.

Thinking: When You Are the Target

Identify the most common way you experience anger from others. Can you ascertain others' styles of anger? Do you think the attackers recognize the purpose of their attacks—to minimize the importance of another individual—to degrade the person so they themselves will seem more important and valuable? Is the goal really to destroy someone who may be seen as a threat, not significant for one's own needs? Or is the one being attacked just a scapegoat for the attacker's own sense of inadequacy, unacceptability, and unworthiness? Keep in your log a record of times when someone gets angry with you. What did you do? Is it necessary to defend yourself each time? Can you think about the other person's stress or his feelings of inadequacy, or his problem? Can you reframe his anger without accepting the insult? Getting to understand one another's anger can help you avoid an escalation or even a serious display of violence. Answering the following questions will help you Hear more effectively and Think about and defuse the other's anger:

> What is the other person upset or worried about?
> Can you let the other person know by words, gestures, or a combination of both that you understand his feelings?
> Can you invite the other person to say what is upsetting?

Activity: Teach these anger management skills to your family, friends, and colleagues. This will help you build and reinforce your skills. Suggest at work, at school, that a support group be set up to deal with anger issues and anger management skills.

When Anger Styles Get Obsolete

Here is an example of an anger style that is not working anymore, but did at one time.

> Jill, at fifteen, controlled her parents by having temper tantrums any time they opposed what she wanted. It succeeded because her parents gave in each time. The pattern had been established when Jill was just two years old and it worked like a charm. She had enormous power over her parents. She thought, "Why should I change my behavior? I get what I want." But then she hesitated, "I'm not so sure anymore. All the kids in my class, all the kids I want for friends seem to avoid me and don't seem to like me. They never pick me for their teams or projects and I don't get invited for parties or sleepovers. I feel miserable."

Jill needed to Rethink what she was doing. It seems that her temper tantrums (translate, anger outbursts) didn't really work every time with her friends. But it is difficult to give up something that has worked so long. It takes a desire to improve relationships that is stronger than the waning success of previous behavior. Ask yourself some tough questions:

> How do people react to me when I express anger?
> Even if I get my way am I losing friendships?
> Do I find myself rejected and isolated?

Do I resolve the argument so that everyone feels satisfied?
Am I aware of the feelings of those with whom I am angry?
Do things run more smoothly after I have expressed my anger?
Do I like myself more after the anger incident?

These questions are difficult to answer truthfully. However if you can acknowledge your impact on others you will be on your way to improved relationship as you use your anger in more creative ways.

Changing One Skill at a Time

If you have doubts about whether your anger style really works for you and want to make some changes, you could start with one of the RETHINK skills and practice it for at least one week, and then select a second skill to practice. One technique that is found to work is to ask the question when you feel angry: "Which RETHINK skill will work here? Or, what combination of skills will work here? Let me take a minute or two to decide what will work." Learning to change the way you think about and respond to provocations, as well as to consider your emotions is never easy. Like any physical fitness program, it takes practice to acquire the skills that you need. It is helpful to isolate each skill and practice until it becomes a strength, very much as you do with muscles.

When you get good at using the skills, you will find more power and have a new understanding of others as you Hear them. Next, you may try another skill like Integrating some respect for the other person as you express your anger. As you practice, you will find you are slower to use anger to control others, but you are not weaker. Rather, managing your anger gives you more control.

As a reminder, you may want to put the list of the RETHINK skills on your desktop or refrigerator door. It is easy to forget that one skill that gives you the most trouble.

Activity: Roleplay a real conflict. Putting the skills together. Ask your best friend if you could practice your new skills with him. Pick a situation from your list of triggers, preferably a pet peeve. Start with a situation that triggers mild anger. Describe the situation in as much detail as possible. Ask your roleplaying partner to take the other person's side. After the roleplay, ask yourself the following questions:

1. What triggered my anger?
2. Were there other feelings? What were they?

3. How does my body alert me I am feeling angry?
4. What kind of self-talk did I use?
5. What else could I have said to myself to defuse the situation?
6. Did I use any calming techniques? What were they?
7. How did the other person communicate his feelings?
8. Was I able to think about the situation from the other person's perspective?
9. Was I able to reframe the situation?
10. Was I able to take and give empathy?
11. Did I use "I" statements?
12. Did I stick to the present situation and not bring up other issues from the past?
13. How would I rate myself in the management of the situation?
14. Am I satisfied?
15. Could I have done anything differently to improve the interaction?

Play it out a couple of times with your friend until your words feel real and the conflict is resolved. Assess the outcome. Frequently, anger does not get resolved in one discussion. It takes time and often many discussions until you can work it out. Did you manage your anger? Did you use the anger energy creatively? What have you learned from the exchange?

Discuss with your roleplay partner your answers to the questions. Now repeat the same exercise and try to improve upon your anger management skills. You are now ready to try to use these skills in your relationships. Learning to handle anger will improve all of your relationships. Remember, mastering these skills takes commitment, patience, and practice, practice, practice!

Activity: Daily workout at the anger gym. Log your anger coping exercises. Practice one step at a time. When you start to change, others may accuse you of extreme behavior and overdoing it in either direction. Frequently we find that things might even get worse before they get better. You may feel stuck, as if in the middle of a tunnel. You can't go back to where you started and you only seem to get into trouble when you move forward. But soon you will start to see the light at the end of the tunnel and know that the change in your behavior is beginning to be helpful.

CHAPTER 13

Regaining a Sense of Personal Power

Forgiving

What is forgiveness? Is it turning the other cheek? Giving in? Giving up? Letting go of past hurts? Making exceptions? Changing the way of thinking? Or, Making an empty promise? And why forgive at all? What do you get out of forgiving except a promise rarely kept?

"Crossroads: A Story of Forgiveness," which was aired on television on the *Hallmark Hall of Fame*, in April 2007 on CBS, is based on the true story of Bruce Murakami. Murakami was enraged and seeking vengeance after a teenage driver, who had been road racing, caused the death of Murakami's wife and daughter. The widower sought a prison term for the young offender and hired a lawyer to assure that all the evidence would be available for the trial. The film shows how the furious husband and father was able to turn a quest for retribution into an act of forgiveness, with a creative outcome of this tragedy. Murakami decided to forgive the teenage driver, and felt Empathy and Compassion for him, as it was clear he was very sad and remorseful. Together they started a campaign to speak to young drivers to alert them to the dangers of road racing. Part of the message in the TV film and their campaign is that automobile accidents are the leading cause of death in children under eighteen. Murakami turned from an angry vengeful man to a person with a mission. His sons could follow his lead in this act of forgiveness.

Another true story involves two brothers who were able to forgive each other after daily encounters with anger.

Arthur and Peter were born eight years apart. Today, they are seven and fifteen years old. The age difference, however, didn't stop them from excessive anger exchanges, ending in repeated fighting with each other. Arthur, the older brother, would call Peter stupid and profess how much he hated him. Anger pervaded the home as Arthur would unmercifully tease his brother. He would push him around, hit him, throw him on the floor, and "wrestle" him, until Peter would bitterly cry in pain. Peter felt brutalized by Arthur. The family situation continued to worsen. The parents felt powerless in stopping the constant fighting between the brothers. They decided to call for some family meetings with a counselor.

In the second session, Peter felt safe enough to speak up and, through his tears, he said to Arthur, "I can't stand it anymore. You are mean, hurtful, and a big bully. Every time you walk into the house you scare me with your meanness."

Arthur first responded that he was only trying to strengthen Peter (Peter is small for his age). "I didn't realize how much I have been hurting you. I am sorry. I promise not to do that again."

Arthur truly meant that he was sorry. He could suddenly see how his actions were damaging his younger brother. Perhaps his aggressive intentions were not all as beneficent as he professed, he admitted only to himself, but he had not intended to injure Peter. Arthur, for the first time, acknowledged his brother's fear and could understand Peter's tremendous resentment toward him. Arthur did not want the fallout from his actions to be so destructive. Although he admitted, again to himself, that he was somewhat jealous of his brother because their parents gave him so much attention, he did not want his brother to hate him.

From that day on, Arthur stopped his physical aggression and teasing of his brother. Having recognized how utterly unloving his actions were toward his brother, he was committed not to hurt him anymore. At the same time Peter agreed to stop annoying his brother. He promised he would not do the things that would trigger his brother's anger, like enter Arthur's room or use his possessions without permission. It has been six months and the brothers have so far kept their promises.

Forgiveness is about letting go of anger and resentment (R. Enright and R. Fitzgibbons, *Helping Clients Forgive: An Empirical Guide for Resolving Anger and Restoring Hope*. Washington, DC: American Psychological Association, 2000). It is an antidote to anger, resentment, hatred, and even bitterness. Forgiveness encompasses compassion, empathy, generosity, and acceptance. Forgiveness is a way of reframing a thought or belief, moving you from resentment to love; from tension to relaxation; from harshness to softness; and to freedom for both the giver and the receiver. It is about improving one's safety as well as one's emotional well-being. Rather than being a sacrifice, forgiveness offers the possibility of improved relationships as well as a strengthened sense of self. There is an opportunity for another chance. During the process of forgiveness (calling for some soul-searching) you realize that a change is important and a commitment to altering your behavior. Sometimes this change involves a radical transformation in your feelings, your thoughts, and your behavior.

The Difficulty of Asking for Forgiveness and Forgiving

Why is it so difficult for many people to forgive? The demand to change our behavior, to say we are sorry, and to let go of anger can be an excruciating journey. It means owning up to our misdeeds, to our mistakes, to the mistakes of others, and letting go of our "righteous indignation." What makes us angry and how we decide to forgive is different for each person and each situation. For some, forgiveness may be difficult for even the slightest provocation. For others it is fairly easy to forgive. Different cultures and different religions express forgiveness in varying ways. Couples, friends, and colleagues also will experience forgiveness in varying degrees and ways. Refusing to forgive means a commitment not only to anger but also to shame, guilt, and a steady state of combat or combat readiness.

Why is it so hard to let go of anger if anger, when not used, channeled, or diffused, is physically and emotionally depleting, as hurtful to the holder as to the receiver? When we are unable to forgive and tenaciously hold on to our anger, we often become inflexible, tight, uncreative, and unproductive. We bind ourselves in a web. Morally grounded anger can become even more resolute, more controlling, and more limiting of our own possibilities. You and everyone around you feel rotten. It is a path of no return.

Most people want to live in a "kinder, gentler" world. They want to be forgiven and even would like to be able to forgive and move forward. Nevertheless, old and new emotional baggage, consisting of our past experiences of anger as well as our needs and our fears, get in our way. We experience holding on to our position as a way of protecting our self-respect rather than seeing the holding-on behavior as self-defeating. We tenaciously remain steadfast to our anger because of our need to avoid blame, or because of our feelings of moral indignation. It is in this state of holding on to one way of thinking that our actions become rigid. The act of forgiveness is particularly difficult in the middle of an argument when your own sense of self-preservation demands that you believe fully that *your way is the one and only way* to think about the situation. But, in truth, holding on tightly and reflexively to one way of thinking may be a signal that something needs to be changed.

For example, when a couple discovers there has been infidelity in the relationship, tremendous anger can be triggered and, in may cases, be highly destructive to the couple's relationship. But, on the other hand, it can serve as a signal for needed change. Infidelity, like other deceptions, when considered out of context, can be misunderstood as ingrained behaviors, fixed traits, or as troubling personality characteristics that exist within the other person, rather than as a response to what may be happening between people. ("I always knew he would one day cheat on me. I knew he was a liar.") Behaviors and our corresponding intentions are complicated and multidetermined. Willingness (as hard as it may be) to understand the behavior, even deceitful behavior, is imperative to saving a marriage or a committed relationship. Frequently, compounding the issue of infidelity is the secrecy that surrounds the affair. Sometimes, a spouse might say that the secret was perpetrated in order to protect the other. Whatever the reason for the secrets, lies, and betrayal, what is most important is the ability to talk about the deception and rebuild the lost trust. Knowing that sexual attraction and even affairs can occur in any relationship (including loving committed relationships), the best thing we can do is agree to openly and honestly discuss taboo thoughts and desires concerning sexual behavior outside a committed relationship. Frequently, a hurtful situation itself is bewildering and must be sorted out. Whenever it happens, forgiveness is usually compounded by ambivalence, reservation, and confusion.

Decisions need to be made about whether we want to do something to change the situation and, if so, what. It takes time to sort out what happened. With each step toward forgiveness we remove the dual weights of anger and hurt so we can move forward. But when forgiveness happens, we reach for openness and honesty, let go of anger, and find compassion, no matter how slowly it happens. It is, more often than not, well worth the effort it takes. Forgiving produces relief and peace of mind. It can be liberating and growth-producing for the giver and the receiver. And relationships can actually be strengthened.

Thinking about Forgiveness

Sometimes, people insist that they are unable to forgive, and that the offense committed was so egregious or violating that forgiving would be impossible and even uncalled for. Acts of violence with permanent consequences come to mind. But luckily, most offenses routinely occurring in daily life are not of that kind. However, even for the most egregious acts, we must guard against insisting that the acts are unforgivable. Keep in mind that *we* determine what *we* think about a situation; *we* create the interpretation; *it is our* perception that impels *our* reaction; *we* decide on our response. Perhaps as seen through the eyes of a so-called objective, independent observer, there might be a different interpretation of the interaction that triggered your anger.

Our perceptions of life experiences can determine our reactions to them. This thought suggests the familiar maxim, "the glass is either half empty or half full, depending on who is looking at it." Realizing and accepting that *you* are *interpreting* every event that you experience, gives you control over your own destiny. But not perfect control: there are situations that are so hurtful they would be considered terrible offenses against humankind, no matter who was observing the situation.

To some extent, our interpretations of potentially provocative events are rooted in our personality as well as influenced by present life circumstances. For instance, if your parents refused to forgive each other after a fight, then you probably doubt that amicable resolution of conflict is possible. This, of course, is *your* way of interpreting. It may be all you have or know, but the result is to limit your growth and produce stagnation. Each person in a conflict situation has a point of view. Most of the time, each believes he or she is ABSOLUTELY RIGHT; each offended person declaring with certainly that he or she is justified in the behaviors.

Bonnie had an argument with her son, Jared. Jared was angry because he thought his mother was inconsiderate by taking the car to work when she knew (or should have known!) that Jared needed it. After all, he bemoaned, "Your office is only a few blocks away. If you planned it right, you could have walked."

Bonnie replied that she was running late and needed to drive the car to make a scheduled appointment. And anyway, her office was only a few blocks away and why couldn't he just walk over and pick up the car?

The truth is, both were right, and if they held on to their different points of view without recognizing the legitimacy of the other's position, it would have been a standoff, with each walking away feeling angry, disrespected, unloved, and just downright awful. When Bonnie was able to say: "I can see why you were upset. If I planned my morning with you in mind, I would have left with enough time to walk to work and then the car would have been immediately available to you."

Jared was responding to feeling disregarded. Of course, this was not Bonnie's intention, and she was happy to have the opportunity to ask for forgiveness.

But could Jared understand the situation from his mother's perspective? For forgiveness to be optimal, both people need to be willing to move from their original perspective and see the situation from the other's viewpoint. In this situation, Jared needed to understand that his mother actually intended for him to have the car for the day but took it because she did not know Jared's schedule.

Mother and son successfully resolved the conflict. But it took time, tears, and the honest expression of anger to reach forgiveness. It is not easy to stand and argue something out with a loved one. At one time or another each person may have the impulse to walk away, or go for the jugular, or both! However, if willing to use the RETHINK skills such as Empathy and Listening, you can move to a place of understanding and forgiveness that ultimately is much more rewarding than just winning the battle in the short run. As you learn to RETHINK your anger, you will also be moving toward a more compassionate way of living with the people most important to you.

Using the RETHINK skills will lessen emotional tightness that frequently finds physical expression as well. Paying attention to our physical responses (N—Notice) gives us information and cues that we can rely on and trust to Recognize our own anger and attempt to Think and examine and reexamine our own interpretation of a provocation. Progress means that our focus is broadened and we explore all aspects of the difficulty so we can move toward forgiveness and resolution. Always our ultimate goal is to *do no harm* to a relationship. This means a focus on how we handle the argument and how to move to forgiveness rather than simply winning. Realistically, years from now you won't remember what the argument was about, but you will certainly remember the experience and the quality of the relationship with your fellow combatant. Using the RETHINK skills on a daily basis with even the most minor irritating events, will lead to less stress, fewer arguments, and greater possibilities of resolution and forgiveness. Learning how to forgive *yourself* for an angry outburst is as important as learning how to forgive others. Think of a time when you had an angry outburst and you felt out of control. What happened? Now, practice forgiving yourself, out loud. Tell yourself, "It's okay." Many times we just lose control. We react without thinking. Then we feel guilt, shame, and/or remorse. We didn't intend to hurt another's feelings, but something set us off. See if you can gain some insight into the thought and the feeling as well as the need that was threatened. In this way you will be moving yourself from being a victim to a person in control. Remember, once you are able to forgive yourself, and gain some insight into the situation, you can always return to the person you have verbally injured and say you are sorry. Also, with insight, the next time you are in a similar situation, you can practice more self-control and instead of being verbally aggressive toward the other, you can struggle to try some of the RETHINK skills.

Rita shared a room at college with Florence and they had become good friends. But, Rita had a habit of borrowing the books Florence bought for class and forgetting to return them. They had discussed this problem from time to time and it seemed Rita finally got the message. At least the books were always there when Florence needed them. Then, one day, none of the books was in the room and Florence was livid. She knew perfectly well that Rita had taken them and she was waiting for her to come back to the room to really tell her what she thought of such behavior. Rita did return and knew the books were not there. She saw Florence's face and realized how angry Florence was. With great difficulty, Rita explained that her boyfriend needed to review material for a test and the material was only in the books Florence had. So she took the books at night when Florence was asleep and gave them to her boyfriend. He was to return them at about 5:30 in the morning so they would be there when Florence woke up. But, unfortunately, he didn't wake up after studying most of the night and so the books stayed in his room. Now Florence was livid! Her roommate could not be trusted! And she expressed her anger with sharp words and a few insults. And Florence insisted that Rita move out of the room; she didn't want to see her ever again. Rita did just that.

Months went by, and Florence began to think of the situation from Rita's perspective. While taking the books couldn't be justified, especially with their agreement, it was understandable how much Rita wanted to help her boyfriend. And, in all honesty, if Rita had told her of her need to lend the books to the boyfriend, she would have permitted it. It was the lack of informing her of what was going on that was so bothersome. But, she really liked Rita and missed her. So she called Rita and suggested having coffee together. Rita accepted and they started with some chitchat, but Florence soon moved into what she was feeling about what had happened and wanted to restore their relationship. If Rita ever needed something, like to borrow books, she should explain what her need is and why and Florence promised she would do what she could to help. Rita understood her request and understood what made Florence so angry. She said she was sorry and that she would be more upfront with her requests.

Think of a time when a friend was angry with you and you reacted by rejecting your friendship.

What happened?
What did the person do to indicate rejection of you?
How did you deal with it?
Was the relationship ever restored?
How did that happen?
Is it too late to restore a relationship that was damaged by anger?

Now, think of a time when you were angry with someone because of something that person had done to really upset you. Can you remember how you felt? Ask yourself: Why does this situation create such intense feelings in me? What can I learn so that when a similar incident occurs again I will be able to handle it with more composure and control? The more you know about yourself, the more you can take responsibility for your own feelings, and the more you will be able to forgive both yourself and the other. Ninety percent of getting more control over the anger experience is personal insight; that is, recognizing what actually caused the anger and seeing what changes are needed to restore harmony. Using the RETHINK skills will help you discover the insight that you need and will guide the accompanying behavior. If you can figure out what is going on emotionally, then you will be better positioned to address your behavior.

To get free of the continuing impact of past experiences, it is important to confront old hurts and unmet needs, rather than disguising these feelings with anger or denial. With reexperiencing these old hurts you free yourself to forgive and take control of your own life. Then you have a choice about whether and how you will respond to a provocation. In giving up feeling like a victim, you will gain a sense of personal power and worth that is sincere and long-lasting. Recognizing that the anger and the hurt come from your own unique way of thinking, from your perceptions, and from your belief system, gives you ultimate command over your life, your reactions, and your behavior. Unless you are a magician or a hypnotist, you cannot control someone else's behavior or emotions. Even those people can control your behavior but briefly. What you really can control are your own feelings and behavior.

Forgiveness can function from a preventive approach to destructive behaviors. Forgiving takes strength, wisdom, and a strong desire to keep the relationship. It does not mean that you pretend that you weren't offended, hurt, or angry by the behavior. Forgiving *does* mean you decide to RETHINK—first about yourself and your own behavior and then attempt to figure out why the other person behaved as he did. The use of Empathy and Compassion for another implies understanding the other's behavior, especially in light of their human vulnerabilities, and moving toward forgiveness, despite the unjust act.

In order for forgiveness to have meaning it is best if you can address the source of the grievance and talk to the other person (or perpetrator) about the incident. Clarifying what about their behavior felt injurious to you and discussing each person's understanding of the situation, can serve to clear up hurt feelings, make amends, and ultimately improve the relationship. If you cannot talk to the individual directly, then talk to a confidante about the insult, the hurt, and the promise not kept. Once you are able to achieve insight and a keener awareness of the problem, you can go back to the offender and try to resolve the difficulty. The goal is for relationships with your spouse, colleagues, family, friends, and acquaintances, to grow and be strengthened rather than destroyed.

Refusal to Forgive

One of the saddest occurrences is lack of forgiveness in families. Over and over again we have seen families splitting and refusing to talk to one another. Words are powerful. They have consequences. If you use words to hurt others, your victims will find ways to return the hurt. Words can devastate a relationship or can heal a relationship. By understanding the skills in this book, you are learning how to think and use your words to improve and when necessary, heal connections.

Robert had a terrible two years. First his mother died; then his favorite cousin was caught stealing from the supermarket; then his sister was diagnosed with a rare chronic disease; and then his father got sick and died. So many losses in such a short amount of time created a feeling of hopelessness. His best friend of fifteen years, Tom, helped in whatever way he could. But when he was unable to follow through on an important request, Robert became furious and refused to continue the relationship. Robert expressed deep hurt that his best friend couldn't write the necessary letter to a lawyer for his cousin. "Yes," he said, "it would have required meeting with the cousin and spending a good deal of precious time, but I would have done it for Tom." "How selfish and cruel you are!" he shouted at Tom, and he refused to see him again.

Sometimes people get stuck in their anger and can't forgive because their anger concerns something else. In the example, Robert was angry about all his losses. He, of course, was justified to feel the tremendous anger that we all feel around the loss of loved ones. He also had a justified need for a letter to be written for his cousin, who was in a time crunch with a case he was working on. However, in such a time of upset, rather than having an honest and open dialogue with his best friend, he never allowed Tom the chance to write the letter later, as Tom was willing to do. Instead, he projected his feelings of loss onto his best friend and created another loss and disappointment.

After the death of a loved one, anger is frequently misplaced and families, as a result, may never speak to each other again.

George and his father (Sam) always had a contentious relationship, but when the mother/wife died things got worse. George decided to leave the town he grew up in and trek in Nepal and there make his home with Buddhist monks. His father, furious about this life choice, said he would disown him. But George, committed to his life choice, followed his dream and his passion. From that day on, father and son never had contact. When George was notified of his father's death, a great sadness overcame him. He decided to go to Israel and try to reconnect with his father and his roots. When in Israel, he went to the Wailing Wall and wrote a note to his deceased father that said, "Dear Dad, I am sorry for our deep disagreement. I wish I could have said this before you died but I hope you can forgive me. Love, George." As he placed his note onto the wall, another note fell out. He picked it up and read it. "To my deeply beloved son, George: Please forgive me for my inability to accept you as you are. It was the greatest mistake of my lifetime. Love, your father for always, Sam.

Without understanding why, we know that negative words and actions have a longer lasting impact than the positive. It is much more difficult to undo the hurt than to cause the hurt.

David picked up four children, including Sally, to drive to school each day. It was invariably a chore because it always made him late for work. But he figured it was part of the good neighborly thing to do and he wasn't going to complain. Luckily, however, on this particular day, it was his turn to pick up *after* school. He arrived on time at the school, and picked up three of the children in the car pool, when Sally came to the car expecting to be taken home. David explained that today her Mom was picking her up. No, Sally was sure she was supposed to go home in the car pool. He had her get into the car, waited to see if her Mom was coming for her, but finally left when no more cars were coming for pick up. He assumed Sally was correct and he had confused the instructions.

Since he was not in a rush, he decided to stop and get the kids a snack. All were in a good mood. When David arrived at Sally's house, her mother was angrily waiting outside. Rushing toward David, she was screaming: "How could you kidnap my child like this? I was scared to death. You have no right to take my child. You are an irresponsible person. I never want you near my daughter or to drive her again!"

The insult was more than David could bear. How dare she talk like that to him, especially in front of the children? He did not respond. He let Sally out of the car and drove away, vowing never to speak to that woman again. It has been three years and David continues to refuse to speak to his neighbor.

How could all of these good intentions go so awry? David set out to be a good neighbor and ended being an enemy of his neighbor. This scenario happens time and again between well-intentioned people whose behavior is misinterpreted. To resolve this standoff, one of the neighbors would need to say, "I'm sorry for the misunderstanding." At this point it could be either David or Sally's mother. But the difficulty in uttering those words, the need for self-protection that each savors, and the stinginess people feel with uttering the words, "I'm sorry," is notorious. Even when people want to acknowledge their wrongdoing, gratitude, or sorrow, frequently they will get tongue-tied. Perhaps, when our Empathy for the other person becomes penetrated enough, it will move us to say the most difficult of words: "I'm sorry. Please forgive me."

How to Forgive

There are some basic rules of forgiveness. To ask for forgiveness requires several steps:

a. Recognize that you did something wrong.
b. Feel sincere remorse.
c. Apologize to all those you hurt.
d. When the opportunity to react in the same way arises again, resolve not to do it.

True forgiveness takes a good deal of inner personal strength, humility, discipline, and willingness to take a risk and make a commitment to the relationship. To be able to forgive means putting our emotional baggage aside, or at least put it in the overhead bin, experiencing regret for our past behavior, and finding a way to incorporate Empathy, Compassion, and RETHINKing skills. Forgiveness doesn't happen all at once. Rather it develops over time, usually in a series of small steps. Adults are more likely to forgive than adolescents, and elderly people are more likely to forgive than younger adults. Age is clearly a factor in the capacity to forgive.

Overall, we suggest the advice given to medical students when they enter the hospital to practice their newly learned skills: First, as we have stated before, is the obligation to do no harm. In this context we recognize that forgiveness is about using the head (cognitive behavior) as well as the heart (emotional behavior). As we know, the intellect needs the emotions to work at its best.

When we want to forgive, we need to be able to use our own feelings to guide our response, while being sensitive to the other person's feelings and moods. It is achieving the balance between our thoughts and our feelings that is important and difficult.

As we have suggested, anger, a signal for change, can be a signal for forgiveness as well. Instead of ruminating about past hurts and pains or remaining arrogant, movement toward forgiveness can be energizing. It is a pledge to abandon past mistakes, resolve not to act that way again, and make peace with a fellow person, and thus rebuild connections. The whole notion of possible progression toward a kinder and gentler world is very reassuring and hopeful. It is a gift for us to use in our everyday interactions. We have a chance for changing the course of our lives. It is the highest level of choice and freedom.

Accepting Forgiveness

Expressing the words of forgiveness may be difficult enough, but what if your words are not accepted? Sometimes we will need to say I am sorry again and again until the words of forgiveness can be acknowledged. Frequently, our first attempts are awkward, clumsy, and frightening to the other person. On the receiving end, it can be difficult to accept another's apology. Often we do not trust the apology or feel so hurt that we want to continue to protect ourselves. We can also decide to hold on to our anger because holding on gives us power. Or there can be a denial of angry feelings, the assumption that one did nothing wrong. This denial might be a signal that the person is uncomfortable expressing anger or that the situation is too painful to revisit.

Beyond Anger

Make no mistake; it is not easy to get beyond anger, especially when the source of the anger has far-reaching implications. The event that triggered your anger was one of those rare, but objectively and truly unforgivable things: the drunk driver who seriously injures your child; the mugger who steals your purse and pushes you to the ground, breaking and permanently injuring your tennis hand; the uncle who sexually abused your child; a spouse whose affair was known to everyone but you; or a teacher who humiliated and failed you unfairly. Anger in these and similar situations is a constantly active force that you can feel throughout your body. What can you do? How can you move beyond the anger? Can *you* transcend anger? Is it possible when you cannot forgive, to move beyond anger? To all these questions, the answer is a resounding "YES." But how?

Other Feelings

The story of Felix Zandman as he relates in his autobiography (*Never the Last Journey*, Shocken Books, New York, 1995), demonstrates how anger can be transcended even in the most austere circumstances. Felix had plenty to be angry about. He was only fifteen years old when the Nazis marched into his courtyard. He was suddenly thrown out of his school, his home, and his neighborhood. In the Warsaw Ghetto, his mother and father were abruptly summoned and shipped out, he knew not where. The Warsaw uprising he and his uncle had participated in had proved futile. They fled and found refuge in a cellar of his Nannie's home, a raw earthen dugout of a cellar. There were five of them crowded together for what turned out to be a year and a half. Felix was entitled to be angry, furious, and of course, sad—but to what end? Anger at this point could not be used as a tool for change. His uncle pointed out that justice would eventually prevail: the Nazis would be defeated by the allies—the United States, England, and the USSR. What he was implying was that they must find a purpose beyond anger and self-pity to be ready for the time after the allied victory. And, as a math teacher, he worked to get Felix prepared to enter the university. They had no paper, no books, and no light; but what they did have was an intense concentration and the power of visualization. And two other adults, a couple who had also been teachers, had other subject matter to teach Felix—literature and history.

When victory finally came, Felix could, in a short time, gain entry to a French university and get started on a brilliant and lucrative career. He became the President of a Fortune 500 company. By getting beyond his anger and getting focused on a purposeful project, Felix was able to grow during a tragically oppressive period. Only the RETHINK skills needed were among the five, and they were more concerned about studies and survival than anger.

Confident that a more powerful group would avenge him, Felix found a way to transcend his anger and even become happy and successful despite the horrendous experiences. Focusing on what you can do can help you transcend your anger. Sometimes, just taking the steps to do something new and challenging is more reparative than the actual steps you take.

Focus on a Specific Goal

Concrete goals give purpose and meaning to our lives and obstruct our tendency to obsess about what is making us angry. During her treatment for cancer, Sally's husband left her for a younger woman. She was furious that he could exploit her physical and emotional vulnerability in such a craven way, and thought about taking revenge by ruining his career. She would make this sordid episode public! She realized, however, that doing so would be extremely harmful to the children; so, instead, she decided to get herself back into shape, return to her art work, and find a partner who was a better match.

The Reverend Martin Luther King transcended the anger resulting from the racial inequality that he and many African Americans daily experienced in American life by developing and implementing a carefully conceived political strategy and a series of sequential goals to change the racial situation in America.

> Jerry was hit and permanently injured by a stray bullet from a drive-by gang shooting. He had every reason to be enraged at having to spend the rest of his life in a wheelchair, especially when he had avoided the gang life in his neighborhood, and was injured in a freakish way. He knew that he could never truly forgive the person who shot him, but he stuck to his dreams to get an education and then work within his own community. Once in college, he transcended his anger about his disability by focusing on learning about the legislative system that gave equal access to handicapped people in educational settings. He had long, hard fights in the legislature—but ultimately succeeded, with the help of many others, to change the laws and transcend his anger for the good of the larger society as well as for the good of his own community.

A parent whose child was struck by a drunk driver started Mothers against Drunk Driving (MADD). The parents of a son who contracted AIDS through unprotected sex were furious at their child's negligence, but joined a political movement to get more research money for the cure of AIDS.

For the last ten years, millions of Latinos from many different countries have entered the United States. These immigrants face tremendous hardships: lack of education, racism, poverty, poor housing, and limited English, all of which arouse anger. However, the strength of the family, and the enormous commitment to their children, created a clear purpose to achieve a better life for the next generation. The person who is able to transcend his anger realizes that the hardships and chaos experienced take a backseat to the higher purposes of being a good parent.

In each of these instances, the angry person recognizes the futility of his or her anger, while realizing that RETHINKing involves transforming the anger to help make the world a safer and more manageable place for others. Your own ability to transcend anger is restorative, not destructive. In this process it also means finding compassion for others. The stories provided here exemplify how people turned their attention outward and accomplished remarkable things. Transcending anger happens when we are able to commit to something greater than ourselves. And, ironically, sacrifice and concern for others are the best things we can do for ourselves. Solidifying our human ties sustains us in the time of greatest need and angst.

Reframe

We have a lot of old sayings for the concept of reframing. "Everything happens for the best," and "Every cloud has a silver lining," are a couple of colloquial expressions that embody a healthy way of seeing even extreme adversity from a different perspective. Using self-talk to help transcend anger such as, "I am strong and am able to transcend and heal my wounds." Or as Henry Wadsworth Longfellow said, "It has done me good to be somewhat parched by the heat and drenched by the rain of life."

Sally was a Yale graduate and did her Ph.D. from Stanford in French Litera- ture. She applied, in vain, for over a hundred tenure track-teaching positions in colleges and universities throughout America. While initially angry at the rejection, she began to view her experience as an indication that she needed to look elsewhere—that maybe academia was not the place for her and some- one with her skills could thrive outside the university setting. Sally answered an ad and took a position as personal assistant to an executive in a startup dot-com company that had international business in French-speaking coun- tries. Her stock options are now worth more than several years' salary as a full professor and she is having the time of her life!

In order to reframe our thinking, it is often helpful to communicate with others about what is making us angry. It is important to ask for opinions and help in sorting out our thoughts. Putting feelings into words, recognizing that others feel the same way, and learning that our reactions are not so "crazy" can be liberating. The old adage that "misery loves company" may be true. We want to see ourselves as no more upset than others would be under similar circumstances. Few individuals can face overwhelming anger alone, and the moral support and good advice others offer can help us feel more in control and move us forward.

Another method of reframing is prayer and/or a belief in a greater force, which can also help in dealing with overwhelming anger.

John was a POW for five years. When asked how he survived the torture and inhumane treatment, he explained that he would pray most of the day. When he woke he would say his morning prayers. After eating his meager lunch of one slice of bread and one-half cup of dirty water he would say grace over his meal; and before he went to sleep, he recited the same bedtime prayers his mother would say with him when he was a very young boy. He believed in a just God who would keep him safe and bring him home to his family. And he believed that his captors would suffer their own pain in the world to come.

It not only helps to pray for oneself, but praying for others can also help to transcend anger. In the worst of times when people pray for the health and well-being of others, even those we feel angry toward, it helps us transcend the anger. And the belief, "I am my brother's keeper," can lift our spirits and help us rise above the anger.

Refusing to take the "bait" even when someone is being insulting, mean spirited, and/or extremely upsetting, is an accomplishment! Anybody would feel angry. But you can say to yourself such things as: "So be it. In the long run it's not so important." Or, "I am not going down that road," or "It's just words—what he says does not have to destroy me." Or, "I do not like that part of her but I do like other parts of her. Nobody is expected to be perfect. I am just going to ignore the negative and focus on the positive."

Learning how to transcend your anger is as important as any skill you will master. You will, however, need the desire to do so, the heart to do so, and the courage to feel your feelings and not get stuck. There are many reasons to try to transcend anger, as crises, trauma, and deep painful losses, are facts of life. They are the times when we have an opportunity to learn from and see these difficult experiences as challenges and perhaps even grow from them.

Why struggle to transcend anger in the face of devastating circumstance when you can't forgive? Principally, because it is better for you both physically and emotionally. As discussed in other chapters, holding on to your anger is bad for your emotional and physical health. Rage boomerangs. When we carry anger around, we frequently are ready to erupt at any moment and can explode at inopportune times. In a way, rather than protecting us, the anger can get the best of us. Anger is toxic when we hold on to it so resolutely.

By staying with the anger, we also sacrifice insight and reflection. We can only learn from a situation when we are open to it. And there is always something to learn, even from the worst of experiences.

If we are unable to transcend the anger, we can become frozen. Attempting to protect ourselves from the pain and anger, we are also numbing ourselves from friendship, intimacy, and closeness. We lack generosity, empathy, and caring. We are suspended in time with a hardened heart. What feels like a protective armor will separate us from people and the important human connections that we all need.

If we become so absorbed in the negative, in the mistakes and horrors that others can perform, we will miss the blessings and the wonder that also surround us. A growing number of scientists are studying the impact of optimism on health as well as on behavior. Optimism works! Try to recognize the good in others, even if it is only a part of the other. This moves us to a sense of well-being and pleasure. Being able to be flexible and positive propels us toward growth and an expanded vision of our universe. Transcending anger is a choice. You are the only one who can decide to do it. This ability—to do what you choose to do—is what gives you a true promise of managing your anger.

Some Final Questions

What are the most important things you have learned from reading this book?

How have you changed your behavior as you deal with anger-provoking situations?

What RETHINK skills have been most helpful to you? And in what combination?

What changes have you noticed in your interactions with people at home, at the workplace, and in the community?

Have you been able to forgive someone for doing something bad to you? How did that happen?

We wish you well!

Further Reading

Anger Management and Controlling Anger: www.selfgrowth.com/anger.html.

Anger Management Self-Help Material: www.articles911.com/.

Baugh, Terri (2002). Education Forum on Adolescent Health: Youth Bullying.

Cornelius, Helena (1998). *The Gentle Revolution: Men and Women at Work. Conflict Resolution Network*. Australia: Simon and Schuster.

Froschl, Merle, Barbara Sprung, and Nancy Mullin-Rindler (1998). *Quit It! A Teacher's Guide on Teasing and Bullying for Use with Students in Grades K–3*, NEA Professional Library.

Gentry, W. Doyle (1999). *Anger Free: Ten Basic Steps to Managing Your Anger*. New York: William Morrow & Co., Inc.

Hot Stuff to Help Kids Chill Out. The Anger Management Book: www.angeronline.com/html/kidsbooks.html.

Middelton-Moz, Jane, Lisa Tener, and Peace Todd (1999). *The Ultimate Guide to Transforming Anger: Dynamic Tools for Healthy Relationships*. Health Communication, Inc.

Paleg, Kim, and Mathew McKay (1998). *When Anger Hurts Your Relationship: 10 Simple Solutions for Couples Who Fight*. Oakland, CA: New Harbinger, Inc.

Potter-Efron, Ronald T. (2005). *Handbook on Anger Management: Individual, Couple, Family, and Group Aproaches*. New York: Hawthorn Press.

Index

Abuse: of children, 171–72; human needs violated, 60; spouse inflicting violence as, 171

ACTH. *See* Adrenocorticotropin

Active listening skills: attention to specific situation in, 138; feelings behind anger, empathized with, 138; hearing to summarize situation, 138; interpersonal relationship needing, 138–39; listening without criticizing, 138; pick up on emotional content in, 138; what is said, clarified by, 138

Adolescence anger, 119–20

Adrenaline, 32

Adrenocorticotropin (ACTH), 22–23

Adult development stages, 55–56

Aggression: human being basic part of, 37; workplace bullying as, 139–40

Anger: abusive spouse inflicting violence in, 171; Americans abroad causing, 188–89; anticipating, 206–7; basic human emotion of, 22; behavior of young children, 114; behavioral reaction of, 4; blaming on others, 198–99; body reactions to, 22–23; change coming with practice, 197–214; cognitive reaction to, 4; in community, 155–61; components of, 4; in couples, 87–105; creative approaches to, 146; creative use of, 1; dangerous level of, 62–63; denial of, 204–5; emotional health developed by, 25; emotion of, 1; emotional paralysis from, 199–202; energy in, 1, 36; exchange planned for, 207–8; extreme danger in job causing, 140–43; family and, 108–10; feelings modified by perspective, 3; feelings of denied, 205–6; focus on specific goal transcending, 228–29; toward friend, 147; friends distract from, 154–55; generated from culture difference, 181; hearing and empathizing, 210; illegal immigrants facing, 189; illnesses

Anger (*cont.*)
developing from, 28–31; improving
relationship, 87; inexpressible
emotions covered-up by, 103; inside
infant, 111, 113–14; letting go of,
8–9; list of what not to do resolving,
17; management of, 24–25;
mismanagement of, 21; obsolete
style of, 212–13; obstacles to,
197–206; as paralyzing emotion,
202; physiological reaction to, 4;
primitive responses to, 61; protects
from making scary changes, 103;
reacting to, 23; reaction to negative
influences, 169; reactions of, 52–54;
recognized in others, 64; responding
to, 24; in school age children,
115–18; self-calming practices for,
209–10; self-protection from,
203–4; signs of, 64; style of, 209;
thinking as target of, 211–12;
thinking reframed managing,
229–31; thoughts fueling of, 22; tool
for change in, 24–25; transcending
of, 226–27; tyranny of, 202–3;
universal emotion of, 2; unresolved,
major factor in child abuse, 171–72;
unspoken expectations violated
with, 98; well-managed enables
health, 21; workplace, challenge
expressing, 127–28; workplace
discrimination causing, 145. *See also*
Community; Couples; Family;
Friends; Workplace
Anger exchange: living through,
208–9; planning of, 207–8;
predesign possible solutions to,
207–8; problem identified, 207;
rehearsing discussion of, 208; taking
action to resolve, 208
Anger expression: blamer style of,
69–70; chipstackers style of, 69;
exploder style as, 67–68; imploder
style of, 68–69; styles of, 66–71;
transformers style of, 70–71

Anger-health connection: energy
source used in, 36; services for, 33
Anger management: adolescents used,
51–52; discriminated women use,
145–46; special creativity in,
145–46; teenagers learning, 52–54;
teens develop creative, 53–54; teens
use time out as, 51–52; workplace
positioning with, 130; workshops
for, 141
Anger triggers: participation in
decision-making lacking, 130;
responding to, 60–63; RETHINK
skills for, 64–66; things making
angry, 57; work failing to challenge
as, 132; workplace related,
128–39
Anger-Violence connection: gang
violence as, 168; genetic explanation
to, 173; male gender more prone to,
173–74; negative consequence of,
163; rampage killing as, 165;
rampage killing by teens, 165–66;
recognizing feeling in, 174–75;
serious problem in society, 179;
vicarious experience of, 163–64
Arguments: connected to family belief
system, 102; issues camouflaged in,
102, 151–52
Attitude: body posture expressing, 2;
workplace anger shown in, 136–37
Autonomy: basic human need of, 58;
personal threatened, 130
Autonomy vs. shame: developmental
stage of, 38, 42–45; limited freedom
resulting in, 44; limits of behavior
and freedom in, 44; stage gaining
self/environment control, 42–43;
unlimited freedom resulting in, 44

Beck, Aaron T., vii–viii
Behavior limits: cultural differences in,
183–84; in friendship, 149–50;
trusted person setting, 40
Behavior management, 47–48

Blake, William, 147, 148
Blamer, 69–70
Body chemistry, 31
Brainstorming, 16
Bullying: anger in schools, 2; in workplace, 139–40

Cellularbiochemical reactions, 31
Central nervous system, 22–23
Change, 24
Child abuse: domestic violence in, 171–72; violence in home, 170
Children: anger in, 110–11; violence against, 171–72; young, 115
Chipstacker, 69
Cho Seung Hui, 167–68
Chronic anger reaction, 26
Columbine killings, 166–67
Communication: cultural barriers crossed by, 187–89; Latino immigrant families lacking, 191; workplace discouraging of, 132
Community: anger, fear, and terror in, 157–59; anger festering in, 159; anger in, 155–61; anonymity arousing anger in, 155; interactions causing anger in, 155–57; the journalist, anger in, 157–58; promoting constructiveness of anger, 161; the snipers, terrorizing, 158–59; stressful interaction in, 155–57
Compassion, 79–81
Confidante, 151–54
Conflicts, in couples, 88
Couples: bullying in, 99–101; creative use of anger benefiting, 87–105; destructive anger in, 93–94; family beliefs cause arguments, 102; hard work being in, 105; imbalance of power in, creating anger, 99; misinterpretations result in anger, 88; responsibility for conflict shared, 92; RETHINK skills for, 93; RETHINKing conflicts of, 95–105; rewriting scripted anger, 95–105; risk in changing spouse, 99; self-help questions for, 105; transforming of, 88–93; tyranny in, 104; unspoken expectations adopted as rules, 97; wishes asserted by, 101–2. *See* Relationships, couples
The Criteria of Emotional Maturity (Menninger), 25
Cultural differences: Americans abroad offending, 188–89; assimilation difficult for, 196; behaviors clashing in, 192–93; behavior variations triggering fear, 183; challenge in understanding of, 182; child protecting parent as, 193–94; communication styles as, 185; competitive vs. cooperative as, 186–87; fear and anger generated by, 181; fear roused by, 195; gender roles defined as, 185–86; Latino groups studied for, 189–90; major and basic dimensions differing in, 183; men gathering in groups as, 184; nuances of subcultures as, 188; people categorized in stereotyping, 184–87; people standing close as, 183; people touching others as, 183–84; subcultures differ unexpectedly, 187–88; value systems not inflexible in, 187
Culture: acquiring of, 181–82; assimilation difficulty of, 196; immigrant fears in new, 189; practices of different, rousing fear of, 182

Decision-making, 130
Defusing trigger words, 81–82
Depersonalize situation, 7
Despair. *See* Integrity vs. despair stage

Destructive anger: inhibition of feelings causing rage, 94; own anger feared in, 94

Developmental stage: autonomy vs. shame, 38, 42–45; Erikson's model of, 37, 38; generativity vs. self-absorption, 38, 55; identity vs. role confusion, 38, 50–52; industry vs. inferiority, 38, 48–50; initiative vs. guilt, 38, 45–48; integrity vs. despair, 38, 55–56; intimacy vs. isolation, 38, 55–56; level of socialization reaching, 38; skill mastery as final phase, 56; trust vs. mistrust, 38–39

Discretion: checklist for trusting, 42; trustworthiness assessed by, 41

Discrimination: emotional support for, 145; resolutions to anger from, 145–46; toward women in workplace, 144–45

Dissembling, 2

Domestic violence, 170

Eastern medicine, 32

Emotion: anger important as, 25; management of, 142

Emotional maturity list, 25–26

Empathy: E in RETHINK, 1; hearing with, 73–86; pain recognized with, 34, 73–74; skill in diffusing anger, 2, 73–74; skill of, 2, 76–77

Erikson, Eric, 37, 38

Exploder style, 67–68

Families, effective: anger in, 123–25; anger management in, 125–26; care and compassion in, 123; communication skills used in, 123–24; crises dealt with together in, 124; do things together in, 124

Family: anger in, 107–46; checklist of angry experience in, 110; children's anger in, 110–11; infant anger, dealing with, 111–13; paradox of, 107–10; training ground for RETHINK, 122–23

Family setting: expect to feel safest in, 107; great disappointments experienced in, 107

Fantasize, 9

Fear: cultural differences creating, 181, 183, 195; culture triggering, 182, 189; destructive anger in, 94; health care professional reinforcing, 33; illegal immigrants living in, 192; intimacy from partners, 88; response to different cultures, 181

Forgiveness: accepting, 226; anger from death needing, 224; antidote to anger, 216; asking for, 217–18; granting of, 217–18; letting go of anger through, 215–17; misunderstandings resolved by, 225; refusal to, 223–24; refusal to offer, 223–25; steps to asking for, 225–26; thinking about, 218–23

Friends: anger with, 147–49; confidantes as, 151–52; goaders inciting violence as, 150–51; humor used on, 151–52; insights from, 152–53; knowing rules of, 149–50; in role of distractor, 154

Gang violence, 168

Generativity vs. self-absorption stage, 55

Get comfortable technique, 82

Goaders, 150–51

Graham, Katherine, 149

Greenspan, Stanley I., viii, 29

Group identity, 132

The Growth of the Mind (Greenspan), viii, 29

Guilt. *See* Initiative vs. guilt

Harassment, 2
Health: anger associated with, 21–36; transcending anger betters, 231
Health care, 34–35
Health care professional: fear reinforced by, 33; patient in submissive role in, 33–34
Hear with Empathy: skill of, 11, 73–74; skills incorporated in, 10–12, 74–77
Hearing: active listening skills summarized, 138; H in RETHINK, 1; listening skill resolving anger, 73; listening to counter anger, 74; techniques for mastering, 74–83; trigger words defused, 81–82
Hearing aids, 82–83
Hearing and Empathizing, 210
Hearing techniques: compassion skill as, 79–81; defusing trigger words skill as, 81–82; get comfortable skill as, 82; hearing aids as, 82–83; hearing with your heart skill, 77–79; the listening perch as, 83; reflective listening skill as, 75–77; RETHINK skills in action, 83–84; skills used in, 84–86
Hearing with your heart, 77–79
High stress, 32
Homeostasis, 33
Human needs, basic: achievements as, 58; autonomy and identity as, 58; competent and in control as, 58; connection to others as, 58; fairness and justice as, 58; hope and confidence as, 58; recognizing, 57–58; respect for self and others as, 58; responsibility of, 58; security most basic of, 57–58; visions of opportunities as, 58
Human needs, violations: abused as, 60; anger triggers as, 58–60; criticized as, 59; lied to or cheated as, 59; negative labeling as, 58–59; not involved in rule-making as, 59; pitied as, 60; poverty as, 59, 190; rejected as, 59; teased as, 59; yelling as, 59
Humor, 10; anger tool friends use, 151; in offsetting anger, 200–202; RETHINKing tool, 2

Identity and the Life Cycle (Erikson), 37
Identity skills, 51
Identity vs. role confusion: adolescence stage in development, 50–52; stage transitioning to adulthood, 50–51
Illness, 28–31
Immigrant: fear and anger facing, 189; Latino groups studied as, 189–90
Imploders style, 68–69
Industry vs. inferiority: developmental stage, 38, 48–50; inferiority in, 49; psychosocial crisis in, 48; school-age developmental stage of, 48–50; task developing social/physical/school skills, 48
Infant anger: developmental reasons for, 113–14; reasons for, 113; solution to, pacifier, 113, 114
Inferiority. See Industry vs. inferiority
Inferiority feeling, 49–50
Initiative vs. guilt: behavior management learned, 47; behaviors hindering promotion, 46–47; development purpose and direction in, 45–46; reasons parents promote initiative, 46; RETHINK used to review experience, 48; stage in development, 38, 45–50; stage of learning initiative, 45–46
Integrate: feelings in "I" statement, 14; I in RETHINK, 1; "I" message in, 210–11; loving and respectful statements used, 14–16
Integrity vs. despair stage, 55–56

Interpersonal relationships: poor
workplace communication
threatening of, 138; workplace
communication in, 130; workplace
communication lacking for, 132;
workplace destroying of, 133

Intimacy: expectations of, 88; partners
desire, yet fear, 88

Intimacy vs. isolation: developmental
stage, 38, 55; partner finding stage,
55

Isolation. *See* Intimacy vs. isolation

"I" statement: anger controlled in,
14–15; feeling directly articulated,
15

Keep: immediate issue focused on, 16,
209; K in RETHINK, 1, 209; in
present situation, 16, 209; problem
defining of, 16; skill of, 16–17

Last straw principle, 14

Latino immigrants: crime and drugs
exposure to, 190–91; difference in
groups of, 194–95; family lacking
communication in, 191; groups
discriminating groups in, 191;
groups studied by location, 189–90;
illegals living in fear as, 192;
language grasping, 190; noninvolved
parenting skills in, 191; parental
problems with, 195; parental role
modeling in, 193; poverty of, 190

Law enforcement: extreme danger
causing anger in, 140–43; extreme
danger in, 140–43; extreme stress
in, 140–41

The listening perch technique, 83

Loyalty, 133

Major health indicator: blood pressure
as, 34; pain as, 34; pulse as, 34;
respiration as, 34; temperature as, 34

Malvo, Lee, 159

Management skills, 134–35

Managing anger, 92

Medical care conflict: controlling
behavior in, 35; medical vs. everyday
language in, 35; objective vs.
subjective focus, 34–35; review
checklist of, 35–36; verbal vs.
nonverbal behavior in, 35

Menninger, William C., 25

Mind/Body connection: eastern
medicine model for, 32; history of,
21–22; homeostasis healing power
of, 33; linkages between, 31;
western medicine model for, 32

Mistrust, 39. *See* Trust vs. mistrust

Monitor on Psychology (Office Bullies),
139, 140

Moose, Charles A., 159

Muhammad, John Allen, 159

Murakami, Bruce, 215

No call technique, 9

Notice: feelings identified by, 13; N in
RETHINK, 1

Office bully: percent of workers victims
of, 140; workplace issue in, 139–40

Optimism, 231

Pain: empathy expressed for, 34, 77;
empathy recognizing, 34, 73–74;
experience not measurable, 34; as
subjective experience, 34

Parents: adolescence anger, handling
of, 119–20; anger in children
responded to, 111–13; child's anger
encouraged by, 112; child's anger
ignored by, 111–12; child's anger
punished by, 112; child's anger
repressed or denied by, 112–13;
initiative vs. guilt promoting, 46;
pre-teens triggering anger in,
118–19; RETHINK school age
children skills promoting, 117–18;

RETHINK skills in children developed, 113
Partners, 88
Passive relationship, 34
Perspective, 10
Physiological relationship, 29
A Poison Tree (Blake), 147
Poverty, 59, 190
Problem solving/reflective thinking, 54–55
Psychosocial crises: in industry vs inferiority stage, 48–49; progressive conflicts, predictably timed, 37

Rage: from anger to, 94–95; destructive force in relationship, 95; expressed externally by exploding, 94; expressed internally by depression, 94; stagnation created in relationships, 95
Rampage killers, 166
Reactions, of body: cardiovascular system on, 30–31; endocrine system on, 31; gastrointestinal system on, 31; musculoskeletal system on, 30; nervous system on, 30; respiratory system on, 30
Recognize: anger and health, relationship of, 5–6; anger detecting signals of, 5; anger in others, 57–71; anger management skills, 64–66; R in RETHINK, 1, 5–6; starting point in skills, 5–6
Redirect energy, 7–8
Reflective listening: anger defused with, 11; hearing techniques skill of, 75–77; skill of, 12; statements phrasing, suggestions, 11–12
Relationships, couples: arguments connected to family beliefs, 102; asserting wishes in, 101–2; being in as hard work, 105; bullying in, 99–101; creative use of anger benefiting, 87–105; destructive

anger in, 93–94; imbalance of power in, creating anger, 99; misinterpretations result in anger, 88; responsibility for conflict shared, 92; RETHINK skills for, 93; RETHINKing conflicts of, 95–105; rewriting scripted anger in, 95–105; risk in changing spouse, 99; self-help questions for, 105; transforming of, 88–93; tyranny in, 104; unspoken expectations adopted as rules, 97
Relationships. *See* Interpersonal relationships
Relationships, teen: challenges with involving anger reactions, 52–54; conflict resolved in, 54; developing skills to help, 54; feeling unconnected in, 52; past cause inferred to now, 54; risk-taking in, 53–54
Relaxation response: angry energy redistributed by body, 32–33; illness antidote to, 33
Relaxation techniques: list of, diffusing anger, 13; skills learned in, 18–19
Resentment, 131–32
Restraint, 8
RETHINK: addressing violence in home with, 172–73; adolescent parenting skills for, 120–21; adolescent parenting skills in, 120–22; anger changing skills listed, 213–14; chronic relationship conflicts resolved with, 95–105; counteracting violence in society, 164–65; disrupting cycle of destructive anger, 87; forgiveness skills used, 221–23; relationship enhanced with, 87; response to anger triggers, 60; school age children skills for parents, 117–18; seven skills of anger management in, 1; situation perspective changed

RETHINK (*cont.*)
with, 3; skills dealing with anger
triggers, 71; skills in community
interaction, 157; skills in final phase
of life, 56; skills moving toward
forgiveness, 220–21; skills putting
together of, 18–19; skills
recognizing anger triggers, 64–66;
skills reviewed for temperament,
27–28; skills taught to children,
111–13; teens with behavioral
problems skills for, 168–69;
workplace control skills in, 135–36
Risk-taking, 53–54
Road rage, 2, 61, 62
Role confusion. *See* Identity vs. role
confusion
Rosenbaum, David, 157, 158
Rouse, Jamie, 166–67

Security, 57–58
Self-absorption stage. *See* Generativity
vs. self-absorption stage
Self-talk: anger channeling use of, 6–7,
14; anticipating anger through, 207;
extreme stress jobs practicing of,
141; transcending anger with, 229
Sense of control: workplace need of,
134–35; work threatening of, 130
Sense of worth: needs and talents
identified as, 131–32; workplace
threatening, 131–32; work violating
need for, 137
Shame. *See* Autonomy vs. shame
Smith, Timothy W., 29
Social-emotional intelligence: teachers
as role models for, 178–79; teachers
emphasizing, 175–76; what it is,
176; workshops in, 177–78
Social interaction: human beings basic
part of, 37; recognition of in
anger-violence connection, 174–75
Socialization process, 47–48

Socialized: becoming, 37–38; factors
associated with expressing anger,
37; people interacting with, 37
Socializing, 132
Stereotyping: flexibility in, 185–87;
people categorized by, 184–87
Stern, Leonard B., vii
Stress: adrenaline stimulated by, 32;
anger as state of, 30; bodily
reactions to, list of, 30–31; extreme
of, 140–41; sense of worth
threatened in workplace, 131–32
Stressors: workplace related, 128–39;
workplace sense of control as,
128–29

Teenager, 120; anger management
learning, 52–54; Anger-Violence
connection of, 165–66; creative
anger management of, 53–54;
parents dealing with, 118–19;
RETHINK skills for, 168–69; time
out for, 51–52. *See also*
Relationships, teens
Temperament: anger reacting on, 26;
case study of, 26–27; familiarity
with personal, 27; natural
disposition is, 26
Think: cornerstone skill in anger
management, 6; reacting after, 6; T
in RETHINK, 1
Transformer style, 70–71
Transforming relationship: anger in
couples, 88–93; RETHINK skills
for, 88–92; RETHINK skills in,
91–92
Trust vs. mistrust: anger energy used
in, 40; development stage, first,
38–39; discretion in, 41–42; limits
to behavior setting, 40–41;
relationships developed in, 39–40;
trust and anger in, 39–40; trust and
limits in, 41

Tyranny: anger used in, 202–3; in couples, 104; in families, 122; in relationships, 104

Use your head practice, 8

Violence: heredity/environment issue involved in, 173; in home, 170–71; previous exposure to, 169; takes little stimulation to trigger, 170; youths acting out with, 164–65
Virginia Tech University killings, 167
Vital signs, 34

Women: anger management by, 145–46; discrimination toward, 144–45; job force advancing of, 143; workplace ambivalence toward, 143–44; workplace discrimination of, 144–45
Workplace: active listening skills in, 138; ambivalence toward women in, 143–44; anger and lack of control in, 135–36; anger complicating life needs in, 127–28; anger expression limited in, 127; anger in, 127–46; anger on job, 133–34; attitude in, 136–37; body language communicating in, 138; conflict threatening loyalty in, 133; discrimination in, 144–45; emotionally literate communication in, 138–39; extreme stress in, 140–41; extreme stress or danger in, 140–43; extreme stress requiring workshops in, 141; interpersonal relationships threatened in, 132–33; job offering security in, 128; job stress experienced more, 128; life autonomy ceded in, 129–30; need for certainty in, 133; office bullying in, 139–40; person continually angry in, 136–37; person's value system placing importance on, 128; poor communication in, 139; RETHINKing skills used in, 134–35; sense of control threatened in, 130; sense of worth unidentified in, 131–32; special issues in, 139–40; stress interfering with health, 128–29; stress threatening sense of worth, 131–32; stressors and anger triggers in, 128–39; stressors building resentment in, 131–32; stressors contributing to anger, 127; verbal communication in, 138; women in, 143–46. *See* Interpersonal relationships

Young children, 115
"You" statement: attacking on personal level, 14–15; sample of, 15

Zandman, Felix, 227–28

About the Authors

RHODA BARUCH is a licensed psychologist and founder of the Institute for Mental Health Initiatives, now integrated into the George Washington University School of Public Health, Department of Prevention and Community Health. She has also served as Associate Dean of Harvard's Center for Research in Careers, and was Director of Career Development at Dartmouth College, New Hampshire. Baruch was also a member of the Advisory Board for WCVB, Channel 5, in Boston. She leads Rethinking Anger seminars nationwide.

EDITH H. GROTBERG is a psychologist and professional lecturer at George Washington University, School of Public Health, Department of Prevention and Community Health. A faculty member at the university's Institute for Mental Health Initiatives, Grotberg is former Director of Research for the Administration of Children, Youth, and Families, for the federal Department of Health and Human Services. She has also been a professor at American University in Washington, DC, and is internationally known for her research on resilience. She is a Fellow of the American Psychological Association and former president of the International Council of Psychologists. She also leads Rethinking Anger workshops.

SUZANNE STUTMAN is a psychotherapist and past director of the Institute for Mental Health Initiatives. Stutman has been a consultant to media including Turner Broadcasting, NBC, MTV, and Fox News Network. She served as the U.S. Representative to the United Nations Conference on Media and Crime Prevention, and, in collaboration with the Pan American Health Organization, she organized an International Conference on Violence Prevention. She also leads Rethinking Anger workshops.